The Strange Case of
# HELLISH NELL

# The Strange Case of
# HELLISH NELL

*The Story of Helen Duncan and the*
*Witch Trial of World War II*

## NINA SHANDLER

**DA CAPO PRESS**
A Member of the Perseus Books Group

NOTE TO READERS: All names, places, dates, and events in
*The Strange Case of Hellish Nell* are true to historical records.
Scenes and dialogue reflect the author's understanding of personalities and events.
The writer's depiction of the witch trial of 1944 incorporates edited
and abridged versions of verbatim transcripts of courtroom proceedings.

Designed by Trish Wilkinson
Set in Fairfield Light by the Perseus Books Group

Library of Congress Cataloging-in-Publication Data

Shandler, Nina.
    The strange case of Hellish Nell : the story of Helen Duncan and the
witch trial of World War II / Nina Shandler.
       p.   cm.
    Includes bibliographical references and index.
    HC: ISBN-13: 978-0-306-81438-9; ISBN-10: 0-306-81438-2
    PB: ISBN-13: 978-0-306-81575-1; ISBN-10: 0-306-81575-3
    1. Duncan, Helen, 1895–1956—Trials, litigation, etc. 2. Trials (Witch-
craft)—Great Britain—History. 3. Women mediums—Great Britain.
4. Mediums—Great Britain. I. Title.
    KD371.W56S53 2006
    345.41'0288—dc22                                              2006022402

First Da Capo Press edition 2006
First Da Capo Press paperback edition 2007

Published by Da Capo Press
A Member of the Perseus Books Group
http://www.dacapopress.com

Da Capo Press books are available at special discounts for bulk
purchases in the U.S. by corporations, institutions, and other organizations.
For more information, please contact the Special Markets Department at the
Perseus Books Group, 2300 Chestnut Street, Suite 200, Philadelphia, PA 19103, or
call (800) 255-1514, or e-mail special.markets@perseusbooks.com.

To Michael with love,
Without your encouragement and support
I never would have written one published word

# Contents

## Part III: Resolutions

# Acknowledgments

F ROM CONCEPTION TO HARDCOVER, THIS WORK HAS BEEN A LONG
HAUL. There are many people to thank. I'll begin near the end.

Bob Pigeon, my editor at Da Capo, took a risk. He accepted my proposal and trusted me to produce a full-fledged manuscript. Along the way, he guided and encouraged me with the enthusiasm of a seasoned mentor.

Jim Levine, my agent at Levine Greenberg Associates, took hold of my proposal with gusto and paraded it to publishing houses with tenacity. No agent could have been more responsive, ethical, and professional.

Betsy Rapoport, my former editor at Crown, has been a loyal support since 1997, when I showed up in her office with a box of tofu chocolates. Betsy welcomed my foray into this historical tale with extreme generosity. Not only did she recommend my agent Jim Levine, but she read a very rough early version of *The Strange Case of Hellish Nell* and edited it with gentle candor.

Along the way, friends read drafts and chapters. I'm particularly grateful to Robin Kasis, Parvati Grais, Vicki and Barry Elson, and Martin and Melly Bock for their time and feedback. Many others have offered unwavering encouragement.

I loved researching *The Strange Case of Hellish Nell*. Mostly, I loved meeting and talking with people who had bits and pieces of information to offer. My most exciting personal moment came when I dialed a number in New Zealand and Stan Worth, the once young lieutenant who testified against Helen Duncan, picked up the receiver. Stan, now a ninety-two-year-old gentleman, remains as sharp, witty, and honest as ever. My conversations with Stan and his wife, Bunty, have spanned five years. Stan told his stories with flare and read, copyedited, added to, and approved of my final manuscript.

Along the way, others offered hospitality and some went the extra mile. In 1999, Dorothy Mahoney in Callander, Scotland, wrote to me repeatedly and introduced me to other helpful citizens of the village. When I sat down to tea with them, all informed me that Helen, with her tomboy antics and weird visions, had been nicknamed and universally known as "Hellish Nell." More specifically, Harvey MacNaughton and his wife spoke with me at length, showed me photographs of old Callander, and gave me photocopies of his uncle's diary—an invaluable source of stories about the bygone days of Nell's childhood and about her family, "The Wild Slaters." Mr. J. K. Dunn, President of the Historical Society, and his wife provided much scenic detail. I attempted to contact Helen Duncan's descendants. Some were unreachable. One relative preferred to remain off the record; others did not respond to my requests for interviews.

On my visits to Portsmouth, I met people immersed in local history and willing to share all they knew. After meeting me in 1999, Terry Swetnam, a retired police officer, took particular interest in my project, tracking down and sending me photographs and service records of Chief Constable Arthur West, Detective Sergeant Fred Ford, and others. In the spring of 2005, I met John Mainwaring at the Portsmouth City Museum. He gave me his impressions of Chief Constable Arthur Charles West and suggested that I contact Jim and Olive Cramer. Jim had worked for Chief Constable West, and Olive had worked at Police Headquarters during World War II. A number of information-packed conversations with this energetic and engaging couple followed.

Another 1999 excursion proved particularly vital to the unfolding story. I wanted to know if Holloway Prison had suffered a direct attack from V-bomb raids while Helen Duncan was imprisoned there. Felicity Ball, at the HMS Prison Museum and Archives, in Rougie, England, dug through archives, unearthed a portfolio of photographs of the now destroyed Holloway Prison, discovered long-forgotten notes of the wartime Holloway Prison Auxiliary, and provided me with copies. The photographs showed V-bomb damage to Cell-Block B, and the Auxiliary notes confirmed the date of the attack: Helen Duncan had been in residence.

Logan Lewis-Proudlock opened the archives of the College of Psychic Studies to me. Together we leafed through documents pertaining to Helen Duncan's séances at 16 Queensbury Street. She shared my excitement at finding the photograph of Helen and Henry Duncan and at reading Dr. Fielding-Ould's assessment of Henry Duncan's avarice and Helen's multiple personalities. Logan filled me in on the reputations of other characters: Miss Mercy Phillimore and Brigadier Roy Firebrace.

Throughout my long years of research, I returned again and again to Britain's archives at the Public Records Office in Kew Gardens, to the British Library in London, and to the Newspaper Archive in Collingdale. I'm indebted to those institutions for preserving history with care and for making it available with such grace.

Finally, Erica Lawrence guided my manuscript with efficiency and grace from one production stage to the next, from loose pages to hardcover book. In that process, Jennifer Swearingen copyedited every sentence and endnote with an astonishingly meticulous eye for detail. I thank them both.

At every stage of this marathon, my family refused to let me drop out. When my energy waned, my daughters, Manju and Sara, read draft after draft, prodding me along: "It's a great story, Mom." "You're a really good writer." "You can do this project." But more than anyone, my husband, Michael, kept me going. His salary supported my research, and his enthusiasm bolstered my courage. To all three, I am inexpressibly grateful.

# Photo Credits

Helen and Henry Duncan compliments of the College of Psychic Studies, 16 Queensbury Street, London, and with special gratitude to Logan Lewis-Proudlock.

Chief Constable Arthur Charles West from Portsmouth public records, with thanks to Terry Swetnam who tracked down and provided the copy.

Harry Price compliments to the Foxearth and District Local Historical Society.

Byculla House, formerly Portsmouth Police Headquarters, photographed by author.

Sergeant Detective Frederick Ford from Portsmouth public records with gratitude to Terry Swetnam who unearthed it and sent it to me.

Lieutenant Stanley Worth generously provided by Stanley Worth.

Holloway Prison with permission from Richard Carling, HM Prison Service, and thanks to Felicity Ball, HM Prison Service Archive, for assisting me in finding a copy of the photograph.

Helen Duncan in 1944 with permission of David Higham Associates from *The Trial of Helen Duncan,* by C. E. Bechhofer Roberts, Jarrolds Publishers, and special thanks to Alice Wilson, Gabrielle White, and Jan Kean for their assistance.

Defense Attorney Charles Loseby with permission of David Higham Associates from *The Trial of Helen Duncan,* by C. E. Bechhofer Roberts, Jarrolds Publishers, and special thanks to Alice Wilson, Gabrielle White, and Jan Kean for their assistance.

King's Counsel John Maude with permission of David Higham Associates from *The Trial of Helen Duncan,* by C. E. Bechhofer Roberts, Jarrolds Publishers, and special thanks to Alice Wilson, Gabrielle White, and Jan Kean for their assistance.

Junior Prosecutor Henry Elam with permission of David Higham Associates from *The Trial of Helen Duncan,* by C. E. Bechhofer Roberts, Jarrolds Publishers, and special thanks to Alice Wilson, Gabrielle White, and Jan Kean for their assistance.

Old Bailey Central Criminal Court with Bomb Damage by permission of David Higham Associates from *The Trial of Helen Duncan,* by C. E. Bechhofer Roberts, Jarrolds Publishers, and special thanks to Alice Wilson, Gabrielle White, and Jan Kean for their assistance.

His Lordship Sir Gerald Dodson, Recorder of London, with permission of David Higham Associates from *The Trial of Helen Duncan,* by C. E. Bechhofer Roberts, Jarrolds Publishers, and special thanks to Alice Wilson, Gabrielle White, and Jan Kean for their assistance.

# Prologue

## Why This Obsolete Tomfoolery?

O N SUNDAY MORNING, APRIL 2, 1944, PRIME MINISTER WINSTON
Churchill woke up at 8:30 sharp, grabbed a cigar, waved it through
the always-ready candle flame, and puffed.[1] After the past week, the
Prime Minister was severely in need of a day of rest. Not only was London ablaze,[2] but a rebellious Parliament had passed some cockamamie
feminist legislation.[3] Of course, the public didn't know the half of it—
Churchill made damn certain the people learned only what was good for
them.[4] The press obediently cheered half-truths: AIR WAR GIGANTIC:
2000 TON BLITZ HITS NUREMBERG, and 600 BOMBERS WARN
BERLIN, "WE'RE COMING."[5]

But in a secret bunker hidden deep beneath London's streets,
Churchill's War Cabinet had grieved the real tally. The Royal Air Force
may have dropped 2,000 tons of explosives on Nuremberg, but 545
British bomber boys died in that raid. Hitler lost only 19 *Luftwaffe* airmen. The sad ratio: twenty-eight British deaths for each Nazi casualty.
German soil was littered with the charred skeletons of British aircraft. Secretly, Churchill conceded that the Battle of Berlin had to be abandoned.

After five years of war, the German air force still triumphed in the skies
over Germany and still bombarded London.[6] This past week, the *Luftwaffe*

1

had attacked with the first-ever cluster bombs, enormous encasements filled with dozens of incendiaries. Lightweight, they floated down from the sky with eerie slowness. Hitting their targets, they instantly burst, spewing fireballs that devoured neighborhoods like kindling. Water did nothing to douse the blue-hot flames.[7]

On top of it all, restive Parliamentarians had hit Churchill with a bombshell of the political sort. Against the Prime Minister's wishes, feminist legislation mandating equal pay for equal work had squeaked into law. Not pleased, Churchill issued an ultimatum: *Reverse the vote, or I will resign.* Labour backed down. There would be no equal pay, not under Winston Churchill's reign. To demonstrate his power, Churchill had paid a visit to the House of Commons. Every last Honorable Member of Parliament had leapt to his feet. In deference and fear, they all applauded.[8]

Now, on the first Sunday in April of 1944, a self-satisfied smirk crossed the Prime Minister's lips. All those distractions—devastating Royal Air Force losses over Germany, cluster bombs setting fire to London, Labour legislation threatening his rule—faded into the past.

On this day of rest, Churchill anticipated focusing on the coming challenge: D-Day, the Allied cross-channel invasion of Nazi-occupied Europe. The Americans were already flooding into the British Isles. His Majesty's Mediterranean fleet had secreted its way back to home port.[9] A decoy fleet had assembled in Edinburgh's harbor.[10] All such highly strategic areas had been banned to visitors.[11] Soon, the greatest seaborne invasion in world history would be launched from Portsmouth. With a pinch of luck and a pound of secrecy, Hitler's forces would be paralyzed. The enormity of the task—saving civilization from barbarism—invigorated Churchill.

The Prime Minister exhaled a blast of cigar smoke, and the smell alerted his staff. Churchill was awake. His butler placed the morning newspapers at his bedside and helped Mr. Churchill into his dressing gown, a green silk kimono embroidered with gold fire-breathing dragons. Ready to read, Churchill settled back into freshly fluffed pillows and opened the oversized pages of London's dailies.[12] Within moments, his teeth gripped the cigar. The corners of his mouth descended to his jowls.

Preposterous news took up space on the front page: a witchcraft trial. This past fortnight, while the nation had waged war and Churchill had battled Parliament, the Old Bailey, Britain's highest criminal court, had been preoccupied with witchcraft.

Grabbing newspaper after newspaper, the Prime Minister confronted the same tale again and again. The *Times,* the most respected newspaper in Britain, ran with the headline: "WITCHCRAFT ACT OFFENCES." The *News of the World* carried the banner: "POLICE REVELATIONS DO NOT SHAKE FOLLOWERS." The *New Chronicle* blared: "MEDIUM DEFIED SASHCORD AND HANDCUFFS." The *Daily Herald* shrieked: 'LIES'—CRY BY MEDIUM."[13] And the *Daily Express,* with laudable irony, printed a cartoon of firefighters training their sights on a witch flying her broomstick over London while the city burned.[14]

Churchill smoldered. A witchcraft trial? What justification could there possibly be for this mockery of justice? Had the police, the Office of Prosecutions, the judiciary, the Home Secretary, all gone mad?

By the next morning, Monday, April 3, 1944, the Prime Minister was ready to dictate common sense. One of his secretaries scurried into his chamber, took her seat at the foot of his bed, and captured his rapid-fire directive.

"HOME SECRETARY

*Let me have a report on why the Witchcraft Act of 1735 was used in a modern Court of Justice.*

*What was the cost of the trial to the state, observing that witnesses were brought from Portsmouth and maintained here in this crowded London for a fortnight, and the Recorder [His Lordship Sir Gerald Dodson] kept busy with all this obsolete tomfoolery . . . "*[15]

Winston Churchill dictated neither a greeting nor a closing. He did not bother to address Home Secretary Herbert Morrison—the member of his War Cabinet in charge of internal security, oversight of the police, MI5, the Office of Prosecutions, the judiciary, media, and censorship—by name.

Churchill's secretary pulled the five-by-seven note from the typewriter. Churchill snatched it from her hand and scribbled his signature. The red ink dripped with disdain.[16]

I held Churchill's note and stared at the red ink.[17] I wasn't supposed to see this curt directive; no one was supposed to lay eyes on this highly classified document for a hundred years.

My fascination with Britain's World War II witch trial had begun two years before I found the Prime Minister's letter to the Home Secretary. Saturday morning, January 31, 1998, was like most of my Saturday mornings. I was in my little black Mazda zooming from store to store, listening to National Public Radio's *Weekend Edition with Scott Simon*. As I turned into the *Stop & Shop* parking lot, Simon announced, "In 1944 the British government tried a forty-six-year-old Scottish mother of six, named Helen Duncan, under the Witchcraft Act of 1735. She became the last person in Britain tried as a witch."[18]

World War II witch trial? In Britain? Unbelievable. I pulled into a parking space, turned off my engine, and turned up the volume. James Mac-Quarrie, cofounder of the British Society of Paranormal Studies, quickly stated the facts: Helen Duncan, a gifted medium, got into grave trouble for channeling spirits during World War II.[19]

War and witchcraft. True crime and the supernatural. Intrigue laced with humor. A mini-movie, a costumed comedy played against the backdrop of World War II, pranced through my mind: As Allied forces prepared to storm the beaches of Normandy, a British barrister, decked out in a long silk robe and sporting a horsehair wig, badgered a witness, "Madame, what evidence do you have that spirits return from the dead?" I giggled, turned off the radio, and headed for the grocery store.

A year later, my youngest daughter flew off to college, and my husband landed a plum position in England. Suddenly, there I was in London—a middle-aged psychologist with an empty nest, no work permit, and nothing better to do than to investigate a witch trial.

Upon the polite advice of a kindly official at Scotland Yard, I hopped on a train and headed for the home of Britain's archives, the charming village of Kew Gardens. I walked down a suburban lane, crossed an empty thoroughfare, and entered the grounds of the Public Records Office. The whole scene was far more agreeable than I had expected: a tasteful modern building, not too square, lots of glass. In front, park benches surrounded a pond. I strolled by ducks bobbing on the water, appreciating how the British preserve their heritage.

I stepped up to the glass entrance. A security guard opened the door wide, greeting me like a long-awaited guest. "Welcome. Do you have an identification card? Well, you simply must get one. Step this way."

I sat down. A woman in a gray suit looked up, smiling. "What do you intend to research?"

Suddenly self-conscious, I blushed. *Would this woman think I was a ghost-crazed American quack on a witch-hunt? A cult-enthusiast unworthy of archival research?* Trying to sound as legitimate as possible, I recited my resumé, "I'm a licensed psychologist and a published author."

"How nice," she commented, nodding quizzically, and then repeated her question, "What do you wish to research?"

I confessed, "I'm looking for records of a witch trial during World War II."

"Quite," she said without raising an eyebrow. Then, as though my investigation was most mundane, she handed me an entry card, smiled warmly, and added, "I do wish you luck and hope to see you again."

Officially approved, I settled down in front of a computer screen, typed "HELEN DUNCAN," and pressed ENTER. I wished for a witch trial transcript and two file numbers appeared. I ordered the first: a criminal document. My request was approved. The document was due to arrive within the hour. I ordered the second. The computer screen flashed a message: DOCUMENT UNAVAILABLE.

Confused, I looked for a research librarian. With great civility, a bookish woman explained why the file might be out of reach. "Often documents, especially criminal documents, are closed to the public view for fifty years. You understand? To protect their families from embarrassment."

With those words—"their families"—she gently opened my eyes to a side of the Helen Duncan witch trial I had failed to consider. This trial had impacted a mother, a father, and children.

The librarian turned to consult her computer. A quiet moment later, her head tilted and, with a curious pout, she whispered, "Oh my. How odd. This file was sealed for a century."

Apparently, my furrowed brow and American accent clued her into the need for further explanation. She spoke slowly, as though to a child: "The closed file is not a criminal file. It's an HO file issued by the Home Office. Our Home Office is charged with internal intelligence. Normally, documents are closed for a hundred years only in matters of national security."

A *closed file,* sealed for reasons of national security. Now *that* certainly piqued my curiosity. Was Helen Duncan a kind of psychic spymaster who used her power against the Allied cause? Did British bobbies and barristers morph into ghost-busters, obsessed with smoking out phantom moles?

With the door to official documents slammed in my face, I scoured the libraries of London, looking for clues. I dusted off out-of-print treasures: a verbatim transcript of the witchcraft trial,[20] a biographical tribute written by Helen Duncan's daughter,[21] a meticulous examination of eyewitness accounts of Helen Duncan's séances,[22] a fellow medium's contemporaneous account of the trial,[23] a callous description of quasi-scientific experiments performed on Helen Duncan,[24] the judge's autobiography,[25] articles in weathered Spiritualist journals, and accounts in wartime newspapers turned sepia with age.

Then, I traced Helen Duncan's footsteps. I traveled to Callander, the quaint Scottish village where the town folk nicknamed her Hellish Nell; to Edinburgh, where she, with scant help from her sickly husband, managed to support her six children; to Portsmouth, where her séances led to her arrest; and to the Old Bailey, Central Criminal Court in London, where she stood trial charged under the Witchcraft Act of 1735.

Month after month, I unearthed more and more information, and the intrigues swirling round the case of Helen Duncan multiplied. This complex, feisty, broken, and ultimately triumphant woman attracted controversy. Her detractors believed her to be a callous and self-serving fraud. Her devotees believed her to be an extraordinary channel to the Beyond. I questioned who had done her more harm. Those who loved her? Or those who despised her? And still I wondered: Why did the British government get embroiled in a paranormal dispute? I wanted to get my hands on that *closed file.*

I returned to the Public Records Office. Sitting at the same computer terminal and expecting renewed frustration, I typed the code for the sealed Home Office document. While the computer searched, I looked down and jotted a quick note on a piece of thin-lined paper. I glanced back at the computer screen and saw the words: DOCUMENT ORDERED. My heart beat faster. I waited, paralyzed, afraid one false move would alert a clerical guardian of official secrets that a closed file had been ordered.

My beeper buzzed summoning me to collect my illicit archives, and I strode up to the counter, trying to look nonchalant. A young man sporting a T-shirt and gelled hair, looking not one bit inclined to protect state secrets, handed me a stack of fading brown folders, held together with a matching cotton ribbon. In the upper right corner of the top folder, a green sticker threatened to thwart my mission. It read: CLOSED UNTIL 2046.

With friendly banter and a "Thanks so much," I placed my palm over the green sticker and carried my forbidden treasure to my assigned seat. I untied the fraying ribbon and found a scrapbook devoted to the case of Helen Duncan: police reports in blue folders; tattered newspaper clippings; notes that had passed between the Home Office, the Office of Public Prosecutions, and the Portsmouth police; letters written by hand on linen stationery—some imploring Eleanor Rathborne, the first woman in Parliament, to take pity on Helen Duncan, and some instructing officials of the government to prosecute her vigorously. After hours of careful inspection, I picked up a five-by-seven note, and my investigative interest turned to starstruck awe. On a scrap of stationery embossed with the return address 10 Downing Street, Whitehall, and stamped "PRIME MINISTER'S PERSONAL MINUTE," I read Winston Churchill's complaint to the Home Secretary—his brusque assessment of the witch trial of World War II: "obsolete tomfoolery."[26]

Apparently, the Prime Minister wasn't privy to the same national security concerns as Military Intelligence, the police, and the Office of Public Prosecutions.

Part I

MISSIONS

# 1

# Prophecies

V ICTORIA HELEN MACFARLANE WASN'T LIKE THE OTHER GIRLS OF HER Highland village; she hated petticoats and talked to dead people. Her tomboy antics and ghoulish visions earned her a nickname: Hellish Nell. That's what the town folk called her.[1] No one could put the fear of God in that child, though her mother, Isabella, certainly tried.[2]

The charms of Callander conspired against Isabella, however, and she fought a losing battle. Just beyond the MacFarlanes' whitewashed cottage, Nell entered a land of ancient magic where any imaginative child might see spirits and where mischief beckoned. Just a hop down the muddy lane, "God so loved the World" was engraved on a cream marble slab mounted over the doorway of the mission church.[3] That was where Nell swore everlasting devotion to Jesus Christ in exchange for tea biscuits and party games.[4] Farther along the lane, just over the bridge, stood the cemetery wall. For a girl like Nell, not a shy and proper girl but a girl in search of adventure, that stone wall with moss creeping into its crevices, begged to be climbed. Once over the top, the cemetery, with its rough tombstones, hid ghosts, ready to rise from the damp earth, howling or whimpering.

Beyond the burial ground, the haunting got even better.[5] A hillock swelled up from the flat earth where prehistoric ancestors had piled load after load of chocolaty Highland dirt to make Tomnachessaig. At its summit, Highland legends come alive. This is where Saint Toma pointed his black Bible to the sun, as its rays streamed through clouds and rain. At his feet fairies baked bread and sang squeaky tunes.[6]

Some days Rob Roy MacGregor himself, in his blazing yellow shirt and his red plaid kilt, returned. The Highland hero and his clan huddled next to Nell, listening to the *tap, tap, rat ta ta tap,* as English redcoats marched into view. Rob Roy pulled his sword from his sheath and, along with his tribe, swooped down, swords flailing, and scattered the invaders. English corpses lay bleeding, their souls rising through the river mist.[7]

Running down Tomnachessaig, whooping and hollering, pretending to be one of Rob Roy's band,[8] Nell stopped short, suddenly emerging from her imaginative vision. Looking about, she shouted, "Where's Pate? Where's my big brother got to?"[9]

Pate was Nellie's own personal Rob Roy. The village folk called her heroic brother Pate the Homer, because he had a way of finding things and bringing them home. In his own small way, Pate redistributed the wealth of Callander. Armed with that righteous calling, and with Nellie close be-hind, Pate snuck around town on the lookout for booty. The two stealthy thieves—the ruffian and the tomboy—crept into the minister's garden, scurried up his apple trees, and skulked off with bulging sacks of juicy Macintoshes. Pate and Nell, the Highland hunters, stalked wayward bun-nies, nabbing the greedy pests as they munched on the cabbage heads planted in village gardens. Nell and Pate made sure the furry plunderers got their just desserts, roasting the long-eared buggers over an open fire.[10]

On the most daring MacFarlane raid of all, the bounty-bent duo eyed a freight train, piled high with coal. Actually, it wasn't a whole train; it was just one lone freight car parked in the railroad yard. Pate and Nellie scaled up its side, unhitched the latches on its back end, and freed the coal, which poured out like lava. The coal dust rose up like a cloud of smoke, and the MacFarlane co-conspirators came up black. Of course they got caught. The stationmaster sentenced them to hard labor: "You scallywags pick up every last lump of coal."[11]

On hot summer days when the sun stayed up to near midnight, Pate was sure to be stationed on the bank of the Lena, the village swimming hole.[12] If your name was MacFarlane, you swam in that pool. Stop any-one on any street in Callander, and every single person would surely tell you, "The MacFarlanes are great swimmers."[13] Of the Archie MacFarlanes, Pate was the champion. Pate was the god of the Lena.

Sure enough, Pate stood, stripped to his underwear, self-employed as Callander's unofficial swimming instructor. Lads Nellie's age, six years or so, ran around on the emerald grass, playing tag and yelping for fun. One strayed just a bit from the pack and Pate struck. Leaping from the water's edge, he grabbed and threw the shrieking child over his shoulder and darted for the Lena. Then, with one heave, Pate threw the squirming boy into the deepest part of the pool. The water swallowed the boy. Most boys surfaced, arms and legs flailing, gasping for breath, and learned to swim. But this particular lad wasn't made for swimming; he sank. Pate watched and counted.

"One," Pate screamed as the child went under.

"Two," he shouted, as the boy's head disappeared for the second time.

"Nellie," Pate shouted, looking away from the drowning lad and waving to his little sister.

"Three," he bellowed as the boy sank one last time.

Pate jumped in, saved the hapless lad, and laid his wee bedraggled carcass on the grass. The lad coughed and shivered as Pate assured him, "You'll do better next time. I'll teach your sorry arse to swim yet, I will."

Pate did his civic duty, taught many a Callander boy to swim, and saved many a Callander boy's life.[14]

Nellie was a great swimmer, too, especially for a girl. Of course, girls weren't allowed to swim. But stupid rules about what girls could or couldn't do never stopped Nellie from doing anything. Swimming was no exception. Other Callander girls stayed away from Pate, crossing the street to avoid his dark stares.[15] Not Nellie. Nellie and Pate stole off, stripped under the bridge, racing and play fighting for hours.[16]

But no matter where they were or what they were up to, Nell had a nose for fresh goodies. When she sensed that Mum was about to bake scones or make candy, she scurried home, skipping circles around the fresh cow patties.[17] If she managed to make it home without getting stink on her shoes, Mum would be certain to give her a bowl to lick clean.

One such day, little Nell rested her chin on the kitchen table, watching and waiting, studying how Mummy made "tablet," a favorite treat:

butter, sugar, and thick cream boiled into fudge.[18] With a spatula in hand, Mummy had dug butter from a crock and scraped it into a measuring cup. Then, she had plopped the butter into a big bowl without messing up her fingers. Not one blob of yucky grease had gotten on Mummy's face or on her dress. Mummy was perfect; every hair was pulled tightly into a knot, and her collar was starched stiff. With Mummy everything had its proper place.[19] Not Nellie. For her, everything spilled out and ran together. Nellie just couldn't keep things separate—the Presbyterian part just couldn't chase off the tomboy part or scare off her spirit friends.

Mummy looked up from her mixing bowl and said, "Nellie, I swear you look like the bonniest lad in the whole of the Highlands."

Nellie knew Mummy was making fun of her, but the rebellious tyke set her jaw, steeled her dark eyes. She had nagged until Mum set her on a chair, placed a pottery bowl on her head, and clipped a straight cut round the edge. Nellie had a boy's haircut, and she loved looking like a boy. Whenever she could, she played dress-up in Pate's best Sunday suit, white-collared shirt, and tie.[20]

"I wish I was a boy," grumbled Nellie. "I'd sooner dress in Pate's pants."[21]

Mummy sneered, "Even with your short locks, you're too pretty to be a boy. That button nose and those inch-long eyelashes give you away.[22] Make no mistake about it, Nellie, I'll be making a proper young lady out of you yet."[23]

Then, just as Nellie's mouth started watering, she saw a Spirit Visitor. Maybe it was the smell of sugar or the warmth of the stove that called Johnny from the Other Side. Nellie didn't know why he came. She did see him clearly, hovering next to Mummy, all dressed up in his soldier's uniform: a plaid kilt, socks up to his knees, gold buttons, all polished bright. A Scotsman, standing proud—a Highlander.

Mummy totally ignored Johnny, acting like he didn't exist, pretending like she didn't see him. Even when Johnny talked, Mum didn't listen. Johnny spoke Gaelic like old-time Callander folk. Gentle rolling R's bubbled out of his mouth like the River Teith, but Mummy paid him no mind. So Nellie talked for him.

"Mummy?" Nell said. Mummy looked down at her. "Johnny's here, Mummy. He's really happy. He wants you to know he's happy."

Mummy dropped the wooden spatula. The messy thing smeared grease on her clean apron before it hit the floor. Her eyes popped wide as saucers. Then, in a flash, Mummy turned into a witch. Her eyes narrowed to slits and her lips shrank to thin lines.

"Victoria Helen MacFarlane. Johnny is dead. That boy was killed before you were born. You don't know him. I don't know where you heard about him. Johnny is not here and you are not talking to him. You will not be doing wicked work. No child of mine is possessed."

With each word sounding sharp, like a wicked spell aimed to pierce Nell's brain, Mum made her three prophecies.

"You'll be thrown in a dungeon. You'll be tried as a witch.[24] You'll be burned alive in a hell fire."[25]

Little Nellie felt the flush rise to her face, and she ran away. Alone, crouching on a stone stoop at the back of the cottage, she clasped both hands over her mouth to keep her sobs from bursting into heartbroken howls. When the heaving of her small chest calmed, she folded her hands in prayer and whimpered softly, "I did see him. I did." The chickens looked up from their pecking and cocked their heads. Then, wee Nellie MacFarlane heard a voice whispering in the gentle wind, blowing down from Ben Ledi, from the Hill of God itself, and across the River Teith, come to comfort her. "Nell. You did see him. In time, many will believe in you."

Nell felt calm descend over her. Mummy didn't believe her, but God knew better. So. That was that.[26]

# 2

# The Seer

THIRTY-FOUR YEARS LATER, IN A STRANGER'S DRESSING ROOM, NELL'S husband, Henry, spoke soothingly, coaxing her to undress.[1] She unbuttoned her frock and let it drop to the floor. Henry watched. Nell lifted her arms and took the pins from her matronly bun. A raven lock fell between her shoulders. She shook her head from side to side, freeing her thick mane.[2] Next, she untied the laces of her corset and guided her brassier straps down her arms. Henry's eyes latched onto her nipples, but he didn't move toward her. Nell peeled off her stockings and pushed down her bloomers. Naked, she perched on a chair.[3] Finally, Henry came close, stood over her, lifted her chin, and stared down at her affectionately, as though he had never betrayed her.[4] He placed a cigarette in her mouth and lit it. Nell inhaled. At least her husband was good for something.

Henry turned and walked out of the bedroom.[5]

Alone, Nell exhaled smoke and looked down at her body. How had her life come to this? It was the summer of 1940. Nell sat naked in another woman's posh bedroom,[6] feeling about as comfortable as a mother walrus on a bird's nest, and that's what she looked like. Nine pregnancies will do that to any woman—leave her breasts resting on her permanently bloated belly and that belly melting into her tree trunk legs.[7] Nell had only six grown children to show for those nine pregnancies, but she refused to feel sorry for herself. Nell held stubbornly to her belief that the children who

16

survived and the deaths of the others—her joy and her suffering—were all part of a divine plan.[8]

The door flung open, and three women gaped at Nell. Helen Duncan's séances invariably began with an inspection of her naked body, a regime designed to ascertain that no hidden piece of paper, bit of memorabilia, or scrap of cloth might be used to fake her psychic powers.[9] The ladies gawked at Nell, and Nell wondered at their astonishment. *Hadn't they ever seen a fat woman before?* Then, ever alert to the judgments of others, Nell sized up her inspectors one at a time. Today, one was a kindly sort who took pity on the humiliation of Nell's nakedness; another, a reverent devotee of spiritual communication; and the third, Mrs. Marion Gray, a vixen so repulsed by Nell's weight as to be rendered incapable of appreciating her gift.

Mrs. Gray's mouth drooped in involuntary disgust as she issued a command, "Stand up, Mrs. Duncan."

Nell stood and pirouetted round like a circus elephant performing for her trainer. Mrs. Gray looked Nell up and down. Nell craned her neck, keeping her eyes glued to Mrs. Gray. The frozen cold judgment etched into this woman's face unleashed a flood of insecurities. This séance was yet another nightmarish test, and Mrs. Gray the latest in a lifelong series of holier-than-thou inquisitors: Nell's own dead mother, the village preacher, the school inspector,[10] and that devil of a man, Harry Price. All had suspected her of cheating.[11]

Anxious and fearing that Albert,[12] her Spirit Guide, might abandon her, Nell pleaded for a reassurance, "Oh, what should I do if Albert doesn't come?"

Mrs. Gray offered not a word of comfort but did come to a reluctant verdict: "I see nothing amiss." The other two ladies nodded in agreement, and Mrs. Gray pronounced a final order, "Put on your séance costume, Mrs. Duncan."[13]

Nell obeyed, slowly, very slowly. Nell usually obeyed, but she always moved at her own pace. A bear of a woman, Nell had been trained to perform, but just below the surface of her compliance a growl rumbled.[14] She inserted one arm at a time into her séance costume, held both arms over her head, and let the black frock drop over her naked body. Still standing, she pulled black knickers up her legs and over her rump. Next, she lowered her backside onto the chair and wiggled her right and then her left foot into her comfy black tennis shoes.[15] Once dressed, she shuffled out of the bedroom and into the séance parlor. There, without looking at her audience, she forced her trembling flesh past the small congregation and onto a makeshift stage.[16]

This simple stage—a pair of curtains hung from a ceiling and were pulled open with an armchair placed between them—was sacred space to believers in spirit communication. On this hallowed spot departed souls re-entered this world and spoke with grieving loved ones. Spiritualists called this informal arrangement a "Cabinet,"[17] and to Helen Duncan, who was claustrophobic and afraid of the dark, it felt literally like a cabinet, like a place where she'd be locked up and suffocated.[18]

By 1940, Helen Duncan was the most widely traveled and talked-about medium in Britain.[19] As the Nazi war machine threatened to invade by sea and pummel by air, Spiritualism, a religion devoted to communication with the dead, took root and flourished. Séance circles, an estimated 50,000 of them, sprang up all over the British Isles.[20] Nell's performances became so popular that she could hardly keep pace with demand.[21] But despite her success, Nell did not relish her work. Truth be known, she didn't have a taste for channeling the dead. But like it or not, Nell had come to believe that she bore a martyr's destiny, and she didn't let any amount of trepidation or any number of doubters stand in her way.[22]

Nell squeezed into the chair at center stage. The bottoms of her feet prickled and fear, like an electric current, crawled up her legs.

The audience prayed. "Our Father, who art in Heaven, hallowed be Thy name. Thy kingdom come, Thy will be done, on earth as it is in Heaven. . . ."[23]

Chest pounding, Nell fixed her eyes on the glowing ceiling lamp and thanked God it was still lit. Was she more afraid of failure and humiliation or darkness and isolation? There was no time for her to tease out the difference, not now, not in front of these sitters. The race was on. She had to force herself into a trance before they turned off that light, pulled the cabinet curtains shut, and trapped her in blackness. Ghosts lurked in the shadows ready to take control of her body.[24]

Nell searched the room for her husband. Henry stood at the back, next to the gramophone. He smiled sympathetically and set the music playing.[25] The sitters joined in:

*South of the border, down Mexico way,*
*That's where I fell in love, where stars above came out to play . . .* [26]

Nell held back a desire to scream. If they closed the curtain or turned off the light before she was ready, she'd rise up like a threatened grizzly, pull down the curtain, and shriek like a banshee. She'd done it before and she'd do it again.[27] Teetering on the edge of panic,[28] Nell latched on to Henry's eyes, and Henry kept his gaze steady as the gramophone played on:

*South of the border, I rode back one day.*
*There in a veil of white, by candlelight, she knelt to pray.*
*The mission bells told me, that I shouldn't stay,*
*South of the border, down Mexico way.*
*Ay, ay, ay, ay (Ay, ay, ay, ay)*
*Good bye, good bye.*[29]

Nell surrendered to Henry's spell.[30] Clinging to a belief that her husband loved her, Nell's spirit lifted, and she fell into a trance.[31]

An hour later, Nell suddenly awoke to find herself enclosed behind the curtain and trapped in the dark. Disoriented, she stumbled out of the cabinet and collapsed into a waiting chair. Her body quaked as it had in childbirth, and she moaned Henry's name.[32]

Henry knelt by her side and waved smelling salts under her nose.[33] Nell's head snapped back. She tried to focus on her husband's face and asked him, "Did Albert come?"

"Albert came," he assured her.

Encircled by sitters, Nell pleaded for approval. "Were you satisfied?"[34]

Mrs. Gray withheld her praise.[35] Others applauded: "Wonderful!" "Brilliant!" "Extraordinary!" Henry put a cigarette in her mouth,[36] and the séance hostess brought her tea. Sitting amid the chatter, Nell listened to the guests marvel.[37]

The metamorphosis of Mrs. Helen Duncan into her Spirit Guide, Albert Stewart, was viewed as one of the most extraordinary transformations in Spiritualism. While Mrs. Duncan, a Highland peasant, muttered in a Scottish brogue so thick that proper Englishmen could hardly decipher her meaning, Albert, a well-traveled gentleman of good breeding, spoke with a proper Oxford accent, 100 percent BBC. Her voice was a guttural baritone, gravelly from cigarette smoking, mill dust, and tuberculosis; Albert's voice was higher pitched, with an effeminate lilt. Mrs. Duncan, sullen and shy, hardly conversed; Albert, the life of the party, acted like a master of ceremonies to the nether world; he spouted wisdom, joked, offered hope, and ushered in a parade of spirit visitors.[38] At Albert's invitation, dead relatives and friends, speaking in different voices and diverse dialects, crossed over and reunited with sitters. In intimate conversations, the spirit visitors revealed personal details and delivered proof of eternal life.[39]

But, in the summer of 1940, after Britain's retreat from Dunkirk and France's surrender to the Nazis, even the most reverent of Albert's devotees found his prophecies preposterous. The German war machine had trampled every nation in northern Europe. Hitler was now free to subjugate Britain, an island nation without allies. Yet, contrary to common sense, Albert predicted that Germany would not invade. When Stalin and Hitler professed their undying loyalty to one another and signed a nonaggression pact, Albert had the audacity to suggest that the Soviets and the Brits would become allies. As military experts issued dark predictions of a quick Axis victory, Albert predicted a protracted conflict, lasting six years. And while Brits lamented America's resolve to stay out of this European conflict, Albert insisted that this war would encircle the globe, from the United States to Japan. Most cryptic of all, Albert prophesied that hostilities would end only after two big bangs. Of course, his audiences ridiculed these inconceivable forecasts.[40] Even Nell hoped Albert's predictions would prove false; she prayed that her two sons-in-law would return home safe and that her two sons would not be pulled into battle and sent overseas.[41]

As for this summer night, Nell's ordeal was over. On the other side of the séance room, the organizer placed a stack of bills in Henry's outstretched hand. He bowed, thanking her, and tucked the payment into his jacket pocket. Catching Nell's eye, he grinned approvingly.[42]

Mrs. Gray moved sulkily toward the door.

# 3

# The Psychic Investigator

I N THE SUMMER HEAT OF 1940, HARRY PRICE HAD TAKEN TO REMINISCING with a pen in one hand and a loaded Colt automatic at his elbow. These days his nostalgia and his weapon served divergent purposes: His memories provided ammunition for his next book, an autobiography titled *Search for Truth*; his revolver kept him alert to his present obligation to shoot any German paratroopers who descended on his village.[1] Price committed himself with unbridled enthusiasm to the first task and with guarded reluctance to the second. He thoroughly enjoyed perpetrating an embellished version of his life story,[2] while he found the thought of killing Arian lads distasteful.[3]

Price liked Germany. The University of Bonn had honored him, and Adolf Hitler had entertained him for a day. In truth, he hadn't actually met Herr Hitler, but the Fuehrer had arranged for Price to be wined and dined in style.[4] If the nations were not at war, Price would have still preferred the company of Nazi psychic investigators to English Spiritualists.[5] Given a choice, he'd sooner topple the likes of Helen Duncan than the Third Reich.[6]

The mailman dropped a stack of letters on Price's doorstep, each one addressed to The Honorable President of the National Laboratory of Psychical Research. He inspected an envelope with a Portsmouth return address.[7] He did not know the sender, but he often received fan mail,[8] especially from ladies.[9]

Harry Price possessed undeniable charisma. The stark baldness of his perfectly oval head accentuated the cool strength of his features: a jaw set with determination, a straight, prominent nose, and large, penetrating eyes. Price wore tailored suits, cashmere overcoats, silk ties, and hats from London's finest haberdasheries.[10]

Picking up an exquisitely sharpened scalpel, he slashed open the envelope, and a venomous note from Mrs. Marion Gray spilled out.

"A coarse and immensely fat woman, naked, was sitting on a chair smoking a fag. The very sight of her revolted me. She fixed me with a persistent stare—muttering all the while, 'Oh, what shall I do if Albert does not come tonight?'"[11]

His lip curled at this bittersweet reminder, and he read on. "Don't you think something should be done to stop these harpies from battening on the misery of others?"[12]

Absentmindedly filling his Sherlock Holmes–style pipe with tobacco,[13] he churned up vivid recollections.

Nearly ten years ago, in the early 1930s, Price had been obsessed with Mrs. Victoria Helen Duncan.[14] He'd first seen her at 16 Queensbury Street, a pristine white-columned Edwardian owned by the London Spiritualist Alliance, the nation's premier paranormal society.[15] At the time, Price's laboratory occupied the top floor of that building, but dealings with his landlords had soured.[16] One memorable day, as he crept up the staircase, the doorbell rang. Turning, he saw Mrs. Duncan, the toast of the Spiritualist elite, walk into the foyer.[17] She'd camouflaged her girth and her lowly pedigree with well-chosen accessories: a little fox stole and fashionable felt hat. Her husband, a man whose horse-like head seemed too large for his skinny frame, stood by her side.[18]

Miss Mercy Phillimore, the grande dame of Spiritualism, welcomed Mr. and Mrs. Duncan. With her usual haughty reserve, Miss Mercy led the couple along the entry hall.[19] As Mrs. Duncan followed, she looked up, noticed Price, tugged at her husband's sleeve, and with a suspicious upward glance, directed his attention to the stairwell.

Noticing the gesture, Miss Mercy explained frigidly, "That's Mr. Harry Price."[20]

Obviously impressed, Mr. Duncan blurted out, "Really. Harry Price himself? The Director of the National Laboratory of Psychical Research?"[21]

Pleased by Mr. Duncan's response, Price touched the brim of his fedora.

Mercy Phillimore glared up at Price and grumbled loudly. "That man is becoming quite famous at our expense, but that arrangement will end soon enough."[22]

In an obvious huff, Miss Mercy took Mrs. Duncan's hand and briskly pulled her toward the séance parlor. Price peered intently after the medium. He coveted Mr. Duncan's wife, though not in the usual sense. His interest was purely scientific: Price wanted to sweep Mrs. Duncan off her feet and drag her roly-poly body up to his laboratory.

Mr. Duncan lagged behind the two women, staring beseechingly up at Price.

Price, always ready to capitalize on his magnetism, smiled invitingly. Then, just as Mr. Duncan began to mount the stairs, Dr. Robert Fielding-Ould, President of the London Spiritualist Alliance, rushed in to rescue the mesmerized husband.[23]

As Dr. Fielding-Ould guided Mr. Duncan away, Price was peeved at his missed opportunity. Everyone who was anyone wanted to observe Mrs. Duncan's phenomenal powers. She, like no other medium, could attract the proper strata of society and elevate Price to scientific supremacy. With Mrs. Duncan at his side, Mr. Harry Price would stand alone as Britain's preeminent psychic investigator. Mrs. Duncan was ripe for milking, and Harry Price did not intend to allow the Spiritualists to suck her dry before he got a go at the bovine darling.[24]

Of course, Price was willing to share, and earlier, the Spiritualists would have granted his every desire. A fickle lot, they had once showered as much adoration on him as they bestowed on Mrs. Duncan. These same Spiritualists had lured him to their premises with offers of ample laboratory space and unfettered access to psychic phenomena. Price had moved into their attic, bringing his library, his equipment, and his passion for objective verification of the supernatural. In return, they had showed him off like a debutant, inviting him to their séances and parading him before the crème de la crème of society.

All had gone swimmingly, until Price asserted his independence. He'd mentioned to Sir Arthur Conan Doyle (and, of course, to the *Sunday Chronicle*) that "the history of Spiritualism was one long trail of fraud, folly and credulity." And with that one observation, Conan Doyle and his Spiritualist family had turned on Price, treating him like a parasite that had wormed his way into their household. Doyle, the great and gullible, the fatherly idealist and the famed creator of Sherlock Holmes, had thrown Price out of his heart and recommended Price's eviction from 16 Queensbury.[25]

Then, in a twist of fate that Price found fiercely pleasurable, his lease had outlived Sir Arthur Conan Doyle.[26] He had read the obituaries for Britain's premier mystery writer while lounging in a leather chair at 16 Queensbury Street. As *The People Below* (a term Price coined to capture his disdain for the Spiritualists[27]) had grieved, Price continued to nest above them, chuckling, "He who laughs last."[28]

As Doyle had lain silent in his crypt, the Spiritualists had moved on to plan this night's event: Mrs. Duncan's gala debut. From Price's roost on the stairwell, he watched the arrival of men in dinner jackets and women in cocktail gowns. The guest list read like a *Who's Who* of the society pages: Sir Oliver Lodge, Madame Destrees, Major and Mrs. J. S. Swayne, Lady Harris and her daughter, Lady Culme Seymour, the Honorable Mrs. Wild, Susan, Countess of Malmesbury, the Countess Ahlefeldt Lauring, Major Stewart, the Countess de Lavradio, Lady Doreen Knatchbull, Dr. E. S. Reid, the Honorable Mrs. Cooper, Baron von Pohl, and Brigadier Roy Firebrace. Mr. Harry Price, Honorable President of the National Laboratory of Psychical Research, had been told that his presence was not required.[29]

Nursing his bruised ego, Price watched Mrs. Duncan and saw her look back and give an unexpectedly subservient glance toward her husband. Mr. Duncan, impressed by his own newly acquired social status and oblivious to his wife's insecurity, wandered off with Dr. Fielding-Ould, the reigning president of the spook worshippers. In that instant, Price divined a useful truth: Mrs. Duncan had a vulnerable underbelly—she trusted her husband.[30]

Impressed by his powers of observation and deduction, Price continued his walk up the stairs of 16 Queensbury. He opened the door to his attic quarters. His equipment was boxed, and his books bound with rope. Hearing spontaneous gasps, cheers, and applause emanating from Mrs. Duncan's exclusive séance,[31] he relished his impending move to a proper and independent facility—his own National Laboratory of Psychic Research on Roland Gardens, just a block south of Queensbury Street. It would soon prove far enough for independence and close enough for clandestine contact with the talented Mrs. Duncan and her sycophantic husband.[32]

But all that was ten years ago; today, in the midsummer of 1940, Harry Price pursued more lucrative avenues. His campaign to debunk Mrs. Duncan had taught him a valuable lesson: The public prefers belief to disbelief. He no longer wasted his energy trying to free believers of their delusions. These days, he made certain his investigations confirmed the supernatural: a glittering coach and stallions, headless apparitions, ladies in white, ominous footsteps, and shrieks in the night. He didn't exactly forge his results; he merely paid "independent" investigators for their observations, focused on paranormal evidence, and avoided mundane explanations.[33] This enlightened approach reaped a handsome payoff. His most recent book *The Most Haunted House in Britain* was a runaway best-seller.[34]

The war proved to be particularly good for the poltergeist business. With *Blitzkrieg* knocking at the door and the grim reaper shadowing the populace, Brits had gone batty, flying helter-skelter from séance to séance, eager to snatch a peek at eternal life before eternal life snatched them. One in four British citizens professed belief in paranormal phenomena.[35] Even top military brass and members of the War Cabinet consorted with ghosts.[36] Harry Price congratulated himself on exploiting this burgeoning fascination to maximum benefit.

Picking up the envelope containing Mrs. Gray's complaint, Price walked to his file cabinet and placed the note in a tattered folder marked: DUNCAN, Helen. Though he maintained a personal distaste for Mrs. Duncan, he wasn't about to get ensnared in a rat's nest with dubious rewards. For him to revisit the Duncan fiasco would require an entreaty from someone of more consequence than one dissatisfied old lady. Harry Price finally understood: Power begets power.[37]

# 4

# The Chief Constable

ON AUGUST 13, 1940, CHIEF CONSTABLE ARTHUR CHARLES WEST
walked through the early mist across Portsmouth Town Square.
On that summer morning, Arthur West had no inkling that a Scottish
medium named Helen Duncan posed a danger to his city. West focused
on the obvious threat: Across the English Channel, just twenty-two miles
away, German soldiers swaggered through the towns and villages of
northern France. The Nazi swastika flew over every country in continental Europe; only Britain, a nation without allies, stood in the way of Hitler's perverse ambition. Portsmouth, the premier naval port of the British
Empire, braced for *Blitzkrieg*.

West looked up at Guildhall; above its marble stairs and columns,
through the haze, he could make out its dome. The fog would burn off today.[1] West turned, took the stairs to the basement, and entered Police
Headquarters. As he walked down the long hall toward his office, on-duty
officers, alert and busy, greeted him with informal salutes and "Morning,
Chief." This underground station, below Lord Mayor Denis Daley's office
and the offices of town government, was action-central. Twenty-four
hours a day, seven days a week, West's men monitored the pulse of Portsmouth.[2] *His* city, *his* duty, *his* men, and *his* rank: It was all so new. Arthur
West had taken the helm of law enforcement at His Majesty's premiere
naval port just thirteen days earlier.[3]

Some said Arthur was too young for the job, but competence had taken precedence over seniority. Portsmouth could not abide an Agatha Christie stereotype—an aging, blundering bobby—in the role of Chief Constable. With Hitler's spies lurking in alleyways and *Blitzkrieg* about to be unleashed, the city required a chief of police adept at moving among top military brass, jurists, and politicians and skilled at demanding the most of his men while giving the utmost to the citizenry. Arthur West might have been young, but he was just such a man. When he had joined the Portsmouth constabulary at twenty-two, the men on the force told him, "Expect one rank per decade; that's the rule."[4] Arthur had broken that rule: Sergeant at twenty-seven, Inspector at thirty-one, Superintendent at thirty-seven, and Chief Constable at forty-one. West had worked his way up the ladder at double speed—four promotions in nineteen years. One rank every five years—that was Arthur's rule.[5]

By afternoon, the fog had indeed burnt off.[6] On this pristine day, Chief Constable Arthur Charles West set out to tour his territory. With long strides and a regal demeanor, West approached a waiting police cruiser, a fantastic specimen of a vehicle: sleek, glossy black with chrome shined to a mirror, humped back wheels, and bulging headlights. One of his men, uniformed in polished buttons and a visor hat, swung the passenger door open.[7] Bestowing a friendly nod toward the officer, West put one foot on the running board and stepped inside.

As his man drove, West took in the scenes that passed by his window. His city and the military meshed. Civilians and sailors scurried back and forth between the Navy's installations and Portsmouth's neighborhoods. Men in uniform strolled the streets; men in overalls worked on the docks. Everywhere preparations for the Nazi onslaught were afoot. In backyards, men dug trench shelters (holes reinforced with concrete and covered with sod) and constructed Anderson shelters (caves made of bent corrugated metal). Most importantly, the dirigibles were in place; gigantic hydrogen balloons, like shining gray whales the size of a tenement block, floated above the city, masking strategic assets. All over town, sandbags blocked entrances to public buildings. Along the rail tracks near Farlington, coffins and shovels waited for emergency burials.[8]

On the outskirts of town, England's beloved countryside had turned ugly. Large-scale rubbish, junked cars, buses, carts, and bedsteads littered every meadow, hillside, and golf course. Not a scrap of open space remained for German transport planes to land and let loose hundreds of marauding Nazi infantrymen.[9] Chief Constable West ordered his driver to head toward Portsmouth's coast.

Along the waterfront, the boardwalk waited for battle. The arcades and cotton-candy stands that lined the shore were now boarded up, and waves licked coils of barbed wire. On beaches, where children had built sand castles, masons now laid concrete barriers. Where mothers and fathers had watched boys and girls frolic, guard towers, like skeletons of steel, watched over the sea. In the harbor, battleships cast shadows on still water. The town must have looked as crisp as a reconnaissance photograph.[10] Arthur West saw it all. Sometimes a sunny day is a curse.

At 4:20 PM, the sirens blared. West sprinted to his cruiser and ordered his driver to floor it. Careening from one location to the next, the Chief Constable supervised the emergency response.[11] As instructed, civilians—mothers, children, and the elderly—scurried into underground trench shelters or packed into the metal Anderson shelters.[12] The military activated its well-practiced routine. Double-decker buses screeched to a halt in front of the naval barracks and armed sailors rushed on board. The buses dashed at breakneck speed to Southsea.[13] The young recruits jumped behind sandbag embankments. All artillery pointed skyward.

On the easterly horizon, a hundred Nazi bombers, perhaps more, appeared, flying high, too high. No weapon on earth could reach planes at that altitude. There was nothing to do but watch. The *Luftwaffe* spared the naval installations, headed straight for the city of Portsmouth, and dropped its payload on shops and houses. Explosions shook the ground and set the city on fire. Most horrifically, the bomb shelters failed: Trench shelters collapsed on women, children, and the elderly; Anderson metal shelters blew apart.

At 4:25, the German bombers turned and flew back to the continent. The attack lasted five minutes. Hitler had ordered *Adler Tag,* Eagle Day; the Battle of Britain began with an attack on Portsmouth.

In the days that followed, the smoke died down and the wreckage cooled. Chief Constable West walked the streets of Portsmouth, assessing the damage and offering sympathy. Like mourners looking for keepsakes, citizens picked through piles of rubble. A young mother, her hair neatly curled in a pageboy, an old grandmother, wearing her Sunday best hat, an elderly gentleman, dressed in his most respectable suit: all of them made pilgrimages. The rooms where these good people had cooked and slept and made love and given birth and taken their daily tea, lay in ruins at their feet. They stepped carefully over piles of bricks, beams, and doors, looking down, searching for blankets, clothes, a pot, an unsoiled canister of tea, a salvable bicycle, a child's favorite doll, a hairbrush. They wrapped any surviving personal possessions in bundles and carried them like precious babies back to the rest houses. These law-abiding citizens of Portsmouth, the Chief Constable's neighbors, retreated to the emergency shelters they now shared with other homeless residents.[14]

Day after day, week after week, month after month, sirens sounded. The German war machine filled the skies over southern England with bombers and turned the earth below into an inferno. In Portsmouth, Southampton, Brighton, Dover, Coventry, South Wales, and London—especially in London—civilians died by the thousands. In September 1940, 6,954 people died.[15] In October, 6,350 died.[16] In November, 4,588 died.[17] In December, another 3,793 died.[18] Between summer and Christmas of 1940, the *Luftwaffe's* merciless bombardment killed 21,685 civilians—mostly the old and the young, mostly women and children. The southeast quadrant of England earned a new name: Hellfire Corner.[19]

The Blitz had a way of leveling people; it humbled the upper classes and elevated the lowly born, especially if the working blokes happened to be extremely competent. When the King, or the Queen or Winston Churchill came to Portsmouth, Chief Constable Arthur Charles West escorted them around the rubble. In no time, the Chief Constable and the Lord Mayor Sir Denis Daley became great friends.[20]

As he did quite often, Arthur West climbed the marble staircase of Guildhall and knocked on the Lord Mayor's parlor door.[21] Sir Denis, a tall, balding gentleman with a small surprisingly impish face,[22] peeked up from behind his newspaper, studied the Chief Constable, and asked, "Arthur, did anyone ever tell you? You look just like King Edward—so handsome, so debonair. . . ."[23]

"So Arian," West interrupted. "Not exactly a compliment, Denis. The man abdicated the throne for a love affair with a divorced American."

"Just your looks, Arthur. I wasn't speaking of character. You're not the type to cede power, not one ounce of it."[24] As West settled into an armchair, Sir Denis changed the subject. "What do you think of the news?"

"Tighter security regulations, the Treachery Act, the Official Secrets Act—I'm just starting to get the power I need," West gloated. "With that old mule Churchill back in the saddle, Parliament is finally getting some proper work done."[25]

"No, no," chided Sir Denis, "I was thinking of the big news. Look here in the *Daily Sketch*."

West moved to look at the mayor's newspaper. Sir Denis pointed to a story captioned, "Spies Attend Séances."[26]

West read the article, concentrating on every detail.

Sir Denis chuckled, "Heaven's Light Our Guide—isn't that the Portsmouth constabulary's motto?[27] Maybe you should trot off to a séance and open yourself to the guidance of the Spirit World? How about it? You could kill two birds with one stone: interrogate the gossiping ghosts while enriching your spiritual life? See if any officials secrets are being let loose before their time. I hear there's a Spiritual Church on Copnor Road, the Master Temple."[28]

"Not funny," scowled the Chief Constable. He had no problem with his constabulary's motto. In fact, he was wholeheartedly behind it. West believed, without doubt, that police work, *his* work, was blessed by and guided by Heaven. *By Heaven*, not by loud-mouthed ghost conjurers with ungodly access to classified information. Arthur West was no Spiritualist.[29]

"Arthur, if you say 'Not funny,' then it's not funny," conceded the mayor. Even Sir Denis Daley knew that Chief Constable Arthur Charles West, with his ties growing to Navy Command and Military Intelligence, was on the verge of becoming the *real* authority in wartime Portsmouth.[30]

On the night of January 10, 1941, five months after Hitler's first air attack on Portsmouth, Chief Constable West left his basement office in Guildhall. Detective Sergeant Fred Ford, one of Portsmouth's more awkward plainclothes sleuths, tipped his trilby hat and said, "Have a peaceful evening, Chief. All's quiet. They're saying it's a winter lull in the Blitz; hasn't been an air raid since Christmas Eve."

West noticed Sergeant Ford's bushy mustache give a twitch. Did he intimidate Fred, or was Fred Ford just a nervous sort of bloke?[31] The Chief Constable kept that question to himself. He asked, "Do you really think Portsmouth has fallen off the Fuehrer's radar screen, Fred?"[32]

Sergeant Ford made no reply.

Weary, but refusing to show any sign of weakness, West straightened his back and walked briskly up the stairs and into Town Square. It was already dark, completely dark. At night, any light seen from above, any sign of life, became a target for the *Luftwaffe*. The bulbs had been taken out of every street lamp. Every window in Portsmouth was painted black or hung with black curtains to prevent even a flicker from escaping. Even the headlights on West's police cruiser were covered with black canvas.[33] He drove slowly through the streets and looked forward to a quiet evening with his motherly wife, Ida.[34]

The Chief Constable arrived home just in time to wish his teenage son, Michael,[35] pleasant dreams. Arthur collapsed in a chair and Ida brought him tea. The couple chatted in their darkened cave. As Arthur stirred sugar into his cup, the sirens blared. "It's probably a false alarm," he grumbled.

Ida smiled, in her comforting way, and agreed, "Probably."

West looked toward the front door.

Ida said, "Go, Arthur. You know you won't sleep. And there's not one thing you can do to protect me or Michael."

West kissed her and left.

Within minutes, street corners all over Portsmouth exploded. A molten glow filled the night sky.[36] With this too-familiar eerie radiance lighting the streets, West sped, full throttle, through tidal waves of flame, back to Police Headquarters.

Swerving into Town Square, he saw Guildhall erupt. The right wing blew sky high and burnt like a gargantuan torch. The ground quaked, and his men rushed up from the basement into the square.

That night 140 tons of high explosives, 50,000 firebombs, rained down on Portsmouth. In the cruelest strike of all, the principal water main ruptured. With no water to dowse the fires, West and his men stood by helplessly. The insides of Guildhall, Police Headquarters included, turned to charcoal.[37]

# 5

# In Morning Light

O N THE MORNING OF MAY 24, 1941, NELL LAY IN BED, EYES STILL
closed. An eerie premonition floated through the fog of her half-
sleep: some calamity in the north.[1] Then a sudden jab at her cheek
shocked her into consciousness. Nell opened her eyes and saw Dawn,
her pint-sized granddaughter, staring over the edge of the bed. And for a
moment, Nell thought Dawn's face explained her foreboding. A terrible
tragedy *had* happened in the north; Dawn's daddy, a gunner with the
Royal Air Force had died—shot out of the sky—and was buried in Norway. Now Dawn's mother, Lilian, stricken with grief and suffering from
tuberculosis, was quarantined in a sanatorium. Dawn and her newborn
sister, Joan, lived with their Grandma Nell, Grandpa Henry, aunts, and
uncles.[2]

Nell asked her granddaughter, "Do you want your granny to make you
special mealy pudding for breakfast?"[3]

Dawn broke into a grin, but that grin didn't erase Nell's apprehension.
Even in the kitchen, as Nell wrapped herself in an apron and dropped a
chunk of bacon fat into boiling water,[4] a feeling of catastrophe clung to
her. Then infant Joan wailed for her bottle. Auntie Gena—Nell's
youngest—rushed to pick up the baby. Auntie Nan—Nell's second
child—scurried in to warm the bottle. Grandpa Henry stumbled in asking for a morning cup of tea. Uncle Harry and Uncle Peter—Nell's two

sons—pulled up to the table and announced, "We're starving." As the cottage filled with activity, the sense of doom slipped out of Nell's mind.

Sometimes even Nell had trouble keeping track of her own children. Little Dawn must have been terribly confused by all these Duncans— Grandma and Grandpa, two aunts and two uncles. Only Dawn's hospitalized mother, Lilian, and Nell's oldest daughter, Bella, weren't crammed into the bungalow.[5]

Bella turned out to be one of the lucky ones. A year ago, her husband had been reported missing in the evacuation of Dunkirk. Then, it turned out that an English fisherman had pulled him out of the ocean and tossed him onto a pile of soldiers, all of them gasping for breath like Dover sole. The trawler dumped him off in the seaside village of Folkestone. Since their happy reunion, Bella's family lived on their own.[6] Even without Bella and Lilian, Nell had seven mouths clamoring to be fed.

By midmorning, Nell escaped the din and headed for work in the cobblestone section of Edinburgh. She knocked on the downstairs delivery door of Mrs. Waymark's fine home. All mediums, at least all lower-class mediums, came and left séances through service entrances.[7]

A servant swung wide the unpolished door, and Nell wedged herself through its opening. Once inside, she hung her coat on a downstairs hook. Gripping the handrail, she forced herself up one step at a time to Mrs. Waymark's living quarters.

Cowering like a lowly wallflower at the back of the foyer,[8] Nell watched other guests arrive through Mrs. Waymark's freshly scrubbed front door and recognized Brigadier Roy Firebrace from her days in London. Even in his civilian suit and tie, the Brigadier looked like military. Tall and broad, he carried himself ramrod straight and moved in the most elite psychic circles.[9] But Firebrace, unlike many of his class, did not hold himself aloof. He was notoriously genial, kind, and fun loving.[10] As soon as he caught sight of Nell, he walked right over and greeted her. "Mrs. Duncan, after all these years, I'm terribly glad to see you. I expect great things from this séance."

The Brigadier took Nell by the arm and escorted her into Mrs. Waymark's parlor.[11] There Nell took her place at the mouth of the séance circle.

With no Cabinet to frighten her,[12] light streaming through the windows, and the sweet hymns of the sitters lulling her, Nell slipped into a trance as guileless as a babe in a cradle.

An hour later, when Nell's body gave a shiver and she returned from her altered state, Firebrace's behavior had changed. Avoiding Nell, the Brigadier thanked Mrs. Waymark for hosting a fine display of clairvoyance, backed out the front entrance, closed the door firmly, and scurried off as though on some pressing mission.[13]

# 6

## A Breach of Intelligence

CHIEF CONSTABLE ARTHUR WEST TAPPED HIS FINGERS ON THE POLISHED surface of his mahogany desk. On this day in December of 1941, West anxiously awaited the arrival of a gentleman from Military Intelligence, Division 5.[1] A secret of vital strategic importance had escaped.[2]

West swiveled in his chair, gazed out the windowed alcove of his office, and surveyed the view. The dormant lotus pond, the gracefully arched limbs of the fig tree, the sleeping flower beds, the well-tended tennis court, the winter ivy crawling over the brick walls,[3] this scene settled his nerves. Hearing the bustle outside his door—his secretary tapping away on her typewriter, his detectives trooping up the marble stairs and calling out their boisterous greetings—the Chief Constable mused at the incongruity: The most opulent estate in Portsmouth was now Police Headquarters.[4]

This mansion in Tudor style—brick with stucco gables and decorative beams—proved that the late Victorians had an insatiable appetite for beer. Mr. Brickwoods's Brewery had made a fortune, and Mr. Brickwoods had poured his wealth into building this architectural showpiece.[5] Every ornate detail, inside and out, begged to be admired. The entry floor—a mosaic of white, gray, and charcoal marble—spelled out the name Brickwoods, in decorative script. Every spindle, every banister, every doorway, every window frame was fashioned from hardwoods and intricately carved. At the center of this magnificent home stood the ballroom: at one end of it, a mammoth mahogany and green marble hearth worthy of a king's castle; at the other, a wall of intricately cut beveled glass fashioned into leaded windows; above, a balcony of graceful arches, white newels, and pillars with light streaming through yet another wall of windows; and the ceiling, squares of skylights, each held in place by wide moldings painted the color of cream.[6]

The original Brickwoods tycoon relished Byculla House, but his descendants had abandoned it. Byculla's last residents had been a bevy of debutantes. During that era, the ballroom had been put to its intended use. Then the Blitz pummeled Portsmouth. The proper young ladies evacuated their sumptuous abode and were, presumably, safely ensconced in a country manor.[7]

Byculla House had been bequeathed to the common good. When the *Luftwaffe* firebombed Guildhall, leaving the Portsmouth constabulary without a home base, Chief Constable West laid claim to it and transformed it into his headquarters.[8]

By some ironic twist of fate, the spirit of Brickwoods Brewery had been revived. The ballroom had turned out to be a great place to party. Arthur Charles West loved nothing better than playing host to a good-humored gathering of police officers and navy men. On many an otherwise dismal night, the finest and bravest lifted their flasks, offering raucous toasts and singing round after round of Cardinal Huff. These revelries did more than blow off steam; they cemented the comradery and the cooperation between law enforcement and the military. And of course, the beer flowed freely.[9]

The Chief Constable did not, however, expect his awaited visitor from Military Intelligence to be the type of bloke to grab a pint and let his hair down. Most Regional Security Liaison Officers (RSLOs) considered themselves to be incorruptible leaders of His Majesty's Empire. Born into the aristocracy and bred to display impeccable table manners and a polite disdain for the lower classes, these men of discretion were well versed at making inane chitchat.[10]

These days, come hell or high water, an RSLO dropped by Byculla House for a regular feast of inconsequential tittle-tattle.[11] Most weeks

West endured the hour, all the while wondering when the War Cabinet would defrock these tweedy fellows and elevate real detectives—plain-clothes sleuths capable of digging solid information out of the gutter—to positions of power.[12]

Yet, despite his general opinion of the genteel shortcomings of Military Intelligence officers, West had a way of getting them to eat out of his hand. Donning a stately manner and speaking in the most impeccable English accent, the Chief Constable told them what they wanted to hear, won their trust, and learned what he wanted to know.[13]

Finally, the gentleman from MI5 arrived. West's secretary ushered him into the Chief Constable's spacious office, left, and closed the door tightly behind her. The RSLO took a chair across from West.

Today West did not have his usual patience for pandering; he got straight to the point.

"There's been a potentially dangerous breach of intelligence—a blatant violation of the Official Secrets Act. The Germans haven't even guessed this one.[14] This rumor flared up and spread like wildfire."

West stood, moved toward his MI5 guest, leaned against his desk, and continued.

"Here's what I know. On November 25, three British battleships—HMS *Queen Elizabeth, Valiant,* and *Barham*—along with eight destroyers, were scouring the Mediterranean looking for a Nazi convoy. A German submarine crept up and torpedoed the *Barham.* Then the Nazi U-boat hightailed it off the scene. Four minutes later, the *Barham's* aft magazine exploded, sending her to hell and gone; 395 managed to survive but 861 of our boys died."[15]

West's words trailed off as he imagined the horror: the blast, the tornado of black smoke, the men swallowed by churning tidal waves.

"But," the Chief Constable refocused, "there is one scrap of good news, very good news: The German High Command doesn't know. Apparently, the U-boat captain made a vague assessment of minimal damage. Hitler believes our Mediterranean fleet is still at full strength; that's a real tactical advantage. This secret is so crucial that the Admiralty has gone to great lengths to disguise the *Barham's* demise. Christmas cards, signed, sealed, and postmarked from the deceased crew, have been sent out. Even relatives of dead sailors have received forged holiday greetings."[16]

The RSLO asked with noticeable suspicion and perhaps a touch of envy, "How did you come by this information?"

"The *Barham* was a Portsmouth ship. Let's just say I have connections," the Chief Constable said cryptically. Then he admitted, "But even with my sources, I might not have learned about the *Barham*. The story leaked."[17]

The RSLO arched his back and listened more intently. West continued.

"After the *Barham* blew up, this Scots medium gave a séance at a Spiritualist church on Copnor Road. Rumor has it that a ghost-like creature appeared, wearing a sailor's cap that read HMS *Barham*. The apparition hovered around a young woman and said, 'Sorry Sweetheart, my ship sank in the Mediterranean. I've crossed over to the Other Side.'

"Turns out the poor girl had a husband serving on the *Barham*. Next day, she called the Admiralty and asked if the *Barham* had gone down.

"The widow had hardly put the phone down before two Admiralty officials showed up on her doorstep. They gave her a pep talk, told her not to believe in ghosts, discouraged her from jumping to conclusions, and assured her that if anything were wrong she'd be notified through proper channels.[18] But it was too late to plug up the leak; this town was already awash in speculation."[19]

West paused and directed his power of interrogation at the RSLO. "What do you know about Helen Duncan?"

"Is she from Edinburgh?" the RSLO queried.

"Yes, this woman treks between Edinburgh and Portsmouth on a regular basis," confirmed West.

"From one strategic location to another,"[20] observed the RSLO.

Idling, hand over his lips, the RSLO eyed Arthur West. "Let me think," he began hesitantly. "Arthur, you'll need to be patient while I sort this out. There's a Military Intelligence officer in Scotland: Brigadier Roy Firebrace. Actually he's not just any MI5 operative; he's Chief of Military Intelligence for Scotland. He used to be Military Attaché to the Soviets. In any case, he's fluent in French, Russian, German, and Hindustani,[21] a large gentleman of large ambition with a flair for the clandestine.[22]

"This Brigadier Firebrace works out of Edinburgh," said the RSLO with a bemused snort. "There's always some unspeakable intrigue afoot around Edinburgh. Remember when that German spy 'Werner Walti' was nabbed carrying a suitcase transmitter at Waverly Station?[23] And last spring, when Deputy Fuehrer Rudolf Hess parachuted down on Scotland, claiming to be under orders from Hitler's astrologers?[24] That's Scotland for you, a rat's nest of never-ending rumors: Nazi spies dressed up like nuns, toting top-secret ray guns concealed beneath their habits;[25] German agents attending séances intent on eliciting classified secrets from the dead.[26] And there was . . . "

West interrupted, with a more realistic assessment of the subject at hand. "Edinburgh is a vital port close to Nazi-occupied Norway."[27]

"That, too," the RSLO agreed. "As I was saying, Brigadier Firebrace is trusted by internal security's top brass. But, truth be known, Firebrace is rather an odd duck, fits right into the Edinburgh scene. He's deeply devoted to paranormal research. Objective analysis of psychical phenomena. He claims he's tested the veracity of spirit communication and swears he's spoken with the dead—Sir Arthur Conan Doyle and Sir Lawrence of Arabia among others.[28]

"This Brigadier happens to have considerable respect for Mrs. Duncan's mystical powers. Last spring, he attended one of her séances. And here's the clincher: The Spirit Control, Albert, apparently a rather haughty bastard, announced, 'A great British battleship has just sunk.'[29]

"Hearing Albert's news bulletin, Firebrace could hardly contain his anxiety; that month Churchill had issued the order to keep secret all losses at sea.[30] The Brigadier managed a polite escape, dashed out of the séance, ran to his office, grabbed his secure phone, and dialed the Admiralty.

"An Admiralty officer answered, and Firebrace asked, 'Have any of our battleships gone down this morning?'

"The officer assured Firebrace that nothing was amiss. Relieved, the Brigadier put down the telephone and went about his Saturday business."[31]

The RSLO's eyes narrowed, and he asked a rhetorical question: "Do you know what day that was? It was May 24, 1941."

With that final piece of information, the point of the story struck West like a slap across the face. May 24, 1941, was the date of the World War II's most infamous naval battle.[32]

While the Admiralty officer had been reassuring Brigadier Firebrace that all was well, off the coast of Iceland, amid blazing wreckage, three British sailors straddled life rafts and paddled through oil four inches deep. Just hours earlier, those three had been proud crewmen on the *Mighty Hood*—the preeminent symbol of British naval supremacy. The night before, under the dense fog of the North Sea, the HMS *Hood* had been stalking Hitler's spanking-new technological marvel, the battleship *Bismarck*. As the sun climbed higher, the haze lifted, and the *Hood* had found its prey. The *Mighty Hood* had let fly the first salvo but had missed its mark. The *Bismarck* had retaliated with a fatal blow. The *Hood* had erupted like a seagoing volcano, sending a geyser-like flame heavenward and spewing its shattered remains over the ocean. Only three British sailors had survived; 1,419 others had perished.[33]

While the three survivors of the *Hood*—caked in grime and fighting hypothermia—waited to be rescued,[34] in Edinburgh Brigadier Firebrace drank tea and munched on cream cheese sandwiches. No one, not even the Admiralty, had any idea of what had happened that day.[35]

The RSLO continued with his story, while the Chief Constable listened carefully.

"Later that afternoon, Firebrace's phone rang. Not the house phone, but the scrambler phone. He bolted at the sound of his secure line, rushed to his study, slammed the door, and picked up the receiver.

"A frantic Admiralty officer informed him that the *Hood*—the greatest of battleships—had gone down. Then, in sterner tones, the officer asked, 'Who told you? How on God's good earth did anyone know?'

"Brigadier Firebrace answered, 'Helen Duncan.'"[36]

The RSLO filled the Chief Constable in on follow-up details. The Admiralty officer had jotted down Helen Duncan's name and opened a fresh Military Intelligence file. By now, Scotland Yard had also taken an interest in Mrs. Duncan. Detective Superintendent Percy Worth, or maybe just one of his detectives, had gotten in touch with Brigadier Firebrace. The

Met had wanted Firebrace's advice on how to keep Mrs. Duncan quiet.[37] Firebrace had offered his opinion: "Mrs. Duncan is a splendid medium, splendid but dangerous."[38]

With nothing more to tell, the RSLO assured the Chief Constable that the Military Intelligence officer in charge of investigating rumors would learn about Mrs. Duncan's latest violation of national security.

Once alone in his office, Chief Constable West considered the situation. Not only had Helen Duncan disclosed the demise of the *Barham*, but she'd foretold the sinking of the *Hood*. Who knew what other strategic secrets this woman might reveal? Already she'd trampled security laws and trespassed on West's territory. If he could have it his way, he'd toss this spook conjurer and her loud-mouthed Spirit Guide in a dungeon and keep the ethereal duo in solitary confinement. But his hands were tied. If he arrested Helen Duncan, it would fuel speculation that the *Barham* had indeed sunk.[39] Plus, he might alienate the Spiritualists in high places; that would be politically unwise. Spiritualism was now an official religion of His Majesty's Navy.[40] Three members of the War Cabinet reportedly trotted off to séances.[41] And to make matters more complicated, West had recently received an order from the Home Office: Mediums were not to be arrested unless citizens complained of fraud.[42]

The Chief Constable had no option but to wait; he hated waiting. But in good time, when the moment was right, Arthur Charles West fully intended to show Mrs. Helen Duncan how he channeled *his* power.[43]

# 7

## Changing Fortunes

Nell's luggage waited by the front door. Any minute, she'd leave her cozy cottage and step into the icy winter winds. The south side of Edinburgh had a way of catching more than its share of bluster, and January of 1944 was no exception.[1]

Nell's little granddaughters, Lilian's girls, Dawn and Joan, now five and three years old, peered out the living room window straining to see a black cab come through the sleet.

In the background, Nell heard Gena, her youngest and still adolescent daughter, pleading with Henry, "Daddy, please don't let Mum go. Please. Something bad will happen." Gena fancied herself a psychic, like her mum.[2] Her siblings thought she was loony, a bit of a crackpot.

Lilian, her voice fully restored from her bout with tuberculosis, shouted, "Shut up, Gena."

Ever since Gena had predicted that Lilian's marriage to Angus Douglas wouldn't last long, Lilian didn't have much patience for her snippy little sister's premonitions. When Angus died, an early casualty of the air war over Norway, Lilian's impatience turned to anger.[3]

Henry waited at the table, and Nan quietly fixed his tea. With Henry often sick,[4] it was a blessing that Nan's husband was still stationed in London; Nell couldn't imagine how Henry would get along without his saintly daughter doting on him.

Little Dawn and toddler Joan, still on the lookout for Nell's cab, squealed, "Is coming! Is coming!"

Lilian's girls were growing up so sweet, with no dad to be seen and their mum still grieving.[5]

By 1944, nearly four years since the *Blitz* started, there were no young men in the Duncan home. Nell's strapping older son, Harry, flew with the Royal Air Force over the Middle East, and her frail younger boy, Peter, floated on His Majesty's aircraft carrier, the *Formidable,* in the seas off Japan. All the Duncan girls flitted in and out of the little house, keeping watch over their feeble Dad. That was the fate of families all over Britain; only the women, children, and the old men remained. In that way, the Duncans weren't one bit different from the rest.[6]

Hearing the cab honk, Gena rushed into the living room, blocked the front door, and wailed, "Mummy, you can't go. I had a dream. I had a dream."

"Gena," Nell began, but then Henry came out from the kitchen and interrupted.

"Don't mind Gena, Mum," he said, winking. "She's got a *gift* for gloom and doom; she's blind to the brighter side of life. You have a wonderful time down in Portsmouth."

Gena shrieked, "Who will give Mummy her insulin? She needs you, Daddy. Why don't you go with her? You used to go. She still needs you."[7]

Henry's face turned red from embarrassment or anger—it was hard to tell which. Was Henry's refusal to travel due to his poor health or his jealousy of Albert? Were Henry's bouts with rheumatic fever the real reason he stayed home while Nell worked?[8] Or was Henry sick of playing second fiddle to her Spirit Guide?[9]

Henry seethed, "Gena, stop your hysterics and listen. I've hired a good woman to travel with your mother. Mrs. Brown will keep her injections right on schedule."

Again, the cab honked.

Henry held up Nell's long fur coat and continued growling at Gena.[10] "Your mother has work to do. Remember your Christmas presents? Do you appreciate this house? What about your holiday pudding? Where do you think the money comes from? Albert, that's where. Your Uncle Albert earns the money. And your Uncle Albert will take good care of your Mummy. Now stop your fussing. Kiss Mum and wish her well."[11]

Nell slipped her arms into the satin-lined sleeves and pulled the soft fur coat around her.[12] Forcing the door open against the wind, she lowered her head and plowed into pelting sleet,[13] her suitcase in one hand and her séance bag in the other.

The cab drove off,[14] and Nell looked back. That cozy bungalow was like a little shrine to her accomplishment. Of course, that wasn't how Henry and Albert saw it. Both of the men in her life, her husband and her Spirit Guide, figured Nell was nothing more than a shuttle bus for spirits who wanted to catch a fare back and forth from the Other Side, a reluctant vehicle prone to fits and starts.

During séances, Albert was forever complaining that he couldn't get "The Lady's" rebellious mind under his control.[15] Sometimes he confided to the sitters, "Thank goodness I love her; she's a poor beggar."[16] Or in a less charitable mood, he'd moan about his ethereal assignment. "I don't think much of my medium; she's too fat."[17]

As for Henry, he behaved like a sniveling ass creeper around Albert. He dubbed the cozy bungalow "Albertine," because Albert earned the money to buy it.[18] But in spite of all his indebtedness, Henry did manage to squirrel away some credit for himself.

Nell had heard the story too many times: If Henry hadn't devoted himself to tutoring Nell in the psychic arts, she never would have channeled Albert, never would have become a famous medium, never would have earned a penny.[19]

Even though it was Nell who hauled herself around the United Kingdom to keep her family fed, Albert and Henry did all the crowing. But Nell didn't allow herself to express resentment. Instead she held tight to a secret knowledge: Both men were totally dependent on her. Without Helen Duncan, Albert would be stuck in some disembodied purgatory. Without Nell, Henry would be a shell-shocked duffer living in a one-room tenement on a disability pension. Even now, the neighbors called him a "kettle boiler"[20] and accused him of bullying his wife into earning a living.[21] Calling himself her spiritual teacher gave Henry a bit of pride, and Nell didn't begrudge him that. After all, Henry had married her after her mother had thrown her out, and other men had seen her as unfit to be a wife.[22]

At Waverly Station, women held onto their hats as their wool coats flapped in the wind. Not so long ago, Nell had wrapped herself in a similar coat—only worse, handmade and threadbare.[23] But the war and the surge in the popularity of Spiritualism had rewarded Nell. Now, her long fur coat warmed her as she trudged from the cab to the train. Settling in for the long chug, Nell paid no mind to ladies who looked at her coat with envy. Nell deserved every last pelt; she had made her sacrifices and earned her just desserts.[24] Yes, Mrs. Henry Duncan might have looked like a woman with a wealthy husband, but that was an illusion.

Nell was the breadwinner in her family, and earning even one crust had not always been easy. In times past, she had slaved to feed her children potato broth without meat and not had a penny left over for holiday sweets. On winter days like this one, with icy pellets stinging her face, Nell had hauled bales of linen on her back and out to the bleach fields. Her overalls had frozen to her skin.[25] Never in all those years had Nell's toil won her any admiration.

Even in hard times, it was Nell's *gift* for communing with the dead that brought goodness into her life. One destitute Christmas, she had searched through an old wooden chest, found two ragged sweaters, unraveled the wool, and knit her children socks. As she handed them their presents and lectured them on gratitude—"Baby Jesus was born in a manger; you're lucky to have a roof over your head"—Auntie Mac, Nell's best friend, burst through the door her arms loaded down with gifts like one of the wise men. As the children grabbed their packages and scurried to corners like chipmunks with acorns, Nell read the tag attached to her present: "With love from Llaine and David Mac."[26] Llaine and David, Auntie Mac's husband and son, had both died that year. Their spirits visited Nell, and Nell delivered their messages to Auntie Mac. Slowly, Auntie Mac's grief had given way to gratitude.[27]

That Christmas so long ago, Nell's eyes had welled up, and Auntie Mac had reassured her, "One kindness deserves another."

Now, in this January of 1944, Nell's fur coat was such a kindness, a kindness earned by giving solace to the grieving.

The train pulled to a stop at Sunderland station, and Mrs. Francis Brown—the woman Henry hired to look after Nell—flitted on board. A sparrow of a woman,[28] Francis nestled in right next to Nell.

"Good morning, good morning. What fun, what fun. I'll take such good care of you. I will; I really will. I'd love to be a medium. Really. It would be so grand. What do I need to do to channel spirits of the dead? Professionally, I mean."

Nell took a moment before she answered, "You've got to be born with the *gift*. Have you ever seen a spirit visitor?"

"I could, I bet I could if I tried," Mrs. Brown chirped with enthusiasm.[29]

"Well, then, you just do that; sit still for a bit and see if you have a vision," Nell suggested with a faint smile on her face.

As the train rattled on, closer and closer to Portsmouth, Nell wished that she was still welcome in Callander, the magical Highland village of her childhood where she first communed with spirit visitors.[30]

"I think I see a ghost; I think I do," Francis peeped hopefully. Then she gave up, opened her eyes, and started digging through her purse. "I have spirit photographs, real spirit photographs, genuine ones. I can show what spirit visitors look like. Want to see them?"

"You don't have to show me any photographs. Save those for the unbelievers," Nell advised.[31]

Finally, the train pulled into Portsmouth. Nell lumbered onto the platform, with Francis tiptoeing alongside of her. Inside the station, Nell faced a wartime poster: An aircraft carrier, painted with impressive realism, was on fire, sinking into the sea. The caption warned: "CARELESS WORDS MAY END IN THIS! Many lives were lost in the last war through careless talk. Be on guard! Don't discuss movements of ships or troops."[32] Nell's younger son, Peter, served on just such a ship.[33] Nell looked down and kept walking.

There was nothing to distinguish 301 Copnor Road from the other two-story Tudor-style cottages and shops lining the street.[34] From the sidewalk, Portsmouth's Master Temple appeared to be a pharmacy. An upright iron coin scale stood out front. Over the left display window, VASELINE was carefully lettered above a scalloped white line, and over the right window, bolder print announced, The Great VIROL Body Builder. Both windows were packed tight with products and picture advertisements.[35] Most pedestrians strolled by the drugstore without noticing the sign posted on the door: Séance Tonight.

Arriving at this familiar destination, Nell sighed. "Finally. Here we are."

"What about the Master Temple?" Francis Brown stammered in confusion.

Nell pointed at the second floor to a bay window covered, like every wartime window, in black.[36] "Up there," she answered with a tinge of pride in her voice.

"I thought you were taking me to a proper Spiritualist church," Francis complained, "not to a pharmacy."[37]

Without saying a word, Nell stomped ahead and opened the shop door. The jingle of a bell hanging from the knob alerted Mr. Homer, the pharmacy owner. He walked from behind the counter to greet Nell and Francis Brown. Nell liked Ernest Homer.[38] He couldn't help but remind her of Henry: tall, thin, soft-spoken, and a true believer.[39] Without making much conversation, Mr. Homer pumped her hand and led her up the narrow staircase and into the chapel. Francis Brown followed.

Elizabeth Homer, a portly woman with an effusive nature, rushed toward Nell, chattering up a storm.[40]

"Mrs. Duncan. Welcome. And Mrs. Brown . . . it is Mrs. Brown, isn't it? Welcome. Mrs. Duncan, Helen. Right, Helen. Mr. Homer and I are so thrilled to have you back again. It's so kind of you to appear at our humble Spiritualist church. Thank you. Thank you. I just can't thank you enough. Your Albert puts on such a spectacular show."

Nell smiled; she couldn't help but smile. Elizabeth Homer had a way of helping Nell forget herself. During the First World War, Elizabeth had entertained the troops. The soldiers and sailors had hooted and hollered while Elizabeth had strutted her stuff, sang, and danced. In those days, she had been quite the Welsh beauty with a buxom body and lusty gaze. Not any longer. She had turned hefty with cheeks sagging and lips wrinkled with age. Between the wars Elizabeth had lost her girlish charms, but she had discovered the Spirit World. Blessed with the gift of the gab, she preached the gospel of Spiritualism. Actually, Elizabeth didn't exactly preach; she gossiped about ghosts. With her amazing stories—many of them about Helen Duncan's extraordinary psychic powers—Elizabeth still attracted the boys.[41] A good number of navy lads worshipped at the Master Temple.

"Portsmouth is such a wonderful venue," Elizabeth bragged, sounding like an auctioneer trying to sell a piece of the city. "Ships come and go all the time—every boat packed with boys prepared to meet their maker on the high seas. Those boys leave wives and mothers behind, all of them worried to death. The boys, the wives, the mothers—they all come to my Master Temple looking for answers and for hope."[42]

As Elizabeth spoke, satisfaction enveloped Nell. Her work did good and that pleased her.

"Tonight will be no exception." Elizabeth assured Nell. Then she abruptly clapped her hands and got down to business. "So much for chatter, time to get ready. Mrs. Brown, you can help me set up the chairs—three rows facing the Cabinet. Leonardo's print of the Last Supper needs straightening, the rostrum has to be swept, and the crucifix dusted.[43] My grown-up daughter, Christine, will help you."

Having issued her orders, Elizabeth turned to Nell. "Mrs. Duncan, Helen, you go to the back room and take a little breather. I'll have Mr. Homer bring you a cup of tea straight away. You've got back-to-back séances coming up in the next few days. With all the talk of invading Europe, I'm all sold out."[44]

# 8

# A Material Witness

O<sup>N</sup> JANUARY 15, 1944, A SATURDAY MORNING,[1] CHIEF CONSTABLE
Arthur West leaned back in his chair, preparing to take a moment's
respite from the ever-growing accumulation of documents stamped TOP
SECRET. Each day, he received memoranda from the War Office, direc-
tives from the Home Office, edicts from Scotland Yard, and instructions
from Military Intelligence. By mid-January 1944, the government had finally entrusted the Chief Constable with broad powers and uncensored
information. Arthur Charles West was now the undisputed internal intelligence authority in His Majesty's premier naval port. No other civilian
had access to these files. No one else could use this information to arrest
and detain at will.[2]

West moved to the alcove of windows overlooking the grounds of Byculla House. Even in winter, this lovingly tended garden, with its lotus
pond and fig tree, brought him peace of mind.[3] Not even his great friend
Mayor Sir Denis Daley knew that just beyond the hustle and bustle of
town, His Majesty's Mediterranean Fleet had taken up anchor. Over the
past two months, British battleships and cruisers had steamed home from
Italy, North Africa, Greece, and Palestine. They had come fast and furious:
one ship after another slithering out the mouth of the Mediterranean, past
Gibraltar, their captains praying to evade detection by Nazi listening posts.
Then, jamming their engines full throttle, they had thundered back to

homeport. The British Navy had now unofficially and furtively abandoned the Mediterranean front.

This movement of ships was the most strategic secret yet in this endless war.[4] At Dunkirk, four years earlier, the British Expeditionary Force had evacuated France. Since then, Hitler's storm troopers had feasted on the pleasure of occupation. Soon, if Allied Command could catch the Germans napping, the easy flow of fine wine and soft cheeses would cease.

As Chief Constable West dared to savor that long overdue possibility, he heard the roar of a motorcycle. Lieutenant Stan Worth dropped by for a visit. As usual, Stan's Airedale perched on the gas tank, and his cheek pushed into his dog's woolly coat. Stan pulled up to the front entrance, killed his engine, and kicked down his stand. His curly-haired companion gave his master a wet lick and jumped to the ground, tail wagging. Stan gave the dog a pat on the head and instructions to stay put. The Airedale obediently lay down by his master's machine, and Stan trotted up the steps.[5]

Arthur West felt a particular affection for Lieutenant Stan Worth.[6] In a way, Stan was like a younger version of the Chief Constable—handsome,[7] competent,[8] born to do police work. But Stan's police pedigree was more established; he'd spent his boyhood surrounded by police activity. His Uncle Percy was Detective Superintendent of Scotland Yard.[9] His father was a respected career man with the Met, operating not only out of London and the Home Counties but also in royal dockyards and naval institutions. In 1923, Stan's father had been assigned to a tour of duty in Portsmouth. With battleships anchored in the harbor and sailors swaggering down the streets, the lure of His Majesty's Navy had smitten Stan. While still a lad, he joined the cadets at HMS *Vernon,* the torpedo training school. Then, too abruptly for Stan's taste, his father had been transferred to Middlesex. For a short spell, Stan put his true love on hold and did the expected. He joined the Special Constabulary in Harlington and, in no time at all, was promoted to Sergeant. Then war broke out, and a greater duty called. Stan volunteered for the Navy.[10] Already he had earned a commission and bumped into Winston Churchill on the HMS *Prince of Wales.* But being a navy man didn't keep Stan away from Police Headquarters; he dropped by for the comradery. Despite all the Chief Constable's respect for the lieutenant, these days even Stan caused West some worry. This young man's mother had become fascinated by séances, and he appeared to be following in her footsteps. Lieutenant Stan Worth had taken up with the spook worshippers,[11] and he wasn't alone.

Last November, just as His Majesty's Mediterranean Fleet began secretly popping up in Portsmouth harbor, former Air Chief Marshal Lord Hugh Dowding, Britain's most beloved war hero, rode into town with all the evangelistic fervor of a born-again Spiritualist.[12] West admired Lord Dowding as much as the next man. If not for Dowding's masterful handling of air power during the Blitz, straight-legged storm troopers with swastikas plastered on their biceps would be patrolling the streets of Portsmouth shouting, "Heil Hitler!"[13]

But since being forced into retirement, "Old Stuffy"—as the Royal Air Force fighter boys affectionately called him[14]—had taken leave of his senses. He now claimed to receive spirit messages from airmen "whose souls had been violently torn from their bodies."[15] Convinced that the dead mingled among the living, Dowding had written a book called *Many Mansions* and now toured the country preaching to packed concert halls. The mannerly aristocrat[16] issued an urgent call for mourners to march off to local mediums and collect messages from the Afterlife.[17] Ever since Dowding's lecture in Portsmouth, otherwise levelheaded men, like Lieutenant Stan Worth, had taken to going to the spooks.[18]

As the Chief Constable returned to office chores, he fumed over the Spiritualist kooks and over one particular Spiritualist medium—Helen Duncan. This woman had a history of divulging ship movements and losses. This was no time for a repeat performance.[19] Continuing to review classified documents and filing them in appropriate stacks, West heard ripples of laughter wafting down the staircase from his detectives' offices. As usual, Lieutenant Stan Worth was entertaining West's men. Among his many virtues, Stan Worth could tell a whale of a story.[20]

By the time Chief Constable West padlocked his confidential file cabinets, the laughter had died down, and the Lieutenant had rumbled back to his base. As West cracked the ornately carved door leading to Byculla's ballroom,[21] he paused to scrutinize Detective Sergeant Frederick David

Ford. Fred wandered about the great hall, poking his head into one door after another. Fred was a bit of an odd-looking giraffe—tall, gangling, and long necked, with large doe eyes and protruding ears that made him look permanently in a state of alert. It had taken Fred a full ten years to make Sergeant. That was six years ago, and it didn't look like he'd make Inspector any time soon, if ever.[22] Quite simply, Detective Sergeant Fred Ford was sincere and well liked,[23] but there was nothing stellar about him.

Finally Detective Ford noticed the Chief Constable. "Chief. There you are. Hello. I mean I've been looking for you, sir." Fred's face bore scars from teenage acne, and his kinky brown hair refused to be tamed. He spoke to the Chief Constable like a self-conscious adolescent.

"Now you've found me," observed West.

"Yes. Good. I found you," repeated Fred; his mustached lip giving a characteristic twitch.

West waited. After an awkward minute, he prompted Detective Ford. "Fred, did you have something to tell me?"

"Yes. Yes. I do, Chief." Again, Fred's words trailed off.

Again the Chief Constable coaxed him forward. "What do you want to tell me, Fred?"

"Lieutenant Stan Worth was here," said Fred.

"I know," confirmed the Chief Constable. Assuming Fred had delivered his message, West headed toward the foyer. To his surprise, Fred followed him straight across the mosaic tile.

Then, with uncharacteristic assertiveness Fred blurted out, "It's about Helen Duncan. Stan Worth says he went to this Spiritualist church, partly because his mom's interested in Spiritualism and partly as a lark, just to check out the spooks. He left that séance hopping mad. Stan says Mrs. Duncan swindled him. Stan says her 'spirit guide' is nothing but a ragged sheet. He wants to press charges."[24]

West stopped dead and turned. Staring at Fred Ford, he asked, "Helen Duncan is a fake?"

Now, standing taller than usual, Detective Ford nodded. "That's what Stan Worth said."

West had ordered all his detectives to keep an eye out for any suspicious activity swirling around the gifted Mrs. Duncan. None of them had any inkling that there was a military intelligence motive behind the Chief Constable's distaste for this particular channel to the Nether World.[25]

Suddenly, the Chief Constable saw a very simple way out of the Helen Duncan quagmire. Nab the woman for faking spooks and quietly throw away the key.[26] No one need ever know about her unfortunate ability to accurately forecast military secrets. With a self-satisfied smirk, West issued an order: "Fred, catch the *gifted* Mrs. Duncan red-handed. Get me that sheet."[27]

## 9

# Grasping at Evidence

B Y THE NIGHT OF JANUARY 19, 1944, NELL HAD ALREADY GIVEN FOUR séances at Mrs. Homer's Master Temple. As Nell waited alone in the chapel's adjoining room, she tiptoed to the door and opened it just a sliver. She eavesdropped on the preliminaries and, every once in a while, stole a peek.

Mrs. Homer bubbled with enthusiasm as she led guests to their chairs. "Hello. Welcome. So nice to see you."

A handsome Navy Lieutenant, Stan Worth, returned for a third séance. This time he brought a civilian friend named Rupert Cross. Mrs. Homer clucked over the pair: "Step right this way. I have a special seat for you tonight. Mrs. Duncan will scare the wits out of you." She pointed them to two seats in the second row behind Mr. Homer.

Once everyone settled into place, Mr. Homer begged the audience to give him their flashlights and explained his reason.[1] Spiritualists believed that any sudden flash of light might inflict injury on entranced mediums.[2] Helen Duncan was living proof of that belief. In the past, when Harry Price and other irreverent psychic investigators had taken flash photographs and shone flashlights on her, burn marks had appeared on her face, and she had bled profusely from her nose. Mrs. Duncan was cursed—or blessed, depending on who you asked—with the Spiritualist stigmata.[3]

Three men from the audience handed over their flashlights, and Mr. Homer took his seat in the front row.

Next, Elizabeth Homer trotted to center stage. With vaudevillian gusto, she announced, "I need three gentlemen volunteers."

Lieutenant Stan Worth and two other men jumped at the opportunity.

"Come on up to the Cabinet, and make a thorough search of it boys," Elizabeth enthused.

The Lieutenant headed for the blue drapes lining the corner walls and shook them. Nothing emerged. Pushing the drapes aside, he found no door, no hidden panels, or anything out of the ordinary. Another fellow pulled up the rug. The most suspicious of the three pulled the removable cushion off the Jacobean chair. After examining it, he told Mrs. Homer to cut it open. Mrs. Homer took a knife and slashed the upholstery. The entire audience stood up to watch, but no ghostly material oozed out. The man poked inside, but found no trace of anything strange.

As if the cushion dissection wasn't enough, Elizabeth handed Nell's séance outfit—her black frock, slip, bloomers, and court shoes—to the person at the end of the front row and issued instructions, "Examine Mrs. Duncan's séance clothing. Take care. Take your time. Pass it on to the next sitter. Every one of you is to investigate. Make certain nothing is hidden. There will be no deception at the Master Temple."[4]

When a navy lad fingered Nell's oversized bloomers, she backed away from the cracked dressing room door and sat down. She lit up a nerve-soothing fag as Elizabeth continued revving up the séance regime: "Will three ladies volunteer to go to the adjoining room and meet the talented Mrs. Duncan? Once you are fully satisfied that nothing has been hidden on her person, dress her in these séance clothes. Then escort her to this Cabinet."

Tonight, three very respectable women—Mrs. Gill, Mrs. Lock, and Nurse Jane Rust—walked in on Nell. Mrs. Gill, dressed in a lovely gray fur, carried the stack of black clothes. Nell stood, and Nurse Rust gently undressed her. Then all three ladies helped Nell into her séance clothes. Nell passed the inspection just fine.[5]

Mrs. Gill swung wide the narrow door, and Nell, dressed in her séance costume, shuffled toward the Jacobean chair.

The group recited the Lord's Prayer and sang "South of the Border."[6] Then, as happened at every séance, Nell's hands fell limp to her sides, her head collapsed onto her chest,[7] and her breathing turned into a sonorous moan.[8]

Shocked blind by the sudden flood of light, Nell found herself sprawled on the Master Temple's cold floor, leaning against an overturned chair with one shoe off and one shoe on. Breathing heavily, heart racing, she feared she'd go into diabetic shock. Shading her eyes, she looked up and saw the silhouette of a man in a trilby hat and trench coat. Nell panted, "I need a doctor. I'm a very sick woman."[9]

The man, Detective Fred Ford, scoffed at her, "You'll get one soon enough."[10]

Kind Nurse Rust knelt down and slipped Nell's foot back in her black canvas shoe.[11] Grateful for the sympathetic gesture, Nell slowed her breathing and calmed herself. Then, she noticed all the coppers, shouting at the sitters. "Shut up!" "Sit down!"[12]

Lieutenant Worth's friend, Rupert Cross, stood next to Detective Ford, seething, "Someone's got that cloth." Then he pointed an accusatory finger at Elizabeth Homer's frumpy daughter, Christine, and hissed, "It's you."[13]

Christine Homer jumped to her feet. With her four-inch crucifix dangling from her neck, and her eyes about to pop through her thick round spectacles,[14] she screeched, "You have accused me wrongly. I demand you search me!"[15]

With motherly pride, Elizabeth joined her daughter's rebellion and demanded that everyone be searched.

All the sitters joined in, chanting, "Search me! Search me! Search me!"[16]

Knocked off guard by the general clamor, Detective Ford stammered, "How can I search the women?"

Elizabeth challenged him. "You have a police matron."[17]

The entire room fell silent, waiting for Detective Ford's decision. Ford's doe eyes lowered, and his ruddy face flushed.[18] Gingerly, he ventured a polite request: "If any one of you here has got this sheet or cloth, will you please give it up? Please, so as not to cause any further displeasure."[19]

No one volunteered, and for Detective Ford that was good enough. He ordered Elizabeth's chapel, but not its worshipers, thoroughly searched.

While the band of policemen ripped the séance room apart, Detective Ford inspected Francis Brown's photographs of spirit visitors. When the ransacking was done, not one scrap of white cloth had turned up. Dumbfounded, Detective Ford arrested Nell for nothing more than telling false fortunes, a misdemeanor worthy of at most a ten pound fine.

Nell smirked. Naïvely confident, she told Detective Ford, "I have nothing to worry about."

Part II

TRIALS

# 10

# A Triumph
# of Humiliation

B Y THE WINTER OF 1944, HARRY PRICE'S FOND WISH FOR A RENDEZVOUS
with Herr Hitler had receded. German invincibility was on the
wane, and Price's prestige among his own countrymen was on the ascent. With the publication of his autobiography, ironically titled *Search
for Truth,*[1] Price had not only established himself as Britain's preeminent
journalist on psychic phenomena,[2] but he had buried the shame of his
father's legacy. For his book and in interviews with the BBC, Price con-
cocted a heritage that brought him pride: His father, a wealthy paper
manufacturer, had encouraged and endowed his gentleman's pursuit of
paranormal science. No one had yet uncovered the mortifying truth: His
father had been a corner store grocer who, at age forty-two, had impreg-
nated a fourteen-year-old girl and had only married the child, Price's
mother, under threat of prosecution. The shoddy affair forced the reluctant husband into the life of a traveling salesman and his family into
poverty.[3] Harry Price had learned from his father's troubles; he married
into money. His wife, a plain but wealthy heiress, had funded his ambitions.[4] And in the end, Price's father had bestowed upon his son an invaluable inheritance. Price had no qualms about skewing facts in the
service of a good story.[5]

His publisher assured him that sales of his up-and-coming book, *Poltergeist over England,* could easily soar to 100,000 copies.[6] No longer would he be dependent on handouts from his wife's trust fund. Already he was fully engaged in crafting another book, *The End of Borley Manor.* The public had an insatiable appetite for Borley stories, and Price intended to capitalize on their gluttony. This most haunted house had come to a fiery end under phenomenal circumstances. Its owner, Captain Gregory, had reported that a pile of books had spontaneously flung itself onto an oil lamp, causing the manor's destruction. Yet, the ghoulish visitations continued: Blue-clad women walked above the ruins, graffiti magically embossed itself on one remaining brick wall, a young woman's skull was excavated from beneath the cellar.[7] Collecting such tales had become Price's primary obsession.[8]

Nevertheless, Price did keep in touch with his protégés who remained intent on exposing bogus mediums. All over England, from Cardiff to Yarmouth to Birmingham, debunkers and the police joined forces, setting traps for the spook conjurers and prosecuting the charlatans. Invariably, the authorities arrested disreputable channels to the Spirit World, detained them overnight, fined them twenty pounds, and set them free the next morning.[9] The harassment pleased Price, but none had thrilled him—until the arrest of Helen Duncan.[10]

Price applauded the headline in the *Evening News*—"Constable Grabs 'Spirit': Shocking Things Divulged"—but the article below disappointed him. Albert, Mrs. Duncan's contemptuous alter ego, had slipped through the officers' fingers.[11] Price bemoaned the expected outcome: a small fine[12] accompanied by an invaluable round of publicity. The result would be larger audiences willing to pay an inflated price for admission.[13] If only someone with clout would impose a penalty of consequence, then Price might be tempted to lend his expertise to the cause.[14]

It had been more than a decade since Price had published his book on the medium Helen Duncan, yet it remained the most thorough exposé of her chicanery. Only he had subjected Mrs. Duncan to proper laboratory scrutiny.[15] Yet the book might never have been published, if Mrs. Duncan's Spirit Control, Albert, hadn't bruised her husband's pride.

Back then, in an era that pre-dated Price's celebrity, the Spiritualists at 16 Queensbury had encircled Mrs. Duncan and refused Price entry.[16]

Despite the snub, Price had learned every intriguing, amusing, and sordid detail from his flame-haired friend, Mrs. Molly Goldney.[17]

One evening in the final months of 1930, invited guests took their seats at 16 Queensbury Street.[18] With the velvet-curtained Cabinet at his back and a brilliant chandelier overhead, Dr. Fielding-Ould, President of London Spiritualist Alliance, welcomed his distinguished colleagues. Stationed within a semi-circle of chairs, a designated note taker sat with pen and pad, prepared to capture every detail of Mrs. Duncan's séances for perpetuity.[19]

Miss Mercy Phillimore, Secretary of the Spiritualist Alliance, appeared in front of the Cabinet with yards of black cloth folded across her outstretched arms and a length of rope dangling from her bent elbow. Dr. Fielding-Ould took the material from her and thanked her. Like a magician's assistant, Miss Mercy stepped to one side of the curtain. Dr. Fielding-Ould unfurled the black cotton. It was an enormous sack, large enough to engulf Mrs. Duncan's hefty frame.

Dr. Fielding-Ould knelt at Mrs. Duncan's feet and slipped the bag up to her knees, as the medium steadied herself on Dr. Fielding-Ould's shoulder. He rose slowly, pulling the sack up to Mrs. Duncan's chin and securing it snugly round her neck with a drawstring. Mrs. Duncan shuffled to her throne inside the Cabinet. Fielding-Ould extended his palm, and Miss Mercy placed the rope over his hand. Fielding-Ould walked to the Cabinet, tied one end of the rope to Mrs. Duncan's chair, and then, with cord in hand, he walked around and around, binding and tying Mrs. Duncan to her seat with multiple knots. After the final knot, he once again stretched out his palm. This time Miss Mercy handed the doctor sealing wax and a lighted candle. Dr. Fielding-Ould dripped wax on every knot.[20]

At the back of the room, Mr. Duncan, relegated to the role of organ grinder, turned on the gramophone.[21] To the gay vibrations of happy tunes, Mrs. Duncan fell into a trance.

The room's light was switched to red, and the Cabinet curtains were dropped from their sashes.[22] Within moments Mr. Duncan stopped the music, and the sound of Mrs. Duncan's rhythmic snoring filled the séance parlor.

The sitters waited. If the Spirit Control Albert extricated Mrs. Duncan from her bondage and produced the mythic substance ectoplasm, the Spiritualists would applaud Mrs. Duncan as a true medium blessed with phenomenal powers. If Albert failed, they'd regard her paranormal phenomena with suspicion. This was no easy feat, no sentimental séance for the easily satisfied.

Everyone waited. 6:10, 6:15, 6:20. Nothing happened. Then Miss Mercy squealed, pointed to the floor beneath the curtain, and gasped, "Look there. Some pale thing is creeping out of the Cabinet."

Excitedly, Dr. Fielding-Ould shouted, "Is that you, Albert? Can you show us more ectoplasm, Albert?"

There was only silence: no answer, no voice, only an anemic strand of ectoplasm sneaking tentatively into the room.

The clock ticked, and Spiritualist hopes faded.

Suddenly a voice bellowed, "Good evening!" The sitters nearly jumped out of their skins. Albert, all jocular, playing everyone for the fool, shouted, "I will show you some more ectoplasm, my lad."

To admiring swoons, the curtains parted. Mrs. Duncan sat in her sack, still entranced. A cord of ectoplasm, streamed from her mouth, floated into the air, and formed the Christian symbol of resurrection, the Holy Cross.

Albert took on the persona of a toastmaster at a wine tasting.

"We have here a fine example of your most basic ectoplasm, still being birthed by the medium, pulsating with potential life, not yet built into the form of living being, not yet inhabited by a spirit visitor. Dr. Fielding-Ould, I invite you to touch and smell the raw substance of materialization. Come, dear man. Stand up. Enter this Cabinet. Feel this glistening ectoplasm. Smell its life-giving bouquet."

Dr. Fielding-Ould trotted into the Cabinet and gingerly touched the floating ectoplasm.

Albert told him, "All right old chap, report to the others. What was the ectoplasm's feel? What was the aroma of it?"

"It feels like an ethereal form of the softest merino cloth ever woven. As for its bouquet, I detect no odor what so ever."

Taking Fielding-Ould to task, Albert scolded, "What is wrong with you, sir? Can't you smell properly?"

Dr. Fielding-Ould stammered, "Forgive me Albert. I am a smoker, and I'm afraid tobacco has dulled my sense of smell."

"Well then, sit down. Let others have a go at it."

Dr. Fielding-Ould skulked back to his place. All the sitters, including Mr. Duncan, took turns touching and smelling the cord of ectoplasm. All agreed to the feel of it: soft cloth. As for its smell, most sensed an odor they called pungent.

Miss Mercy piped up, "It's the slightly arid bouquet I've smelled at many materialization séances."

Mr. Duncan, trying to make a helpful contribution, translated her observation into plain English: "Yes, indeed, I've noticed that myself. Ectoplasm smells like an old dish rag."

Suddenly enraged, Albert roared, "Duncan, you're an idiot! The aroma isn't unpleasant. It's much more appealing than that."

Quickly recovering his composure, Albert laughed sardonically.

All the sitters joined Albert in a robust guffaw at Mr. Duncan's expense.

Moments later, with the audience returned to their chairs, the face of a child appeared and hovered next to Mrs. Duncan. Albert didn't allow that particular spirit to speak. Instead he complained, "If only I could get rid of that girl."[23]

After that game of ethereal peek-a-boo, Albert appeared to materialize a baby in a long christening dress, and the Cabinet curtain closed.

From behind the curtain, came clattering and rustling noises as though Mrs. Duncan and Albert were tussling with one another. Mrs. Duncan, as vague-eyed and unsteady on her feet as a sleepwalking toddler, wandered out of the Cabinet. Finally, Albert had freed his medium from the black sack.

Dr. Fielding-Ould rushed into the Cabinet and inspected the vacated bag. He reported with amazement, "The sack is undamaged; the knots still tied."

The audience members, six eminent Spiritualists, mulled over one question: How was Albert able to extricate Mrs. Duncan from the sealed bag and knotted rope?

Mr. Duncan cleared his throat and offered his theory: "I think it's simple, really. Albert temporarily elongates the medium, rearranges the molecules so her body stretches thin."

Presumably, Mr. Duncan imagined his wife's ethereally transformed body floating out the mouth of the sack. Once escaped, her temporarily wispy form plumped out to her normal shape and landed on the floor.

Mr. Duncan's explanation was too far-fetched for Albert. The disgruntled Spirit Guide snarled in disgust, "Nonsense, you fool. You're a perfect ass with your theories."[24]

All the prominent Spiritualists snickered like cruel children siding with the playground bully.

Trying his best to save a little face, Mr. Duncan quipped, "Well now, Albert, you're a funny man, as fine a comedian as George Robey."

George Robey was, without parallel, Britain's most celebrated comic, famed for his outrageous antics. But apparently visitors from the Nether World didn't keep tabs on current forms of earthly entertainment.

"Who's George Robey?" Albert asked.

"You don't know George Robey?" Mr. Duncan responded incredulously.[25] Everyone knew that George Robey worked in vaudeville, went into a trance and channeled an assortment of barnyard animals.

Apparently Mrs. Duncan's Spirit Control took offense at her husband's attempted tribute. In response, Albert made his own suggestion. "Henry. Go lose your self."[26]

That's the way it had gone. For November and December of 1930 and on into the spring of 1931, every Tuesday and Friday, Albert played host to London's Brahmins. Albert's moods switched and changed. Sometimes he grumbled outright, "I wish there was someone here to take this blinking bag off my medium."[27] Sometimes, in a jaunty manner, Albert proposed the ridiculous: "Miss Mercy Phillimore, I'll come to your wedding and play the bagpipes."

On one occasion, amid grunting and complaining, Albert produced a blob of ectoplasm, white and phosphorescent, but formless.

Mr. Duncan observed, "It looks like a baby's head."

Albert, unable to resist any opportunity to publicly berate the husband, said, "It isn't a baby's head. You think I have no brain? You old fathead, I'll twist your blinking neck off."[28]

Poor, self-pitying Henry Duncan merely wanted to serve Albert, but Albert gave the man not a smidgen of appreciation—not one kind word, no sugar to sweeten Henry's tea—just insults and threats. At the back of the room, standing by his gramophone, faithful Henry endured the abuse.[29]

Albert didn't reserve his caustic wit for Mr. Duncan. One night Albert decided that tying Mrs. Duncan's body into a sack wasn't constricting enough. In his most polite and facetious voice, he asked the audience, "Would you prefer to control my lady by nailing her into a coffin?"[30]

Albert's most belittling mistreatment came on March 17, 1931, a Tuesday. Dr. Margaret Vivian, Miss Mercy Phillimore, Mrs. Moffat, a theater producer, a baron from continental Europe, and Military Intelligence attaché Brigadier Roy Firebrace were counted among those present. That particular night, the psychic investigators packed Mrs. Duncan into a newly designed séance suit, stitching it up the back, the neck, and the arms, before lashing her to a chair.

A sprightly spirit named Peggy appeared, dancing and singing, "Baa, baa, black sheep have you any wool? Yes, sir. Yes, sir. Three bags full." All the sitters clapped with delight.

Once little Peggy skipped on back to the Other Side, Albert—not to be upstaged by the ectoplasmic scamp—pulled Mrs. Duncan's séance suit straight off her body and flung it into the audience. Not a stitch of clothing remained on Mrs. Henry Duncan. Only a transparent swathe of ectoplasm veiled her naked body.

Like horny johns at a striptease show, the titillated Spiritualists grabbed for the cast-off garment. Picking up the séance suit off the floor, they checked the seams. Nothing was amiss. Albert was a hero. Mrs. Duncan remained in the Cabinet, still entranced[31] and shivering.

Adding to her husband's humiliation, the incident was published in *The Light,*[32] and word spread far and wide. At Cambridge University, young men spoofed Mrs. Duncan and quoted Wordsworth.[33]

> *Not in entire forgetfulness,*
> *And not in utter nakedness,*
> *But trailing clouds of teleplasm*

Obviously, a good number of Spiritualists didn't give a wit about their pledge of confidentiality. And even though the London Spiritualist Alliance promoted Helen Duncan's séances with promises of the return of loved ones with perfectly recognizable faces,[34] the mounting mockery distressed Mr. Duncan.[35]

Learning of the husband's disgruntlement, Harry Price had laid a trap of flattery laced with bribery. Price had "spontaneously" bumped into Mr. and Mrs. Duncan on Queensbury Street. Within a day or two, Mr. Duncan had dropped his wife on the doorstep of Price's National Laboratory for Psychical Research, and Harry Price began his experiments on the medium and her Spirit Control.[36]

That intrigue, with all its frustrations and humiliations, lay in the distant past. Still, Price held out hope that Mrs. Duncan's current brush with the law would be more satisfying than her previous encounter. Tantalized by the possibility of revenge, Price lifted a copy of his book about Duncan from its shelf and blew off the dust. Should he send the Chief Constable of Portsmouth a copy of his book touting Mrs. Duncan's fakir-like powers of deception? Why not? No one had proven him wrong.[37]

# 11

# At the Chief Constable's Bidding

THE MORNING AFTER HER ARREST, NELL TROMPED INTO PORTSMOUTH Magistrates' Court irked by the disruption of her schedule, ready to cough up twenty pounds, and resume her séance tour. Getting nabbed by the police had not been entirely surprising; a witch-hunt was afoot. The coppers and vigilante ghost-busters set about the country hounding the *gifted* ones, rounding them up like nothing more than common street gypsies. Nell, with her exhausting itinerary and extraordinary séance phenomena, was bound to become a target for such religious persecution.[1]

In court, Detective Ford stumbled through reading the misdemeanor violation:[2] "Every person pretending or professing to tell fortunes, or using any subtle craft or device by palmistry or otherwise, to deceive His Majesty's subjects shall be deemed a rogue and vagabond."[3]

Nell snorted in disgust.[4]

Detective Sergeant Ford shuffled some papers and stammered on. "Your Honor, Chief Constable West has asked me to beg the Court to remand the prisoner in custody without bail."[5]

The magistrate pounded his gavel and said, "Fine. Take her to Holloway."[6]

71

Nell's knees buckled. No prison had a more frightful reputation than Holloway—suffragettes had starved to death in its cells, and spies were still hung from its gallows.[7]

Two constables hustled to her side and pulled her fast across tarnished wood planks, past empty seats, and through the courtroom door. A square black paddy wagon waited outside. The officers swung wide its back doors and hoisted her inside. She crumpled on the hard bench of the windowless van.[8]

Detective Ford leaned in and handed Nell her insulin kit.[9] The engine churned and the driver pulled into traffic. Heading north on Commercial Road, the cruiser picked up speed as it left the crowded streets of Portsmouth business district and wound its way through the countryside toward its ominous destination.

In London, the traffic grew thick as the auto crept up Camden Road toward a medieval fortress, its tower belching clouds of black smoke.[10] The driver quipped: "That's your castle, my lady, an exact replica of Warwick Castle. But don't think any Prince Charming will be scaling those ramparts to rescue you. Those stone walls stand twenty-four feet high."[11]

The cruiser pulled into a mammoth portal and froze inside its dark tunnel. A wooden gate lifted, groaning like a giant jaw inviting its prey to enter. Nell's hearse-like transport crawled into a barren courtyard and stopped.[12] Her police escort unlatched her door, and the stench of coal mixed with sewage welcomed her.[13] Anxious to make his escape, the officer tugged her from her seat and deposited her on the raw dirt.[14]

A woman in a long black cape flew out a dungeon door,[15] swooped toward Nell, and cackled, "Don't just stand there. Follow me."

Nell plodded obediently through the gray smog.

The wardress opened a barred gate and ushered Nell down three concrete steps. Inside, she whipped off her cape and hung it on a peg. Underneath, she was dressed like a nurse, in starched apron and crisp frock.[16] As though transformed into a cheery Miss, the wardress greeted Nell. "Good day, Mrs. Duncan. I'm the registration sister."

By World War II, Holloway Prison had officially entered the enlightened age of rehabilitation. Prisoners were deemed to have a social disease, and prison was the cure for their malady. Jail administrators referred to guards, all of them female, as "sisters."[17]

Nell clarified her own status. "I'm Mrs. Helen Duncan, and I'm no criminal. I'm just here on remand."

"Well, now, that remains to seen, doesn't it?" The wardress twittered. "Come along. I've other sisters to introduce you to."[18]

Nell lumbered behind, down a damp brick passage. As the sister's teeth chattered from the cold, Nell thanked heaven for her fur coat.[19]

The narrow walkway widened to a corridor lined with hanging half-doors like a horse barn. Each stall held a bathtub.[20]

Another sister rested on a chair by a shelf stacked with towels and clothing.[21] With a grumpy "humph," this one ran her eyes over Nell from head to toe.[22] The registration sister left Nell in the care of this scowling guard.

With the bitterness of a woman relegated to dressing in wool, the wardress grabbed the nap of Nell's fur, pulled it off, and tossed it onto the rickety shelf. From the same shelf, she grabbed a towel, threw it at Nell, and pointed in the direction of a bathing cubicle.[23]

Nell understood what was required of her. She walked into a bath stall, nearly tripped over the wooden bathmat in front of the tub, perched on a cold metal corner bench,[24] and removed every stitch of her clothing. Then she dutifully hung her clothes over the half-door and sat in the bathtub like a shivering mass of gelatin.

The wardress kept watch from just outside the bath cubicle and turned on the faucets that fed the tub.

Scalding water jolted Nell, and she bellowed, "The water's too damn hot."

Laughing, the wardress rushed in and dumped a bucket of ice cold over Nell's head. Clearly not every sister at Holloway subscribed to an enlightened ethic of kindness.

Nell huddled there, her lower body burning, while freezing droplets of water dripped from her hair onto her shivering shoulders. Not even her mother had bathed her with such heartless contempt. Trembling, she rose slowly to her feet, stepped from the tub, and wiped her body. Looking toward the stall door, she found her clothes were gone. Nell whimpered.[25] Already, she had learned not to complain.

The sister handed Nell a stack of prison clothing.

Nell pulled a scratchy regulation vest over her breasts and bloomers over her buttocks. She unfolded a blue-and-white-striped prisoner's frock, slipped it over her head, and tugged it down her body. She put on woolen stockings and pushed her feet into flat, strapped shoes.[26]

The sister shoved a piece of paper in her face. "Sign this. It's a list of your belongings. You'll get them back when you leave, whenever that is."

Nell scrawled her name and watched her fur disappear.[27]

In her prison cell, Nell sat, stiff as a tombstone. A wardress stomped in, slammed a pen, a sheet of stationary, and an envelope on the bedside table and informed her, "You're allowed one letter on your first day.[28] Make it good."

Staring at the letterhead—a tiny picture of the King's crown with the return address HM Prison Service, Holloway Prison, London[29]—Nell blanched at the challenge: Write one note to one person who could rescue her. She scrawled her plea, as neatly as her hand allowed, and addressed the envelope to Henry Duncan, 19 Kirkland Drive, Edinburgh, Scotland.[30]

Nell would not have been in this mess if not for Henry. When Nell met Henry, she wanted nothing to do with being a medium. Certainly, she had been born with the gift of second sight and had talked with spirit visitors since childhood, but allowing the dead to enter her body—that she believed to be altogether different. That was the devil's playground.[31]

. Theirs had begun as an ethereal romance; Nell and Henry had met in a dream.[32] But on that night, Nell was not sleeping alone. A baby slept by her side, a baby from a secret seed. Whether made pregnant from a short-lived love or from some far more unspeakable affair, Nell refused to tell. Either way, she was a sinner with a bastard child. At least that's how her God-fearing mother saw it. In an adolescent attempt to win forgiveness, Nell named her fatherless infant after her puritanical mother: Isabella MacFarlane.[33] But the gesture had done no good; Nell remained banished from her family and her village.[34]

An unwed mother, alone without support, Nell needed a husband. But a contagion of patriotism had carried the young men off to the Great War, and husbands—especially ones willing to marry "spoiled goods"— were in short supply.

Two years earlier, before Nell's unplanned pregnancy, she had all the male attention she desired. Her mother had encouraged Nell to move to Dundee, live in a young ladies' hostel, and join the workforce.[35] The mill girls were a fast and fun-loving lot, and Nell fit right in. At five each morning, she had tossed a shoddy shawl around her shoulders and sauntered off to the mills in the good company of other hard-drinking, snuff-chewing, fag-smoking, foul-mouthed adolescents. All day, she slaved, chained to her machine, with clouds of flax dust swirling round her head. At night, free of her mother's regulation, Nell cruised the streets and went pubbing.

With money tucked into her more than ample bosom, Nell had what it took to support those rowdy times. Men, their woolen flat visor caps cocked to one side and their trousers held up with suspenders, gathered on every corner to whistle and catcall. In Dundee, girls had the jobs and the money. The blokes leaning against the storefronts were too clumsy— and their egos too big—for weaving and sewing. The best hope a Dundee man had for a night out on the town was to lure some sexy little number into buying him a drink and giving him a whirl. For a mill girl, the power was intoxicating.[36]

Then World War I broke up the fun. In the summer of 1914, the men of Dundee got over their girl-crazy affliction and came down with a terminal case of war fever. Between the rows of brick factories, the sound of bagpipes beckoned. In pubs, men put down their pints and scurried to the doors. When the pied piper in his infantry kilt came into view, lads by the hundreds fell in behind him. A ragtag parade of the unemployed snaked a path to the recruitment station. The volunteers stood in line for hours. Each man in his turn signed away his freedom for a shilling and walked out standing taller, able to buy a pint of brew and a pack of cigarettes without seducing a mill girl. Of course, it took less to seduce the girls; Dundee men were no longer a penniless lot without prospects.

The sultry boys were the Crown's loyal legion, bravely facing battle. Every lad among them expected to tan the hide of "bloody Jerry" and be home to sing *Silent Night* on Christmas Eve.[37]

Two Christmases later, those boys still slept in lice-infested trenches, while Nell dreamed of a father for her baby girl. One night, she floated off to the war's front lines. Looking from above, she saw a tall frail lad of sixteen, knee-deep in mud. Bombs exploded and the earth shook. The young soldier tried his best to march, struggling to free one foot from the muck, and then the other. His face broke into a sweat, his body went limp, and he collapsed into the rat-infested stench. As delirium engulfed her dream soldier, Nell broke through, and he saw her smiling face. Dragged to the field hospital, he drifted away from the smells of disinfectant and the screams of men with severed limbs and floated toward Nell's comforting image.

Nell spoke to him not in the voice of an angel but in her own husky voice, reassuring him, "You'll be just fine, you will."

Like a shy lad with a schoolboy crush, he whispered, "I like you."

As it turned out, that soldier, Henry Duncan, was the brother of Nell's best friend. The first time they met in the flesh, their eyes locked, and Henry said, "So. We meet at last."[38]

On May 27, 1916, Nell and Henry married.[39] Bella, little Isabella MacFarlane, had a step-daddy, and Nell had a husband. Of course, Nell was grateful, and like other young women of her time, she expected her husband to protect and provide for her. But from the start Henry had other ambitions. Henry intended to make something of her talent.

"Nellie," he cooed, looking down into her trusting face, "I'll teach you one step at a time to be a proper medium."[40]

Nell's eyes narrowed; her husband looked more and more like the evil face of temptation. "Henry Duncan," she told him, "it's a blessed thing to converse with the spirits. It's a wicked and dangerous thing to let all manner of dead folk come in and take over your body. I'm not intending to become possessed."[41]

A quarter of a century had passed. Long after dark, at nine o'clock sharp, a call bellowed from the corridor of Holloway Prison: "Lights out."[42] A steel door weighing 133 pounds[43] banged shut on Nell's cell, a key turned, and the first of her mother's prophecies—*You'll be locked in a dungeon*—rang true.[44]

Nell survived her first sleepless night in Holloway Prison. The morning bell clanged at 6:10 A.M. and she fell into line. By day, she scrubbed whatever she was ordered to clean, ate her allotment of bread and beans, prayed in the Anglican chapel, and trudged in circles around the fortress yard.[45] By night, forced into dark and solitary confinement, she wrestled with her demons. With no word from outside the prison gate,[46] Nell spiraled into deeper and deeper despondency.[47]

Then, four days after her arrest, a guard called out, "Helen Duncan! You have a visitor."

Her heart throbbed with excitement as she rushed to follow the prison sister. The cells of Holloway blurred as one thought consumed her: Nell was about to be reunited with Henry. Finally, the door to the visitors' room swung open, and Nell flew inside. Henry was nowhere to be seen. Instead, a ghoulish shadow in a black overcoat and fedora fixed his blazing eyes on her. Filled with anguish and disappointment, Nell burst into tears.[48]

# 12

# An Extraordinary
# Pack of Lies

B EHIND THE CLOSED DOOR OF HIS OFFICE, CHIEF CONSTABLE WEST
studied a sheaf of papers stamped boldly in red: TOP SECRET. A
few shadowy intelligence strategists had hatched this plan in a secret
bunker beneath the streets of London. Only a very select number of
highly placed law enforcement officials—Chief Constables in the most
strategic locations—received this particularly crucial document. Inspired
by Churchill's famous advice to Stalin, "In wartime, truth is so precious
that she should always be attended by a bodyguard of lies," these name-
less men had titled the document "PLAN 'BODYGUARD'." Its second
line read: "Overall Deception Policy for the War Against the Germans."[1]
Naturally, the Chief Constable of Portsmouth was privy to this blueprint
of the war's most skillfully crafted lies.[2] Arthur West paid meticulous
attention as he read: "The German General Staff . . . already suspect
that large-scale Anglo-American operations will be undertaken in Western Europe sometime in 1944."[3]

Absorbing the meaning of that phrase, West swiveled around in his desk
chair. How things had changed since the *Luftwaffe* had bombarded Guildhall[4] and the police had been forced to occupy Byculla House.[5] Three
years ago, Portsmouth blazed beneath the savage Nazi onslaught, and

Britain stood alone without any hope of allies.[6] But now the Royal Air
Force pummeled Berlin,[7] and the British Empire had two powerful allies:
the Soviet Union, an unreliable but war-savvy collaborator;[8] and the
United States, a trusted but battle-naïve friend.[9] At this moment, Russian
forces were pushing Hitler out of Eastern Europe,[10] and the Americans
were pouring into England.[11] West mumbled, "large-scale Anglo-American
operations." The phrase rang so sweet.

Refocusing, the Chief Constable pondered, distilled, and committed
to memory the essential fictions of Operation Bodyguard.

Military Intelligence intended to convince Hitler that while the Russians attacked from the east, the British-American forces planned as-
saults on three separate Western European fronts later in the year:

Bogus Front #1. From the South: In late spring, or early summer,
British battleships currently docked for repair in Portsmouth harbor
would return to the Mediterranean for a major offensive.

Bogus Front #2. From the North: In late spring, an Allied invasion of
Scandinavia would be launched from waters off Edinburgh, Scotland.

Bogus Front #3. From the West: In late summer, an assault on Calais,
France, would be launched across the channel by General Patton's troops,
now stationed in the Thames estuary.[12]

If Hitler bought this threefold falsehood, Nazi troops would remain
dispersed, waiting in the wrong places at the wrong times. The tide of the
war would finally and irrevocably turn in the Allies favor. If the Fuehrer
suspected otherwise, he'd move all his forces to northern France. The assault on the beaches of Normandy would be a senseless bloodbath, and
Allied victory would be in peril.

To guard against detection of the real Allied plan (one massive invasion
launched from Portsmouth and the southeast coast as early in the spring
of 1944 as possible), every citizen in Britain needed to be deceived; all
gossip had to support the bogus three-front strategy. All leaks had to be or-
chestrated to confirm the illusion.

If Portsmouth's citizens asked, "Why are so many battleships anchored
in the harbor?" the encouraged speculation was: "Those battleships are
home for repairs, getting ready for a big push in the Mediterranean."

If Scotsmen wondered, "What's going on with the buildup of forces around Edinburgh?" the approved rumor was: "The Allies must be planning an attack on Norway or maybe Denmark. I bet for late spring."

If Londoners questioned, "Why do you think General Patton's troops are training at that huge secret base on the Thames?" the acceptable gossip was: "It's the best place to cross the channel. The top brass must be planning a major assault on Calais. I hear the American soldiers aren't trained to fight. They've got to put off that main invasion until late summer."[13]

As long as these lies circulated as truth, the invasion had a fighting chance of success.

There was a tentative knock on West's door. The Chief Constable shoved the TOP SECRET document into his desk drawer, locked it, and shouted, "Come in."

Detective Sergeant Fred Ford cracked the door and stuck his face in.

West cheered Fred's arrival, "Detective Ford, I've been waiting to hear about Mrs. Duncan's quiet little meeting with the magistrates."

Chief Constable West had sent Detective Ford off to Magistrates' Court with one clear instruction: "Do not let Mrs. Duncan free on bail."[14] West didn't have a clue where Mrs. Helen Duncan got her information. He did know the Admiralty wanted her quietly tucked away behind bars.[15] This one-woman rumor mill traveled far too regularly between Edinburgh (where preparations for a bogus assault on Scandinavia were being simulated)[16] and Portsmouth (where undercover preparations for the largest seaborne invasion in history were actually taking place).[17] The Chief Constable had a simple plan for silencing Mrs. Duncan and her host of loose-lipped cheesecloth goblins: Continue to deny bail and make certain the wheels of justice turned at a snail's pace. With a little help from his favorite judge, Chairman of the County Court, His Lordship Sir Grimwood Mears,[18] Mrs. Duncan's appearances before the local magistrates and county bench would ramble on and on without resolution. Spring and summer would come and go with Mrs. Duncan on sabbatical in Holloway Prison. By the time Sir Grimwood levied a twenty-pound fine, the invasion would be history, and Allied forces would be closing in on Hitler's bunker.[19]

From the hallway, West heard someone call, "Hey Fred, nabbed any spooks today?"

Detective Ford chuckled but didn't answer.

West ignored the comment. Fred had been chided and teased enough about his failure to capture the elusive Albert. Instead the Chief Constable did all he could to welcome the chronically self-conscious detective into his office. "Detective Sergeant Ford. Fred, don't stand there. Come in. Sit down."

Fred settled his lanky legs and arms onto a wooden chair, crossed his knees, folded his hands, and looked directly at the floor.[20]

Chief Constable West tapped his fingers on the desk and tried to contain his impatience. "Well . . . ?" he asked, coaxing information.[21]

Fred sneaked a peek at his superior and blurted out, "Mrs. Duncan's free on bail."[22]

West felt the red heat of anger rise to his face. After a few calming breaths, he seethed, "Fred, wasn't it enough that you let the sheet get away? Now the woman's gone free?"

Fred whispered, "It wasn't my fault, Chief."

That lame excuse uncorked West's rage. He shouted, "Tell me about it! Give me the blow by blow! Then I'll decide whose fault it is!"

Fred, sitting stiff, recited his story.

"It was like this, Chief. I go to Magistrates' Court, just like you told me. I'm waiting there for the cruiser to deliver Mrs. Duncan. This old man dressed in black, like he's straight out of a Dracula flick,[23] glides up to me. He stares right through me and growls, 'My name is Mr. Charles Loseby, barrister-at-law. A consortium of distinguished Spiritualists has retained me to represent Mrs. Duncan.'[24]

"Chief, you didn't tell me Mrs. Duncan would have a lawyer."[25]

West spat out, "So this debacle is my fault, Fred?"

"No. No. Not at all, sir. You don't know everything," Fred stumbled over another feeble attempt at ducking responsibility. "Anyway, next thing, I unlock the cruiser door and Loseby muscles in. He takes Mrs. Duncan's arm and escorts her up the court steps. Where did he come from, Chief? What's the fuss over a bogus spook conjurer?"

West didn't bother speculating. He simply prodded Fred on. "What next, Fred?"

"The charge gets read: vagrancy violation, a misdemeanor for pretending to tell fortunes. I do just what you told me, Chief. I say, 'Chief Constable Arthur Charles West has instructed me to request that the defendant, Mrs. Helen Duncan, continue to be held in custody without bail.'[26]

"Loseby flings his arm in the air and yelps, 'Objection!' Then, his voice all raspy, he starts telling the magistrates how he's lodging a complaint with the Home Office. Seems he's all chummy with Home Secretary Morrison, and Morrison made a promise not to arrest Spiritualist mediums. All high and mighty this Loseby character says, 'I have no doubt that the Home Secretary intends to keep his word, but the police have completely ignored his orders.'[27]

"Before I can say anything to defend the constabulary, Loseby tells the magistrates this sob story. Poor Mrs. Duncan. Portsmouth police officers attacked the sickly lady, endangered her life, and dragged her off to prison without cause. By now, Loseby, grandstanding for somebody, says, 'Mrs. Duncan is a woman of distinguished achievement.'[28]

"Not knowing what else to do, I say, 'The police have no objection to bail.' But I set it real high, Chief—one hundred pounds,[29] a fortune. I never thought for one minute that Mrs. Duncan would have that kind of money. But apparently she's got backers with deep pockets. Loseby immediately agreed to put up the cash, and the magistrates set a date for us to come back."[30]

Fred paused for a breath and then offered an opinion. "I know it's none of my business, Chief, but it's just a misdemeanor. Let it go. It's out of your control. There's nothing you can do."

"Out of my control? Nothing I can do? There's *always* something I can do, Fred. Wake up, Fred," bristled the Chief Constable. "I'm the Chief Constable of Portsmouth. I've got emergency powers. I can arrest and detain anybody I want, anytime, for any reason.[31] And I want Mrs. Duncan silenced and behind bars. Am I understood?"

West idled for a moment, and then he realized that he had said too much. Calming his voice and covering his tracks, he justified his ire. "Mrs. Duncan is a bold-faced fraud who profits from grief. It's my job to protect the credulous citizens of Portsmouth from her heartless deception."[32]

"I see what you're getting at, Chief." Fred parroted the Chief Constable's opinion. "It's a nasty con job, alright. We've got to protect the spook worshippers from their own stupidity."

Reassured that he had set Fred on a straight and narrow path, West summarized the situation. "Fred, you've set a swindler loose. Mrs. Duncan's free to prance about the country, manipulating a piece of muslin and deceiving the grief-stricken with phony messages from the Beyond."

"She's out on bail, Chief," Fred reminded West. "She's scared; she'll lie low."

"Don't count on it," West snapped. Fred's reassurances had a way of evoking West's irritation. Fuming, the Chief Constable remembered the clandestine blueprint—Operation Bodyguard—secreted away in his drawer. The bulk of His Majesty's western fleet was docked just beyond his doorstep, and a spook conjurer with an unfortunate penchant for accurate predications was on the loose. Fred was right; West had lost control of Helen Duncan. Normal judicial protocol might well thwart the Chief Constable's plan. The Office of Public Prosecutions would take on the case. A hearing before three Portsmouth magistrates, none professional judges, all respected citizens, would be convened. If the magistrates considered the Prosecution's evidence strong enough, they'd refer *Rex v. Duncan* to the next regularly scheduled session of the County Bench in late spring.[33] By then, the Allied invasion would be in full throttle. Suddenly, with Helen Duncan, a rumor mill of dangerous proportions, on the loose, the sluggish tempo of British justice had turned against West.[34]

Fred Ford continued to study the floor as West studied him. This self-conscious, large-eared, doe-eyed Sergeant Detective wasn't exactly the brightest bulb in the box.[35] On careful consideration, that's exactly what West needed. A more competent detective might question more and find out too much. Fred took things at face value: The Chief had gone a bit daft, and become a self-righteous crusader hell-bent on ridding Portsmouth of a spook conjurer. That was the public line, and the Chief Constable could count on Fred to perpetuate that propaganda. West decided to leave Fred Ford on the Helen Duncan case.[36]

"Fred," said West in a conciliatory tone, "I know this hocus-pocus only seems like a twenty-pound fine, nothing worthy of my concern. You're right. I can't let this case take too much of my time. That's why I need you, Fred. I want you to gather enough evidence to convince Mr. Loseby that Mrs. Duncan is as guilty as sin. I want the Spiritualists to see her as an embarrassment and drop her like a hot potato. Here's what I want you to do.

"First, write a full report and send it directly to the Director of Public Prosecutions.[37]

"Second, get in touch with the Edinburgh Police. Look for previous trouble with the law, financial irregularities, and disgruntled séance sitters. Focus on fake phenomena. Find out if anyone has ever nabbed a sheet, cheesecloth, or any white material. Stay away from predictions and messages; they're irrelevant.[38]

"Third, scour Portsmouth for disillusioned Spiritualists.[39]

"Fourth, stay close to Lieutenant Worth. Take him to a pub. Take him out on your fishing boat.[40] Right now, that young man's testimony is our most convincing weapon.[41]

"Get going, Fred. Get to work."

Once Fred was out the door, Chief Constable West hatched his own shadow operation. He rallied his influential allies, motivating each with tidbits of information and setting them free to do his bidding.

Director of Public Prosecutions Sir Tindall Atkinson learned that due to special circumstances of interest to the Admiralty, Mrs. Helen Duncan required a quick trial and incarceration for no less than nine months. Sir Tindall's assignment: Appoint a crack team of prosecutors, design a sure-fire incarceration strategy, and make certain not to implicate Military Intelligence.[42]

Lord Mayor of Portsmouth Sir Denis Daley, West's great friend, learned that Mrs. Duncan heartlessly preyed on the citizenry of their city. Sir Denis's assignment: to serve as Head Magistrate[43] at the next hearing of the Duncan case and accommodate any Prosecution requests.

For the moment, the Chief Constable kept his most intimidating allies undercover. His favorite judge, His Lordship Grimwood Mears, and psychic investigator Harry Price would be activated when each could provide maximum impact.

# 13

## Conspiracy

O N THE MORNING OF FEBRUARY 29, 1944, A QUEUE OF RESPECTABLE citizens, men and women, mostly women, most attired in woolen suits and Sunday-best hats, waited impatiently on the walkway and steps of Portsmouth Magistrates' Court. Newspapermen, pens and cameras in hand, forced themselves through the crowd trying to stake out a good view. All awaited the arrival of Helen Duncan.[1]

Within the circle of the faithful, Nell's arrest had elevated her to the status of revered martyr. Doling out fines to less prominent, less extraordinary, less well-traveled mediums was bullying. Incarcerating Mrs. Duncan was a travesty. Her detention without bail proved that the Home Office and the Anglican hierarchy, Home Secretary Morrison and Archbishop of Canterbury Lang, were conspiring to strangle the Spiritualist message.[2] The Archbishop had quashed a report written by his own church Committee on Spiritualism.[3] A copy of the report had leaked, however, and the churchmen had concluded: "Experience with mediums make a strong *prima facie* case for survival and for the possibility of spirit communication."[4] As for his part in the plot, Home Secretary Morrison had let loose boorish constables with a vendetta against all evidence of everlasting life. While Spiritualist boys abroad risked their lives for liberty, their religion was under assault at home. What were they fighting for?[5] For Mrs. Duncan, a mother with two sons of her own fighting in His Majesty's armed forces, to be hauled off and thrown in prison? If Helen Duncan could be incarcerated, every medium and every British Spiritualist was in danger of prosecution. At any séance, a zealous band of coppers might march in, wielding nightsticks, and arrest entire congregations.[6] Inspired and paranoid, the Spiritualist faithful contributed money to hire the prestigious defense attorney Charles Loseby.[7] The most sincere believers, hailing from Portsmouth, London, and reaches further west, gathered on the doorstep of Portsmouth Magistrates' Court.

Nell, swathed from neck to ankles in black fur,[8] arrived at the court, escorted by her lawyer. As usual, the sallow-cheeked Charles Loseby wore his black overcoat and fedora, but on this day, he sported a festive touch, a polka-dot ascot.[9] The waiting crowd burst into cheers and flashed V-for-victory signs. Cameras flashed as they captured the scene for the newspapers.[10]

Her committed supporters filed into the courtroom and seated themselves on gallery pews, squished together as closely as churchgoers on Easter morning. Local dignitaries were also in attendance. Chief Constable Arthur Charles West sat next to lowly Detective Ford. The Lord Mayor of Portsmouth, Sir Denis Daley, in a three-piece suit and tie, sat in the head magistrate's chair, flanked by two esteemed citizens, Elsie Berryman and Leonard G. Basby.[11] To Nell's defenders, the Chief Constable's presence and the Lord Mayor's choice to serve as head magistrate proved the government's anti-Spiritualist agenda.

Sir Denis pounded the gavel. A court constable unlatched the gate to the dock[12] and waited for Mrs. Helen Duncan, Mr. Ernest Homer and Mrs. Elizabeth Homer (the Priest and High Priestess of the Master Temple), and Mrs. Francis Brown (Mrs. Duncan's assistant) to step into the dock.

Now there were four defendants.

Since Nell's initial arrest, the case had become more complicated. The police and the Office of Public Prosecutions had decided that a misdemeanor charge wasn't serious enough for Nell. They intended to charge her with a felony. For that, they needed a conspiracy and an exchange of money. They had issued warrants to the most likely accomplices: Mr. and Mrs. Homer, the proprietors of the Master Temple who had collected the cash, and Mrs. Francis Brown, who had declared herself Nell's understudy. Nell had been informed about this flurry of activity.[13]

Nevertheless, when the clerk called out a revised indictment—"Conspiracy"[14]—an audible gasp rippled through the gallery. This was wartime. Conspiracy implied spying, and spying led to hanging. Nell panicked. Head spinning, in confusion and fear, she strained to listen.

As it turned out, the conspiracy charge was not of the spying variety but of the common "conspiracy to cheat and defraud" genre. The government was merely accusing Nell of being a fake, of "pretending to communicate with deceased persons and causing spirits to materialize."[15] According to Detective Ford, Mr. and Mrs. Homer, who collected the cash, and Mrs. Brown, who assisted Nell, were obviously in on the jig. The government was about to present its case against Nell and her three alleged collaborators, but the police didn't have even a scrap of evidence.

# 14

# The Hearing

JUST AS THE SPIRITUALISTS BEGAN ABSORBING THE SHOCK OF THE surprise conspiracy indictment, a dead ringer for George Robey, Britain's most celebrated comic, bolted to his feet. Just the look of this man—his shaggy eyebrows, his cherub cheeks, his broad backside and thin legs[1]—evoked giggles, even from the Spiritualists. Edward Robey, son of the outrageous vaudevillian,[2] whose humor Henry Duncan had long ago equated with Albert's caustic wit,[3] was about to present evidence gathered by Chief Constable West and the Office of Public Prosecutions. Robey's instructions had been made clear: Keep the evidence focused on Mrs. Duncan's phony phenomena. Not even Robey—and certainly not Defense Attorney Loseby nor his Spiritualist backers—need know about the Chief Constable's more pressing security agenda.[4]

Luckily, Ed Robey had no difficulty mustering sincere indignation in service of the indictment. For this particular solicitor, dubious trances and cheesecloth puppetry were an affront to his legacy. Nearly every Brit knew how Ed Robey's father, George, had become an entertainer.

As a young man, George Robey had been comfortably ensconced in his rooms at Cambridge when the Robey family business hit a bad patch. Funds evaporated, and George was thrown out on his arse. There he stood: A well-bred young man with all avenues suited to his pedigree shut down. He took to visiting the Royal Aquarium.

The Royal Aquarium had nothing to do with fish and not much to do with royalty either; it was an entertainment pavilion that covered a Westminster city block and housed two stories of vaudevillian acts. The playbill boasted Professor Wingfield's Performing Dogs, Menotti's Aerial Performance on the High Wire, Offenbach's comic opera "Helen," and magic acts like the Great Maskelyne. For George, the chance to down a pint, smoke a cigar, and watch boisterous amusement provided welcome diversion from his sorry fate.

On one particular outing to the Royal Aquarium, George managed a close-up seat in the grand hall to see "Professor Kennedy, Mesmerist Extraordinaire." The "Professor" called to the audience for an audience volunteer. Even in his youth, George was neither a shrinking violet nor one to be constricted by inhibition, so he leaped onto the stage. "Professor" Kennedy waved a gold watch before the young man's eyes. Within moments, George exhibited a convincing vacancy, a blank-eyed stupefied stare. The "Professor," then instructed him to perform the usual embarrassing antics. Fully cognizant of his opportunity to elicit wails of unbridled laughter and applause, George took the part of the mesmerist's donkey. He strutted about the stage and bellowed his naughty songs, flapped his wings and clucked like a chicken. The rest was history. George Robey became, as billboards bragged, "Britain's Prime Minister of Mirth."[5]

Edward Robey had benefited greatly from the financial rewards of his father's counterfeit trances. His childhood had been peopled by the famed and influential. He boasted an education at Westminster, Cambridge, and the Inner Temple.[6] Edward had a personal quarrel with Helen Duncan: There was nothing that appalled him more than poorly performed vaudeville.

For his opening, Edward Robey restrained his inborn inclination. Stonefaced, he began, "This case has aroused much public interest. I want to make this perfectly clear: The issue at stake is not whether there is life after death, or whether departed spirits can communicate, or whether dead persons can materialize. The real issue is: All the defendants conspired and pretended that Mrs. Duncan could cause spirits of the dead to materialize."[7]

With that quick concession to Spiritualist quackery complete, Robey faced the magistrates and jumped into a more entertaining personae.

With his father's signature hilarity written all over his every gesture, he scratched his chin with his stubby pointer finger, shuffled his feet, tilted his head, raised his bushy brows,[8] and laid out the case, "So what do we have here? A show. A performance. A con job. Here's how it went: On January 16, Lieutenant Stanley Worth and Surgeon-Lieutenant Fowler bought tickets. The two naval officers paid a dockworker's daily wage to see the dead return to life. They walked into the séance room. The stage was set. Mrs. Duncan fell into what was called a trance."[9]

Imitating the trance, Edward feigned a vacant stare, let his head fall limp, and then snapped his neck back again. With eyes popping, his voice turned slow and spooky, "Then, in the glow of a single red light bulb, the congregation intoned some sort of prayer."[10]

Charles Loseby, Nell's Defense Attorney, swallowed the bait and growled, "It was the Lord's Prayer."[11]

Robey countered, "That makes it all the worse."[12]

Having clipped Loseby down to size, Robey added his own pet peeve: "The conjuring act was overpriced and poorly performed. Nothing like the magic shows of the Great Jasper Maskelyne."[13]

Chief Constable West squirmed. Without knowing it, Robey had hit a sensitive spot. For a few men with access to matters of national security, comparing Jasper Maskelyne[14] to Helen Duncan bordered between a military intelligence gaff and a masterful inside joke. With the outbreak of war, Maskelyne, Britain's most famous living magician, had renounced the stage and joined His Majesty's Expeditionary Force. Paid no more than a Major's salary, the illusionist had used lights, mirrors, wood, and fires to trick the Germans into attacking decoy targets. The Allied victories in North Africa owed a great debt to Maskelyne's wizardry.[15] Closer to home, thanks to the magician's techniques, the *Luftwaffe* had once bombed the nearly uninhabited Hayling Island and left Portsmouth in peace.[16] The Chief Constable considered Jasper Maskelyne a selfless patriot. Helen Duncan, on the other hand, was a parasite who grew fat off war's grief[17] and endangered Allied victory.[18]

Dispensing with his allusion to Maskelyne, Robey quickly ran through the sequence of events leading to Helen Duncan's arrest: Lieutenant

Worth's first Helen Duncan séance, his disillusionment, complaint to the police, and subsequent séances.[19]

Then, slowing his words for emphasis, Robey described a culminating travesty: "When the final séance was over and Mrs. Duncan was properly in police custody, this Mrs. Brown, who stands in the dock today"—Robey pointed to the skinny Mrs. Brown—"this co-conspirator, addressed those sincerely gathered Spiritualists and said, 'Jesus suffered like this.'" Robey shook his head in self-righteous disbelief, looked into the eyes of the Lord Mayor, and concluded his opening remarks: "To trickery is added blasphemy."[20]

The clerk announced the first witness, "Lieutenant Stanley Worth."[21]

In dress uniform—double-breasted navy blazer, gold buttons, spit-polished shoes, and officer's hat tucked respectfully beneath his armpit[22]—Stan Worth looked nothing like the fun-seeking motorcycle rider who rumbled between the Master Temple and Police Headquarters.[23]

Robey posed the Prosecution's first question. "Lieutenant Worth, please tell us about the events that led you to lodge a complaint against the defendants."[24]

Stan cleared his throat and began stating the facts. "In December, 1943, I had a conversation with the defendant, Mrs. Homer. She told me that Mrs. Duncan would be coming along in January of this year to hold a materialization séance."[25]

Robey asked, "Materialization séance?"

The Lieutenant smirked, before explaining, "Mrs. Homer said Mrs. Duncan could produce spirits of past relatives who would come out into the room for everyone to see."

Robey furrowed his brow, inviting an explanation. The singsong lyrics from Frank Loesser's wartime tune trickled into the courtroom from some nearby pub.[26]

*Down went the gunner, a bullet was his fate*
*Down went the gunner, and then the gunner's mate*
*Up jumped the sky pilot, gave the boys a look*

*And manned the gun himself as he laid aside The Book, shouting*
*Praise the Lord and pass the ammunition!*
*Praise the Lord and pass the ammunition, and we'll all stay free.*[27]

Another squadron of fighter planes roared overhead.[28]

Lieutenant Worth could no longer repress his talent for telling a good tale. Stan did more than quote Mrs. Homer. With Mrs. Homer's theatrical bluster and a Welsh lilt to his voice, he reenacted her sales pitch: "Mrs. Duncan is a *wonderful* woman! The ectoplasm issues from her body and forms into the shape of a spirit. Quite definitely! You will see spirits of the dead! Mrs. Duncan's Control stands right next to her, and other spirits walk out into the room! The cost is twelve shillings and six pence. It's worth every penny. I have to refuse hundreds, but I will let you come, as a special favor."

At Robey's bidding, the Lieutenant entertained the court with impromptu impressions[29] of an entire parade of floating white apparitions: Albert; a mutilated soldier who had been wounded and died in Singapore; a young man who was missing in service; a meowing cat that had been drowned in a bathtub; a Scottish child named "Peggy" who sang "Loch Lomond"; a policeman who retreated to the Nether World in search of his lost helmet; and Mrs. Homer's singing granny. Stan apologized for not knowing Welsh well enough to serenade the spectators with the granny's song.[30]

Chief Constable West settled back in sheer admiration: Put that young man in a darkened room with a sheet, and he'd give any bona fide medium a run for her money.

Summing up his testimony, the witness complained, "The spirits were fat and clammy, undoubtedly human, with nothing ethereal and no ectoplasm about them."[31]

Lieutenant Stan Worth had earned his billing as star witness for the Prosecution.

Less stellar but adequate Prosecution witnesses followed. War Reserve Constable Rupert Cross reviewed his ambush on the illusive ghost. Detective Sergeant Fred Ford admitted that a posse of eight constables ransacked the premises and found no white cloth. A local medium complained that the Homers had a money racket going. Disillusioned Spiritualist Bessie Lock grew teary as she spoke of her dashed hopes.[32]

The Prosecution's case petered out, and on instructions from Charles Loseby, her high-priced lawyer, Helen Duncan, blushing with embarrassment, mumbled her rehearsed response. "I do not wish to give evidence or call witnesses today."[33]

Each defendant in their turn—Mr. Homer, Mrs. Homer, and Mrs. Brown—repeated that line verbatim.[34]

Chief Constable West beamed with satisfaction. This charade was proceeding according to plan. The Office of Public Prosecutions had instructed West's ally, Lord Mayor Sir Denis Daley to refer *Rex v. Duncan* directly to the highest criminal court in Britain, the Old Bailey, for the speediest possible trial.[35] This outcome was sure to send Defense Counsel Loseby reeling, forcing him to negotiate a face-saving prison sentence for the *gifted* Mrs. Duncan.

After a short recess, the entire cast—Mrs. Duncan, her co-defendants, witnesses, policemen, and the clerk—piled back into the courtroom. The Lord Mayor Sir Denis Daley looked over the crowd and announced the magistrates' decision: "This case presents a matter of substance and we the magistrates of Portsmouth recommend it be given a full hearing before a jury at Central Criminal Court in London."[36]

Calls of "Hear, Hear" rumbled joyfully through the Spiritualist gallery.

The unexpected jubilation unnerved Chief Constable West. Had the Office of Public Prosecutions marched into a Defense ambush? Clearly, Loseby wasn't on the verge of surrender.

The true believers had gotten exactly what they wanted. Women hugged. Men shook hands. All rushed to congratulate Mr. Loseby. His ghoulish eyes sparkled. The Spiritualist cause would have its day. Spirit communication would be proved in a court of law—and not just any court. The Old Bailey was Britain's highest criminal court.[37] The potential for mass conversions was staggering. In the midst of the celebrating, Helen stood mouth agape with eyes glazed over, a pawn in this Spiritualist crusade.[38]

Chief Constable West surveyed the scene and considered his options. An out-of-court settlement would require increased intimidation. The Chief Constable congratulated himself on his recent efforts to activate the ire of His Lordship Sir Grimwood Mears.[39] The time had come for additional reinforcements. West intended to recruit the most noteworthy ally in his arsenal, psychic investigator Harry Price.[40]

# 15

# A Tempting Invitation

FINALLY, HARRY PRICE RECEIVED AN INVITATION WORTHY OF HIS consideration. Sir Edward Tindall Atkinson, Director of Public Prosecutions had been in touch. With respect for Price's scientific acumen and ever-increasing celebrity, Sir Tindall's Assistant Director had asked Price to lend his expertise, to testify against the artless Mrs. Duncan and her slippery Spirit Guide. Apparently, the invitation had come at the behest of Arthur Charles West, Chief Constable of Britain's premier naval port.[1] As the foremost authority on the Duncan phenomenon, no exposé would be complete without the input from Britain's premier researcher of paranormal experience.

Price rubbed his palms together and salivated with anticipation. He imagined himself holding judge, jury, and galley spellbound as he recounted his escapades with Mr. and Mrs. Duncan. The publicity would be spectacular. Every newspaper in the nation's capital would send reporters. The cameras would flash, reporters would scribble his every word,[2] and he would be the topic of headlines. Even the BBC had interrupted its coverage of Russian advances in Eastern Europe and Allied victories in Italy to announce the arrest of Helen Duncan.[3] Perhaps Price would be interviewed in the same hour as Winston Churchill. Best of all, he'd have another opportunity to defrock that insolent cheesecloth apparition, Albert.

Even now, thirteen years after his last encounter, Price bristled at Albert's innuendo. In the early days of his association with Mr. and Mrs. Duncan, Price could have championed the pitiable medium:[4] a poor peasant, playing host to Albert, a parasitic ghoul who verbally abused her.[5] But then Albert had spoiled Mrs. Duncan's opportunity.

To begin their association, Price had invited the Duncans to his laboratory parlor at 13 Rolland Street and offered ten pounds per séance, substantially outstripping the purse offered by his competitors at the London Spiritualist Alliance. The husband's greedy eyes had bulged. The two gentlemen had shaken hands on the deal, and Mr. Duncan dutifully proceeded to deliver his wife to the highest bidder.[6]

Then, test séance after test séance, Price's investigators searched and straight-jacketed Mrs. Duncan. The lights dimmed and the curtain drew. Ectoplasm played its usual variety of games, streaming from her mouth, spilling onto the floor, and shrouding her body, while Albert chatted up his guests. More ectoplasm, more controls, and no explanation for its origin.[7]

As Albert had done at the London Spiritualist Alliance, he continued to disparage Henry Duncan with an assortment of caustic witticisms.[8] Price found Albert's barbs refreshingly honest—until the audacious goblin stooped to suggest that the investigator and the medium's husband were made from the same cloth.

One night Price found himself in agreement with Mr. Duncan. In response, Albert jibed, "Great fools think alike; fools seldom differ."[9]

At Price's fourth investigative séance, Albert behaved unforgivably. The tubular Spirit Control poked his white head through the velvet curtain and, with a suggestive lilt to his voice, sang, "Hullo! Mr. Price, how are you tonight?"[10]

Taken a bit aback by the excessively familiar tone, Price answered, "I'm all right, but I have been very rushed in the evenings."[11]

Albert ventured a bit of conciliatory advice, "Never mind, put it all to the wind."[12]

Taken off-guard by the apparition's show of concern, Price confided, "I'm so seldom tired. Normally I can work all night without fatigue."[13]

Albert laughed in a bawdy manner and remarked, "Of course it depends upon who you are with!"[14]

This innuendo resonated too closely. Everyone in the room eyed his beautiful protégé, the flame-haired Mrs. Molly Goldney.[15] Embarrassed, Price objected, "That was unkind."[16]

Albert sighed, "We are all very much alike, Mr. Price."[17]

Price found this response beyond the pale and could not help but ask, "Surely you are not like that now? Not in death?"[18]

Albert moaned, "I do not know. I am very much attached to a woman. Bad luck that I did not find a gentleman."[19]

My God, thought Price, I'm conversing with a ghost who lives in a woman's body, confesses to an obsession with a lady, and aspires to homosexuality.[20] What has psychic investigation come to? He assured Albert, "Your fondness for a woman is to your advantage."[21]

"Disadvantage!" Albert asserted without a moment's hesitation. "Ladies can make you do what you don't want to do. Men cannot."[22]

*Touché.* Price had agreed.[23] Albert had won that round, but the fight had just begun. From his corner, Price had vowed to bludgeon and bloody the impertinent Albert. Only Mrs. Duncan's total humiliation could restore Price's dignity.[24]

Once again savoring the sweetness of imagined revenge, Price fingered the invitation from the Assistant Director of Public Prosecutions.[25] All possibilities for mushrooming stardom whet Price's appetite.[26] The fact that this opportunity would be at Mrs. Duncan's expense made it all the more tempting.[27]

# 16

# Behind Closed Doors

O N THE IDES OF MARCH, 1944, CHIEF CONSTABLE ARTHUR WEST motored to London for a discrete meeting. As instructed, he avoided the pillared entry and public foyer of Devonshire House. Instead he tapped on the metal-clad door of the sparsely traveled east entrance.[1] Inside, he walked with assumed nonchalance to the Office of Sir E. H. Tindall Atkinson, the Director of Public Prosecutions.[2]

Arriving in good time, West knocked on the appointed door. Sir Tindall Atkinson peeked out and pulled the Chief Constable into the office. Dispensing with a greeting, Atkinson issued instructions, "Chief Constable West, I see no reason for the Home Secretary to learn of my direct participation in this affair. As a matter of fact, if Morrison asks, I'll deny my contribution."[3]

A moment later, the door squeaked, and two men entered without knocking. This odd couple could have jumped off a cinema screen. The man in the lead swaggered with the suave elegance of a matinee idol;[4] his shadow sulked behind, head slumped, with the mechanized obedience of Frankenstein's monster.[5]

Sir Tindall enthused, "John Cyril Maude, it is good to see you."

The handsome Mr. Maude tipped his head.

The youthful John Maude and the elder Sir Tindall Atkinson shared an old-boy brotherhood: Both were Oxford men, and both had been called to the bar at the Middle Temple.[6]

Recently, Maude had risen to the heights of the legal profession—he had been appointed King's Counsel[7] and traded cotton robes for robes of silk.[8]

Atkinson turned to West. "Chief Constable Arthur Charles West, it's my pleasure to introduce John Cyril Maude, son of Britain's famed actor Cyril Maude and a rising star in his own milieu of jurisprudence."[9]

West and Maude shook hands. The two had met before and not merely in court. The Chief Constable understood Maude's qualifications for this particular case, perhaps more completely than the Director of Public Prosecutions. Beneath the silken robes of King's Counsel, Maude hid a clandestine identity. John Cyril Maude had been a Military Intelligence officer, the RSLO charged with investigating information leaks. Maude had traveled north to Scotland, into Helen Duncan's home territory.[10] Recently his covert prestige had received another boost; Maude had been assigned to the offices of the War Cabinet.[11]

Atkinson cryptically volunteered, "I appointed John because he's especially qualified to handle this unusual case with ability."[12]

West nodded approvingly; the Director of Public Prosecution had taken the Chief Constable's concerns seriously. Normally lesser prosecutors were assigned based on a rotation of the Old Bailey's barrister pool.[13] That would have left West with a less savvy ally.

West and Maude momentarily locked eyes acknowledging their unspoken mission: To incarcerate Mrs. Duncan as quickly as possible, for as long as conceivable, in order to stifle any potential leakage of accurate information about the coming Allied invasion of Europe.

Maude exhaled a noncommittal, "Yes. Right." Then, he turned to introduce the large man hovering beside him. "Chief Constable West, have you met my junior counsel, Henry Elam?"[14]

With relief, West realized that the monstrous man who extended his hand thought this matter involved nothing more than a dirty game of faked hobgoblins. Elam's appearance fit the case to perfection. Even though Elam measured a good six feet six,[15] his block-like head appeared too large for his body. The Assistant Prosecutor's feathery eyebrows turned up like horns, and his pastel eyes shone oddly flat like nonreflective glass.[16]

Atkinson offered the Junior Prosecutor unsolicited advice: "Pay attention to your lead, Mr. Elam. You'll learn a lot."

The Chief Constable eyed John Maude, and Maude reassured West, "Mr. Elam will learn just enough and not too much."[17]

Just as all four men pulled up armchairs, Ed Robey walked in.[18] With signature aplomb, so characteristic of vaudevillian roots, Robey planted his briefcase on a table and announced, "Here it is gentleman, the evidence for the Prosecution, flimsy though it may be."

"Ahhh," intoned Maude melodramatically. "Not one scrap of material evidence."

Once again, Chief Constable West seethed at the thought of the sheet that got away.

Unfazed, Robey leaned forward and cracked the briefcase. His face lit up in mock delight. His brushy eyebrows reached for his hairline. Then, twisting his fingers to and fro, he plunged his hand in among the papers. Like a magician pulling scarves from a top hat, he slowly drew out a long piece of sheer muslin.

In a rush of excitement, Atkinson jumped to a conclusion: "Ed, you scamp, you found the bogus Albert. Brilliant!"

"No, no, it's not Helen Duncan's Albert," the Chief Constable rushed in to set the record straight. "Ed just tossed it in with the evidence."[19]

West turned to Robey. "Where did you get it? From some vigilante ghost-buster who nabbed it off another medium? From Harry Price?[20] Or did you just buy it at Woolworth's?"[21]

"Arthur, don't be so quick to correct a favorable misimpression," Maude scolded. He motioned for Robey to hand over the cheesecloth. Once he had possession of the Albert look-alike, Maude dangled it from his fingertips and made it dance. "It's not evidence; it's a prop. This cloth has a certain demonstration value. During the trial, just for effect, I'll unleash our very own apparition."[22]

Watching Maude put his inherited skill to good use, Atkinson sagely noted, "Success in theater, success in court—the skills are the same. His Lordship Sir Gerald Dodson would be the perfect choice to adjudicate this case."

Maude laughed, but for Chief Constable West, the in-joke required explanation. Every Chief Constable in England knew that Sir Gerald Dodson ran Central Criminal Court. Seven years earlier, the barristers of the Old Bailey had elected him Recorder of London, and His Lordship Sir Gerald Dodson had become the most powerful arbiter of criminal law in Britain.[23] But Atkinson and Maude knew something about His Lordship's extracurricular passion.

Sir Gerald Dodson reveled in theater. As an amateur thespian, he had written a play, *The Rebel Maid*,[24] and he loved to hobnob with the stars.[25] John Maude's pedigree—son of Cyril Maude, unassailable icon of the stage, manager of the Haymarket Theater, builder of the Playhouse, author of *The Actor in the Room* and *Behind the Scenes with Cyril Maude*[26]—was sure to bedazzle this particular judge.

Without warning, Atkinson turned unexpectedly sober. "Here we are, sitting on a political powder keg, holding a conspiracy indictment. The problem is the conspiracy charge has a hole in it large enough to let your Mrs. Duncan waltz right out the courthouse door, free as a bird."

According to the conspiracy law, conspirators had to knowingly perpetuate a deception: promise to deliver goods or services in exchange for monies and then fail to produce what was promised. To be convicted, it would have to be proved that Mrs. Duncan purposefully duped the public, claiming to manifest spirits of the dead and collecting the fee. Mrs. Duncan made no such promise and never handled the money. The woman hardly appeared to speak. She hadn't breathed a word to the star witness, Lieutenant Worth. Elizabeth Homer, the proprietor of the Master Temple, and Mrs. Francis Brown, the traveling companion, were the only culprits touting Mrs. Duncan's conjuring capacities.[27]

Atkinson sat back, crossed his arms over his chest, and waited. His crack prosecution team sat in silence. Finally, the Director of Public Prosecutions wandered toward a booksh elf, took down a dusty volume, slammed it on the table, and leafed through the brittle pages. He came to an ancient statute and broke into a triumphant grin.[28] He shoved the chosen page under John Maude's nose.

King's Counsel Maude read the salient passage out loud: "If any person shall pretend to exercise or use any kind of witchcraft, sorcery, enchantment, or conjuration, or undertake to tell fortunes, every person so offending shall suffer imprisonment by the space of one whole year without bail."[29] Maude need not have read another word, but satisfaction put him in an impish mood, and he finished the paragraph. "And, on the market day, the convicted shall stand openly on the pillory, by the space of one hour."[30]

# 17

## The Appearance
## of Justice

NELL HUDDLED ON THE BACKSEAT OF A BLACK CAB.[1] HER FEEBLE
husband, Henry, nestled in next to her,[2] and her delicate daughter
Nan[3] balanced on the pull-down bench across from her. The car pulled
up to a stunted arched doorway cut into the Old Bailey's chiseled stone
façade.[4] An orderly queue snaked from that innocuous entrance on New-
gate Street, around the corner, and down Old Bailey Street.[5] Above them,
a gilded statue of Lady Justice crowned the building's majestic dome. Behind them, the elegant Court of the Recorder lay in ruins.[6] That's how the
Blitz had worked: Tragedies and miracles had come within a stone's throw
of one another. And it wasn't over. Many of those in line had spent the
night crammed onto wooden cots in the tunnels of the underground,
waiting for the all-clear to sound. But Hitler's renewal of aerial bombing,
this "Little Blitz,"[7] had not kept a crowd from arriving at the Old Bailey
two hours before its side door opened. Every person on that sidewalk
wanted to watch Nell go on trial.[8]

Nell stepped out of the car and the gathering fell quiet. With Henry
holding her left arm and Nan gripping her right hand, she trundled not
toward the arched doorway but off to the entrance reserved for defendants.[9] A well-wisher called out, "God bless you, Mrs. Duncan."[10] In

front of the iron gate, Nell kissed Henry on the lips and Nan on the cheek. The bars rattled open, Henry and Nan let go of Nell, and she walked on through the gate.[11]

Inside the dungeon-like holding room, Mr. Homer, Mrs. Homer, and Mrs. Brown waited, stoop-shouldered. Off to the side, a court sheriff studied his watch. After a few moments, he led the four of them through a slender door. Nell placed one foot on the first step of the grimy stairwell and began the climb from the crypt of the Old Bailey to Courtroom #4, an ascent of seven flights.[12] The tight passage echoed with the sound of hammering. Even while the bombs still fell on London, workmen stubbornly went about rebuilding the Old Bailey.[13] By the time she saw an opening above her head, she heaved with every breath, and beads of sweat trickled from her brow. Holding tight to the railing, she heard the clerk bellow, "Bring in the prisoners."[14]

Last night, Nell had been an honored guest in a lovely house in Merton Park.[15] Now as the clerk roared, "Prisoners," the court sheriff prodded her. Nell pulled her fur tight around her body and forced herself up a final step. She shuffled, a disgraced bear of a woman, into the dock[16]— a raised stage enclosed by a solid half-wall, topped by four feet of thick glass, framed in brass piping. The entire court—judge, jury, barristers, and spectators—stared.[17] Nell hung her head.

Her codefendants—Mr. Ernest Homer, in dark tie, white shirt, vest, suit, and herringbone gray overcoat; Mrs. Elizabeth Homer, in felt hat with black net veil and fur coat brightened by a chrysanthemum pinned to the lapel;[18] and Mrs. Francis Brown, in a feathery fur jacket—fell in behind Nell.[19]

The clerk unfurled a scroll and called out the final version of a much-revised indictment.

"You four conspired together, and with persons unknown, to pretend to exercise some kind of conjuration, that through the agency of the said Helen Duncan, spirits of deceased persons should appear, and were communicating with living persons contrary to the Witchcraft Act of 1735."[20]

Nell trembled. The second of her mother's prophecies—"You'll be tried as a witch"—had come to pass.[21]

# 18

# Opening the Prosecution

A WHISPERED ECHO OF ONE WORD—WITCHCRAFT—TRAVELED FROM one set of disbelieving lips to the next, and Chief Constable West settled more comfortably on his hard bench. The Director of Public Prosecutions had fashioned a legal stranglehold designed to snare the slippery Mrs. Duncan and her vulture-like lawyer. Not only had the Director of Public Prosecutions framed the indictment, but he had successfully manipulated His Lordship Sir Gerald Dodson into presiding over this witch trial. Atkinson had composed a personal note to Sir Gerald. In bold letters, he had stamped it PRIVATE AND CONFIDENTIAL. With appropriate deference, the Director had suggested that Sir Gerald might assign himself to this delicate case of "bogus Spiritualist séances." To undercut any prudish fidelity to an independent judiciary, Atkinson had assured His Lordship, the Recorder of London, that the Office of Public Prosecutions "naturally had no right or desire to interfere with the allocation of cases" at Sir Gerald's court and trusted Sir Gerald would not "take amiss at this interposition on his part."[1] The solicitous message had charmed the judge, who now sat enthroned above the court.

In his shoulder-length silver wig, silk robe, and starched Puritan collar, His Lordship Sir Gerald Dodson was the embodiment of stern imperial justice.[2] But lurking behind his austere façade, and despite his soft spot for the theatrical pedigree of Prosecutor John Maude,[3] Sir Gerald harbored tendencies that distressed Chief Constable West. His Lordship, a devout Christian,[4] prided himself on his paternal affection for those below his station and tended toward lenient sentences for humble repentant folk.[5] Standing in the dock, head bowed, Helen Duncan resembled the kindly, plump nurse-governess of his childhood.[6]

The clerk's voice rang out, "Helen Duncan, are you guilty or not guilty?"[7]

The grandmotherly Scot's voice cracked, as she struggled to say, "Not guilty, sir."[8]

That deferential "sir" did not please the Chief Constable. Such an initial show of subservience was sure to activate the sympathetic side of this judge's prejudices.

As Chief Constable West shifted nervously in his seat, Prosecutor John Maude, unerringly suave in wig and silk,[9] took to the podium, bowed with ceremonial flare, and introduced the cast of characters.

"May it please your Lordship and members of the jury: I appear with my learned friend Mr. Elam to prosecute these four persons. We appear for the Crown, and my learned friend Mr. Loseby appears for the Defense of all four prisoners."[10]

Preliminaries out of the way, Maude turned his full attention to the wartime jury of one woman and six men.[11] In the calm and unhurried tones of a seductive conversationalist,[12] he mused, "I daresay you noticed: When the indictment was read out, the Witchcraft Act was mentioned. It is an old Act; it is two hundred years old, a little more. Sometimes that law is thought to be foolish, sometimes it is not quite such an ass."[13]

In unison, the members of the jury snickered, and Chief Constable West smirked. Maude had read the jurors' minds and used their language. All seven were ready to follow this pied piper anywhere he might choose to lead them.[14]

"In the olden days," Maude explained, "it was popular to chase poor deluded creatures who were thought to be witches. Indeed, sometimes they may have believed themselves to be witches."[15]

Maude cast a chauvinistic glance in Helen Duncan's direction, then leaned in the direction of the jury, as though to share an incredulous bit of gossip.

"The public believed in that sort of thing. But witchcraft was not the only means known in those times of playing upon the imagination of the public. There was sorcery, enchantment, spells, and one particular thing which was called conjuration, conjuring up of spirits."[16]

Squaring his shoulders, Maude waved his hand, as though to be rid of a pesky fly.

"Times changed, and our forefathers began to think it was all nonsense, utterly impossible."

Continuing his history lesson, Maude clarified that while the enlightened strata of eighteenth-century English society had no longer believed in witches, lawmakers worried about the ignorant credulous portion of the population. "You would then give rein to tiresome people who pretended they could turn the village idiot into an animal, or something like that," he said.[17]

His Lordship peered over his spectacles in the direction of the gallery.[18] Maude had just dismissed Spiritualism as "utterly impossible" and equated Britain's fastest-growing religion with "turning the village idiot into an animal."[19] Were the ardent believers in spirit communication taking offense? The Home Office and Members of Parliament had received untold numbers of letters and petitions complaining of religious persecution.[20]

As though sensing the gathering ire of the Spiritualists, Maude followed the judge's lead, swiveled left, and addressed the gallery.

"No doubt today Spiritualists would be the warmest supporters of any measure by the State against fraudulent and deplorable activities of pretending to call back the dead so that they shall be visible and audible."

Maude stopped and gathered an affirmative nod or two among the spectators. Then, motioning to the four defendants and shaking his head in disgust, his voice boomed with indignation.

"These people caused money to be paid for false pretenses, for the pretense that Helen Duncan was in a position to bring about the appearance of spirits of the dead. At this time, in wartime, when the dead are anxiously sought by persons who have lost their boys, such conduct is a false and hollow lie."[21]

With the righteous nature of the Crown's case hanging in the air, Maude launched into the tale of the crime.

"We are concerned with a small house in Portsmouth; No. 301 Copnor Road, where if you went today, you would find Mr. Homer's drugstore. Mr. Homer is the man in the dock."[22]

All heads turned to see only one man seated among the defendants, holding his fedora in his hand, his thin lower lip trembling in humiliation.

"Next to him, is Mrs. Elizabeth Jones, who is known in this case as Mrs. Homer. Although they are known as Mr. and Mrs. Homer, she is not his wife."[23]

Exposed as a weather-beaten mistress, Mrs. Homer sobbed into a hanky. West cheered; no amount of shame could erase the flaw in her character. This sniffling defendant had already proven herself capable of misrepresentation.

Satisfied that his initial jab had inflicted injury, Maude turned to the scene of the crime, a shoddy room over a chemist shop with "the attractive title: The Master Temple."[24] As the Prosecutor told his version of the tale, Lieutenant Stan Worth emerged in the marquee role as Prince Charming, setting free all the innocents who had come under Helen Duncan's wicked spell.[25]

In closing, Maude zeroed in on the jury. Using the full impact of his celebrity visage and speaking with mesmerizing power, he instructed the members of the jury.

"You have the paraphernalia of fraud: the dark room, the red light, the voices of Albert and Peggy. You must find the defendants guilty, and the mockery of the dead will cease in the little room over Mr. Homer's shop."[26]

# 19

𝕰~☙~𝕰

# The Irreverent Witness

MAUDE BOWED AND RUSHED OUT OF COURTROOM #4,[1] OFF TO defend Harold Loughans, an emotionally unstable petty criminal who had confessed to another Portsmouth crime—the gruesome murder and rape of a beerhouse grande dame. In a bizarre twist, Loughans now claimed his confession had been a gag designed to irritate "his enemy," the police.[2] The poor sod was probably innocent, but that didn't mean he would escape the hangman's noose.[3] Chief Constable West had pitied the feckless thief,[4] and Maude had agreed to defend him.[5] Still, as the Chief Constable watched Maude fly out the rear door, he worried. The examination of the Prosecution's star witness now rested on the stooped shoulders of the freakishly large Junior Prosecutor, Henry Elam.[6]

Stan Worth, in dress whites and lieutenant's stripes, made a good impression,[7] as he placed his hand on the Bible and vowed to tell the truth.

Henry Elam, all six feet and six inches of him in black cotton robe and starched collar and tightly curled rug balancing on his square head,[8] stood and posed question after question to the affable Lieutenant Worth.[9]

Stan got down to details, describing the séance room, routine, and goings-on.[10] He gloated about purposely misidentifying an initial apparition as his living aunt. Then the ghost of his uncle had appeared, and his nonexistent baby sister popped out of the Cabinet.[11]

Finished with manifesting Lieutenant Worth's relatives, Albert had moved on to materializing forms for more reverent sitters. A man seated in the second row, named Taylor Ineson, had called to a disembodied voice, "Is that you, Jarvis?"[12]

Stan described the encounter for the jury.

"This white shrouded figure came out from between the curtains, leaned over the first row, and shook hands with Taylor Ineson. Mr. Ineson said, 'Hullo, Jarvis, how are you?' They had a jovial sort of conversation. Then the ghost looked around and asked, 'Why have you got all these people with you? Why don't you come here?' The Jarvis spirit motioned to the Cabinet. Taylor Ineson said he could not go in the Cabinet. There was some muttered conversation between the two of them, as though they were having a private joke. I distinctly caught the words: bloody twister."[13]

Given British sensibilities during World War II, a spirit appearing at a séance and calling a sitter "bloody twister" was equivalent to an angel appearing at vespers and shouting obscenities. Even the Spiritualists clucked in disapproval.

Incredulous, His Lordship interrupted. "Lieutenant Worth, you caught the words 'bloody twister'? Jarvis swore at Mr. Ineson? You heard that?"[14]

Stan answered with absolute certainty, "Yes, My Lord."[15]

Leaving the tale of the foul-mouthed émigré from the Nether Regions, Lieutenant Worth leapt from descriptions of one apparition to the next. Fed up with the chicanery, he told judge and jury, he'd lodged a complaint at Police Headquarters. At his final séance, he blew a whistle, the signal for Detective Ford and his posse of police officers to rush into the Master Temple.[16]

Junior Prosecutor Elam had no more questions for his stellar witness.[17]

The time had come for cross-examination. With black robe hanging over his gaunt frame and squirrelly tailed wig bristling on the nape of his neck,[18] Charles Loseby, Mrs. Duncan's vulture-like defender, rose. Bony faced and hollow cheeked, with darkly ghoulish eyes,[19] Loseby stared blisteringly into the fresh-faced sailor.[20]

All in all, Loseby had made a perfect first impression—from the perspective of the Prosecution. Age-pocked Mr. Loseby had the look of a villainous predator, and youthful Lieutenant Stan Worth that of an unblemished prince.

Baring his fangs as though thirsting for blood, Loseby snarled, "You were not a spy, or anything in the nature of a spy, at the Portsmouth séance?"[21]

The boyish witness did not avert his eyes. Instead of wilting like a flower in scorching sun, the Lieutenant lengthened his spine and narrowed his eyes. No pansy, this naval officer; more a red-blooded lad ready for a brawl.[22]

"I beg your pardon," Stan chafed. "I was not a spy for the police. I was spying on my own account, if you prefer to call it *spying*."[23]

Loseby spat back, "I did not use the term 'spying' first; you used that term first."[24]

Stan countered, "You put in it my mouth and I used it."[25]

Loseby turned toward the gallery, preening over his petty victory.

But Lieutenant Worth was not about to cede ground; he corrected his inquisitor: "I prefer to say: I had been defrauded. I wanted to satisfy myself that I had been defrauded."[26]

Stan's measured response hit Loseby like a spitball. The barrister snapped his neck and shouted, "I do not understand why it was necessary to tell so many lies."[27]

This court proceeding was fast turning into a juvenile game of name-calling: "Spy! Spy!" and "Liar! Liar!" And much to the Chief Constable's delight, any advantage Mr. Loseby might claim as an elder was quickly evaporating.

Stan cocked his head and quipped, "Me? Many lies? I do not understand you, sir."[28]

Loseby tossed his head. "For example, when you told Mr. Homer that you thought the séance was 'amazing.' You intended to convey amazingly good."[29]

"Did I?" asked the Lieutenant, raising his eyebrows. Then he sighed indulgently and asked, "Well, sir, don't you know what 'amazing' means?"[30]

Here His Lordship found the lad impertinent and instructed him, "Don't ask counsel questions."[31]

And so Stan, now too much a wise guy for his own good, lost a bit of his sparkle. The sparring between name-callers went on and on. Even

Chief Constable West lost interest—until Loseby framed a dreaded question.

"You were a special police officer before the war, weren't you?"[32]

"Yes, for six months, in Harlington, Middlesex, in the Metropolitan Police,"[33] admitted the Lieutenant.

The Chief Constable scrutinized the faces of the jury. Were they wondering why young Worth hadn't mentioned his connection to Scotland Yard? West certainly wasn't the only man in the courtroom who knew that the young Lieutenant carried the same surname as the Detective Superintendent of the Metropolitan Police.[34] When Percy Worth spoke, every newspaper in the nation reported his ruminations on crime.

Loseby asked, "Were you connected to the police force anywhere else?"[35]

"No, sir," answered Lieutenant Worth.[36]

"Were you by any chance particularly interested in police matters?" queried Loseby.[37]

"No, sir," replied Worth.[38]

Even Chief Constable West saw that Lieutenant Worth's denials strained credibility.

Loseby, more relaxed now, asked, "You did worm yourself thoroughly into the confidence of the Master Temple, did you not?"[39]

"I just went there; I did not intend to seek anyone's confidence at all,"[40] replied Lieutenant Worth.

Loseby smiled. Calmed, as though sure he had undermined the veracity of the witness, the lawyer switched to a more philosophical line of questioning.

"Did you gain knowledge on the whole subject of Spiritualism, and the theories of the universe?"[41]

Chief Constable West waited for Junior Prosecutor Elam to shout, Objection! Irrelevant! But no objection was raised.

"Yes, sir. Well, broadly speaking."[42]

"And this world being intertwined with another world?"[43] Loseby's voice waxed ethereal.

Chief Constable West felt the proceeding slipping into dangerous territory where religious freedom reigns supreme and even the most unbelievable superstitions garner respect.

Lieutenant Worth scoffed, "Not described in that way."[44]

As though not hearing the young man's irreverent interruption, Loseby assured the jury, "The human body has two bodies: a physical body and an etheric body."[45]

Lieutenant Worth responded, although he had not been asked a question.

"All I understood was this: While a person is alive on earth, one's body and soul are together. The moment someone dies, or 'passes over,' as you call it, one's spirit leaves the body. The earthly covering stays on this earth, and the spirit goes somewhere else."[46]

Now, unexpectedly in harmony with the witness, Loseby chimed in, "And that under certain circumstances persons supposed to be dead could communicate? Not only communicate, but make themselves visible? Did you know that materialization séances only have one main point?"[47]

Rolling his eyes, Lieutenant Worth asked, "Such as what?"[48]

Loseby explained, "To provide proof of the continuity of life and survival, that was the main, and almost the only, purpose."[49]

Chief Constable West glared at the judge. Why on God's good earth was the intertwining of this life and the afterlife being addressed in a court of law? Why wasn't His Lordship pounding a gavel and putting an end to all this spooky speculation? Instead, Sir Gerald appeared enthralled by the religious nature of the testimony, as though the reality of eternal life might be adjudicated in his court.

Now in the full flush of inspiration, Loseby continued.

"Do you know this? The theory that the person, the entity, is only enabled to render himself visible through the body of the medium—that was the function of the medium?"[50]

"I had been told," replied Lieutenant Worth, "that ectoplasm comes from the medium and forms into the shape of the spirit."[51]

Loseby enthused, "Really! That out of ectoplasm the person supposed to be dead, but not dead, makes himself or herself visible. Would that be a fair way of putting it?"[52]

An incredulous grimace crossed Lieutenant Worth's face, as he replied, "If you wish, sir."[53]

With this snide quip, the argument again turned petty. With escalating volume, Mr. Loseby and Lieutenant Worth shot accusations at one another, amounting to repetitions of "You're a liar," and "You're a fool."[54] Ultimately, His Lordship tired of the injudicious exchange and interceded.

"Neither of you need raise your voices; we can all hear."[55]

In modified volume, Loseby asked Lieutenant Worth a rhetorical question: "Did you intend to be insulting?"[56]

Between clenched teeth, Lieutenant Worth responded, "No, sir."[57]

"How old are you?"[58] Loseby asked in the tone of an affronted geezer.

Old enough to die for his country, thought Chief Constable West.

"Twenty-eight, sir," [59] seethed Lieutenant Worth.

Treating Lieutenant Worth like an insolent youth and posturing as an aged sage, Loseby commented, "You take great responsibility for yourself?"[60]

Eyes closing derisively, Lieutenant Worth hissed, "I used my common sense, sir."[61]

Loseby issued a challenge, "You decided to denounce Mrs. Duncan to the police. You must have had a theory. If you thought she was a fraud, how did you think it was done?"[62]

Avoiding the trap, the Lieutenant sidestepped Loseby's question and delivered a self-righteous barb of his own. "I had been told, sir, that this was a spiritual meeting whereby good spirits—that is, people who had lived a good life and behaved as Christians should behave—were able to return. I decided there was very little that one could call Christian in what I saw."[63]

Undeterred, Loseby proposed, "Could you think of anything other than Mrs. Duncan playing boogey-boogey with a sheet over her head? That is really what you thought, is it not?"[64]

A sudden sparkle shot from Lieutenant Worth's eyes, and he admitted, "Something along those lines, sir."[65]

Incredulous, Loseby echoed his own question. "Mrs. Duncan playing boogey-boogey with a sheet over her head?"[66]

"Yes, sir," said Lieutenant Worth with unmistakable self-assurance.[67]

Winding their testy interchange to a close, Mr. Loseby summarized, "I am only going to conclude: That, as you know, yours is a completely untrue account."[68]

"Thank you, sir," quipped Lieutenant Worth in mock gratitude.[69]

And on that caustic note, testimony for day one of the witch trial of World War II ended.[70]

# 20

# Indecent Suggestions

O N HER SECOND DAY IN THE DOCK, FRIDAY, MARCH 24, 1944, NELL looked down at the gallery and spotted a former tormentor, the red-haired socialite Mrs. Molly Goldney.[1] Bordering on panic, Nell searched the pews to her left and right. Where was Harry Price? Not in court. Waiting in the wings to testify against her?[2]

As the morning wore on, Mr. Loseby deftly disposed of one prosecution witness after another, while Nell, hands clasped in a prayerful effort to reduce her shaking, waited for the humiliation of an earlier time to be exposed. By midafternoon, she dared to hope that she might escape reliving the public degradation imposed on her by Molly Goldney and Harry Price.[3] Then Detective Fred Ford, the master planner of the bungled assault on the Spirit World, took the stand.[4]

Mr. Loseby fixed his intimidating stare[5] on the ruddy-faced detective[6] and asked, "There were how many agents of the police there for the purpose of searching for this illusive cloth? I put it to you that there were eight of you."[7]

Detective Ford's kinky hair curled tighter, and his burro-like eyes popped wider,[8] as he admitted, "There were eight in all, yes, sir."[9]

Mr. Loseby's tone turned inexplicably sweet as he continued. "I suggest that your plan or scheme—I do not want to say anything disrespectful about it—was, was it not, to take Mrs. Duncan by surprise and catch her red-handed? You, having applied your mind to it and being highly intelligent, would also say the spirit visitors could not appear without apparatus?"[10]

Detective Ford amiably agreed, "Yes, a sheet was apparently necessary."[11]

Eight police officers from the Portsmouth constabulary had ransacked the Master Temple, and they had found no sheet, or cloth, or any such thing. With that admission, Nell felt a surge of joy. There was no evidence against her. The confidence she felt on the night of her arrest came back to her; she had nothing to worry about. That relief might have stayed with Nell, but her lawyer was hungry for more carnage, and he pressed on.

"Did several of the women ask to be searched? There had been a suggestion, had there not, that some in the audience were accomplices in the matter of fraud?"[12]

"Apparently so, yes, sir,"[13] Detective Ford agreed.

"Is it fair to say, you searched nobody?"[14]

From the tip of his weak chin to the top of his freckled forehead, the detective's face turned scarlet. "I still think, it would have taken the assistance of a medical man to have carried out a thorough search of the females in the room."[15]

"Why?"[16] Loseby asked, feigning innocent curiosity.

Detective Ford sputtered in response. "It would have been a medical man's job to do that, to search a woman to the extent that would have been necessary to find a sheet. Police officers could not do it."[17]

In sudden panic, Nell's eyes darted from His Lordship to the jurors and back to His Lordship. Every face registered confusion. They had no idea what Mr. Loseby was getting at or why Detective Ford was stumbling over his words. It took a mind as filthy as Harry Price to imagine such perversity and a woman as heartlessly alluring as Mrs. Molly Goldney to supervise the humiliation.[18]

In the spring of 1933, Nell's husband, Henry, had felt a special kinship with the noted investigator of psychic phenomena, Harry Price.[19] Henry and Price had formed a gentlemen's agreement: Nell became Harry Price's laboratory rat,[20] and Mrs. Molly Goldney was the cheese.[21]

On the second of Price's séances, the rapturous Molly Goldney, all sweetness and smiles, led Nell away from her husband's side, out of Price's séance parlor through double doors and into a laboratory.[22] A doctor's exam table stood in the middle of the room. A man followed and closed the doors behind him.[23]

Quickly soothing Nell's fears, Mrs. Goldney explained, "I'm a nurse, and this is Dr. Brown, a proper medical doctor. We'd like to give you a thorough physical examination."

Mrs. Goldney wrapped a nurse's pinafore over her cocktail dress, and Dr. Brown slipped a lab coat over his dinner jacket. Dr. Brown ordered Nell to take off her knickers. Without objection, Nell pulled down her underwear. Doctor and nurse motioned to the exam settee. Nell complied, hoisting herself onto the padded table. Following orders, she placed her feet in stirrups and splayed her legs.

Looking round at the glass cabinets, tests tubes, and stainless steel instruments,[24] Nell braced herself for the assault. A cold hard speculum was forced into her. Then a rubber-gloved hand poked at her insides. The bold fingers wiggled around as though looking for something. What were they searching for? A lost sanitary napkin? A baby yet unborn? A spirit waiting to cross over? Finally, that wanton hand gave up its search, and Nell relaxed. Just as her body melted like soft butter, stiff fingers jammed up her ass. Shamed by the violation, Nell whimpered, but said nothing.[25]

In a chirrupy voice, Mrs. Goldney ordered Nell to disrobe, as though nothing had happened. The nurse and the doctor watched her every move, while Nell stripped her body bare. Next, Mrs. Goldney offered to help Nell into a newly designed séance outfit.[26] Nell needed a cigarette[27] and a shot of whiskey to calm her frayed nerves,[28] but no compassion was allowed; this was pure science, an objective investigation.

Nell stepped into the large neck opening of the black satin jumpsuit, a full-body straightjacket. The openings for her feet and hands were sewn shut. As a final touch, Mrs. Goldney stitched the back tight round Nell's neck, using a secret colored thread in an undisclosed pattern.[29]

Dr. Brown swung open the double doors, and Nell faced a parlor packed with men and ladies dressed in evening attire. Like a child trying out ice skates for the first time, she slid one slippery satin covered foot in front of the other gliding unsteadily from the laboratory to the Cabinet.

Mr. Price blindfolded Nell with one of Mrs. Goldney's black silk stockings,[30] and Nell fell into trance.

That night, Albert had appeared in all his translucent whiteness. Yet, when the psychic investigators checked the back of her straightjacket, the stitches in their secret code had not been broken.[31]

The third séance had followed the same humiliating pattern.[32]

At the fourth of Harry Price's degrading investigations, the indignity preyed on Nell's mind.[33] Her trance felt more like a fitful sleep than a heavenly escape. Her body retched involuntarily, and blood poured from both her nostrils. Shaking off her trance, she focused on the sneering face of Harry Price. Always duplicitous, the psychic investigator offered a supportive arm and escorted her to the upholstered couch. There she sprawled, trapped in the satin straightjacket, while Mrs. Goldney cleaned the blood from her face.[34]

Price, smiling, posturing, turning on his charm, loosened the stitching around her hands and offered her a cigarette.[35] Nell reached for it; her hand shaking uncontrollably. Like a freed hostage, she inhaled while Price lit the fag and murmured in her ear.

"Mrs. Duncan, thank you so much for your cooperation. We have just one more small procedure. It's quite harmless. The whole business will last only a few minutes. I've invited Dr. Brown, Professor McDougall, Professor Flugel, and Professor Fraser Harris to remain in the room as observers."[36]

Still disoriented, Nell looked up at the men gathered around her. The men parted and the laboratory doors opened, giving Nell a clear view into the examination room. In place of the exam table stood a monstrous machine with transformers, rheostats, coils, and masses of wires.[37] Shivering, Nell shook her head and repeated, "No, no, no, no more. I can't take any more."

Her husband, Henry, rushed to her side and, speaking in fatherly tones, reassured her. "Nellie. Nellie. Everything is all right. There's not a thing to worry about. Mr. Price is your friend. Now you just take Mr. Price's hand, and he'll tell you exactly what you need to do."

Those words mobilized the slumbering bear in Nell. She flushed and screamed; then, raging to her feet, she dealt a smashing blow to Henry's face.[38] Henry fell to the floor, and Nell, showing more triumph than remorse, stepped over him and asked to use the lavatory.[39]

Harry Price pointed in the direction of the hallway. Nell, erect but still costumed in feetless satin, tried to gather her dignity and shuffle toward the hall. Once through the door, out of Harry Price's den, the séance suit tripped her. Catching herself on a hallway chair, she slid to the floor and ripped the cloth from around her feet. Two of her tormentors, the very worst two, Dr. Brown and Molly Goldney, scurried into the foyer and scowled down at her. Looking up, Nell panted like a trapped dog. Taking pity, Dr. Brown said, "I'll get the sorry creature some water."[40]

Dr. Brown moved, and Nell saw the door to the street. She bolted across the room as fast as she could. Not even as a child running with a sack of stolen apples on her back had she run so fast. Molly Goldney fell to the floor. Nell flung the door open and hurled herself down the marble steps into the dark night.[41]

But escape was as cruel as captivity. Nell fell onto the black and white tile footpath leading to Price's establishment,[42] then regained her footing, but stumbled again as she reached the sidewalk. She clung to the iron fencing in front of Harry Price's bay window.[43] The séance suit was now twisted around her legs, and she could not get up again. She tore at her garment, ripping the straightjacket, trying to free herself from the silken cage. All the while, Nell bleated like a lamb going to slaughter.[44]

A crowd of kind and concerned passersby gathered.

Nell pleaded, "Help me. Help me. I'm a sick woman."

Mrs. Goldney, Dr. Brown, Harry Price, and Henry rushed to the sidewalk, joining the crowd.[45]

Henry dropped to his knees, wrapped his arms around her, and crooned, "Nellie. Nellie. Sweet lass. I'm here. It's all right. It's all right."[46]

A bobby in helmet and uniform rushed up, crouched beside Nell, and asked, "Are these men hurting you, love? Do you need an ambulance?"[47]

Nell looked at the crowd but could not find words to explain. Instead, she looked up at Mr. Price and his accomplices and let fly a string of obscenities. Then, she nestled her head on Henry's shoulder and sobbed.

Henry assured the concerned police officer, "She's my wife."

That all had happened before Price hired Dr. X and Dr. Z.[48]

More than a decade had passed; but now, sitting in the dock of Court-room #4, Nell braced herself for another bout of public humiliation.

Mr. Loseby, her own lawyer, asked Detective Ford, "Are you suggest-ing that there is anything beyond stripping and an ordinary search that could possibly be necessary?"[49]

Detective Ford's head bobbed up and down, up and down. "Yes. I still consider that it was a medical man's job."[50]

Loseby placed his fingers on his cheek and furrowed his brow, feign-ing confusion. Then he probed further.

"Tell me what you mean. Why? What could a medical man have done in the direction of discovering any possible getaway for the sheet? What are you suggesting? Where could a medical man have searched? Do not hesitate to say it; we are in a court of law."[51]

Detective Ford gulped between words. "A woman might have secreted the sheet in another part of her body."[52]

Mr. Loseby pouted and pushed on, doing his ultimate best to coax the implausible explanation from the blushing detective's lips—that Nell or perhaps someone else, Mrs. Homer or her daughter or Mrs. Brown, had quickly pushed a full-length sheet up her dress and inserted it up her vagina with eight policemen watching their every move.

Even His Lordship began shifting uncomfortably inside his silk smock.

But Mr. Loseby didn't stop grilling Detective Ford. "What part of a woman's body would not be revealed by stripping? What are you suggesting?"[53]

Finally, His Lordship could stand no more, and he interrupted the questioning.

"These are all speculations, the merest speculation. What more can he say? He has made it as plain as anyone could make it plain without actually putting it into words. There it is."[54]

Deflated, Mr. Loseby sat down.

Prosecutor Maude popped up. In a no-nonsense voice, he asked, "De-tective Ford, how long have you been a police officer."[55]

Detective Ford paused to calculate and then answered, "Seventeen years."[56]

Without hesitation King's Counsel posed a follow-up question, "And, in seventeen years, have you ever found it necessary to employ a medical man to search a woman?"

"No,"[57] came Detective Ford's emphatic reply.

Prosecutor Maude had rescued Detective Ford and given Nell a momentary reprieve. As the detective left the witness stand, Nell braced herself for a final prosecution witness: Mr. Harry Price.

Instead, Prosecutor Maude stood up and announced, "My Lord, that is the case for the Crown."[58]

# 21

# Opening the Defense

O N Monday, March 27, 1944, Chief Constable Arthur West
entered Courtroom #4 still digesting the weekend's events. On Friday, just after midnight, the *Luftwaffe* had bombed the Middle Temple[1]
where his ally Prosecutor John Maude had been called to the bar[2] and continued, occasionally, to take his meals.[3] The deafening blast had shaken the
ground and unleashed a shaft of blue-hot flame that streaked skyward before spewing incendiaries along Temple Lane, some landing dangerously
close to Charles Loseby's chambers.[4] The fire brigade had quickly extinguished nineteen fires, but the roof of the grand Temple Hall blazed on.[5]
That scene was replicated all over London; bombs fell and buildings
burned.[6]

Nevertheless, on Saturday, other events temporarily took priority over
responses to the attack. Barristers, witnesses, and defendants turned out
for Salute to the Soldier celebrations. London's entire war-weary population had scurried onto the underground, rushing to Hyde Park like ants to
their queen. The gala spirit was reminiscent of old times: Street vendors
hawked Union Jacks and tea sellers set up carts on every corner. The
crowds clamored for a front-row view of the military parade. Children
atop their fathers shoulders heard the bagpipes and strained to see the
Scots Guardsmen in their plaid kilts, as they swaggered to the whining
blare. A contingent of tanks grumbled along slowly behind them. The En-

glish Fife and Drum Corps strutted to the rat-ta-tat-tat of their music. Group after group passed: the fresh young gals of the nursing corps, sailors in their yoked shirts and bell bottoms, Royal Air Force fighters in their leather helmets. All marched to the cheers of a grateful multitude. The Choir of the Royal Air Force sang "Onward Christian Soldiers," as the crowd silently bowed their heads.[7] The parade wasn't really a celebration; it was a send-off. Thousands and thousands of these soldiers were going to die.

Sunday evening, the Chief Constable, like nearly every citizen of Britain, had huddled by his radio, listening to the crackling voice of Winston Churchill crow about the approach of the Second Front, a massive Allied invasion the likes of which the world had never seen. Churchill had boasted, "The armies of the United States are here and pouring in." And he had warned, "To deceive and baffle the enemy as well as to exercise the forces, there will be many false alarms, many feints, and dress rehearsals."[8] Of course, this very speech was a ploy to convince the public that the cross-channel invasion would be launched later rather than sooner.[9]

Chief Constable West knew better: Plans were progressing rapidly, and German spy planes were flying over the south coast.[10] Arthur West wanted this trial over and done; he wanted Helen Duncan and Albert, her loud-mouthed cheesecloth puppet, out of circulation; and he wanted to get back to Portsmouth. Nonetheless, the Chief Constable did not think Mrs. Duncan's conviction and incarceration were foregone conclusions.

Chief Constable West expected the queen of the spook worshippers to take the stand by the end of the day.[11] No doubt she'd put on a good performance: poor Nell, head bowed in humble submission, the lowly Scots grandmother,[12] sick with worry over her sons in the services[13] and extending comfort to other grieving folk.[14] That depiction made the Chief Constable sick. He could only hope that Helen Duncan's image would crack under Prosecutor Maude's grilling, that jury and judge would see this woman as the worst kind of criminal: a heartless fraud, callously preying on the inconsolable and profiting from war's misery.[15]

But before the Prosecution got a crack at the old girl, Charles Loseby would take the floor for the Defense.[16]

As it turned out, despite his raptor-like appearance, Charles Loseby, barrister at law, was a force to contend with. His resumé was sterling, and his connections were downright impressive. A sixty-three-year-old gentleman of some distinction, Charles Loseby boasted an entry in *Who's Who*.[17] Born into privilege, young Charles, son of landed gentry, grew up among the famously flowered gardens of Market Bosworth—a stone's throw from where good King Richard III fought the War of the Roses.[18] By the time he reached manhood, Charles was sampling the niceties of colonial life, attending university in South Africa, soaking up the January sunshine, and courteously thanking the Africans who cleaned his rooms. As soon as he graduated, Charles loaded his trunks onto a steamer and headed for London. He settled into the Inns of the Court and commenced the study of law. In 1914, at age twenty-five, Charles was called to the bar but did not take permanent chambers amid the stained-glass windows, the manicured lawns, and the tastefully furnished sitting rooms of Gray's Inn.[19] Patriotism won out; Loseby volunteered for the Great War.[20]

As barrister at law, Charles Loseby used his influence and pulled a commission. Captain Charles Loseby commanded the First Lancashire Fusiliers. During his hellish stint in the lice-infested trenches, he was gassed and wounded. The gas turned his skin sallow and gave his voice its rasp. The bullets left his arm permanently crippled, hanging limply at his side.[21] Loseby returned to England as a war hero and ran for Parliament. His war injuries assured his election.

While in Parliament, Loseby worked closely with Winston Churchill, championing veterans' benefits. During that period, Churchill dropped by Loseby's Kensington home for tea. Later, Loseby played an instrumental part in establishing the Ministry of Health and campaigned for women's emancipation. On his resumé, Loseby claimed a continued friendship with the Prime Minister.[22]

Lately, Loseby had turned his zeal to emancipating the Spirit World. Chief Constable West could only hope that since taking up with the spooks, Loseby had degenerated into a nerve-shaken old man who had burned all his bridges.

Beginning ceremonially, Charles Loseby, his horsehair wig balanced atop his head and its pigtail tied in a bow, bowed to judge and jury. With a slow drawl that failed to smooth out the croaky quality of his voice,[23] Loseby opened his case: "May it please you, my Lord. Members of the jury, the Prosecution has concluded, and the time for the Defense has come. My learned friend Mr. Maude very carefully and, if I may respectfully say so, wisely made reference to a body of people called Spiritualists. Every one of the persons in the dock . . . "

Loseby's voice trailed off; he took a quick glance at the defendants, scratched his forehead, and confessed his first doubts.

". . . I believe, but I am not quite sure, belongs to that body of Spiritualists."[24]

Clearing his throat, the barrister continued.

"My learned friend Mr. Maude said that he should have thought Spiritualists would welcome a trial. My learned friend is quite right, and just as he commenced the Prosecution's case with certain words of courtesy, so I want to do so. It was at the express wish of the Defense that these people were brought to this place; I, having been courteously consulted by the Prosecution, agreed and asked for this course. It is an opportunity long and eagerly awaited by the Spiritualists: a trial by a British jury at the Central Criminal Court, a prosecution undertaken by the Director of Public Prosecutions, and the Prosecution entrusted to my learned friends Mr. Maude and Mr. Elam, representing the highest traditions of the English bar. I would like to say that the Office of Public Prosecutions has granted every possible facility and every possible courtesy; of that there is no doubt."[25]

Attempting a smile in the direction of Prosecutor Maude, Loseby's lips crinkled. John Maude lifted his eyebrows encouragingly.

"There is one matter," Loseby admitted. Then, noticing the jury's attentive stares, he waved the seven men and one woman off dismissively. "It does not concern you."[26]

It did concern the Chief Constable. Arthur West relaxed on his wooden pew and watched Charles Loseby squirm. Apparently West had engineered his behind-the-scenes intimidation successfully. Weeks ago, on that day in late January when Loseby had intimidated the Portsmouth magistrates into granting bail, the overzealous barrister had stood on the court stairs grandstanding for the local press. In his signature black fedora, wool overcoat and polka-dot ascot, Loseby had proclaimed that Home Secretary Herbert Morrison had given his personal assurance that Spiritualist mediums were due immunity from prosecution and that in arresting Helen Duncan, the Portsmouth police had defied the Home Secretary's instructions.[27]

Mr. Loseby's public chastisement had backfired. Chief Constable West had turned the barrister's injudicious boasting into ammunition for the Prosecution. West had expected that his favorite judge, His Lordship Sir Grimwood Mears, would find the Spiritualist assertion of special privilege irksome. Sir Grimwood, a retired gentleman who continued to serve God and country as Chairman of the County Bench, remained a man to be reckoned with. A graduate of Exeter College and Oxford University, called to the bar by the Inner Temple, appointed to investigate German atrocities, Secretary of the Dardanelles Commission and Royal Commission on Irish Rebellion, attaché to America, Chairman of Bombay Back Bay Enquiry Committee, Chief Justice of High Court Allahabad,[28] even now, in the winter of 1944, Sir Grimwood Mears evoked a bit of mystery. He kept his pulse on England's southeast coast from Meonstoke House.[29] This stately brick estate lay a safe distance from the coast, just west of the walled streets and attached stone houses of Meonstoke village.

Though the manor was only a mile down a muddy road from the local pub, the villagers weren't entirely sure who lived there or what went on inside.[30] There were rumors, however. Late in the evening when brew filled heads and loosened lips, the locals whispered: "The big house, it's military now, all top secret and hush, hush."[31] But they were just guessing; none of them really knew.

In his study, overlooking his duck pond, Sir Grimwood had attended to a discretely delivered communication from Chief Constable Arthur West: a personal note with sensitive passages marked "Confidential" and a newspaper clipping from the *Portsmouth News*. By the time Sir Grimwood had finished reading, he had been predictably perturbed with Charles Loseby. Who was this man, this barrister, this believer in ghosts and goblins who claimed influence with the Home Secretary? What were these assurances of special privilege? Right there and then, Sir Grimwood picked up a fountain pen and wrote to the Home Office.[32]

As planned, a disapproving word from Sir Grimwood Mears set the wheels of bureaucracy in motion. In 1916, Mears had served as Secretary on the Dardanelles Commission;[33] the report had laid blame for the military disaster clearly at Churchill's feet. Churchill's military scheme had been ill planned, pitifully executed, fraught with procrastination, dogged by personality clashes, and doomed by lack of ammunition. Mears's Commission of Inquiry had held Churchill, then First Lord of the Admiralty, responsible for the senseless loss of life.[34] For making those observations, Grimwood Mears had been dubbed Knight of the Order of the Crown. And Winston Churchill had lost his job. Everyone with political ambitions remembered and feared Sir Grimwood Mears. Rumor had it that Home Secretary Morrison was positioning himself to unseat Prime Minister Winston Churchill.

Sir Grimwood Mears wanted Charles Loseby sanctioned on the floor of the House of Commons, and he sent that message to Home Secretary Morrison.[35] The Prosecution had apparently offered Mr. Loseby a deal.

West imagined their meeting:

*Maude and Robey corner Loseby at the Garricks, the gentlemen's club to which all three belonged.[36] While other members, famed actors and celebrity lawyers, swirl brandy and smoke fine cigars,[37] Robey, his bushy eyebrows arched, and Maude, his alluring smile on display, make a friendly proposition: "Charles, remember Sir Grimwood Mears? The old boy wants Secretary Morrison to denounce you in Parliament. But we're prepared to offer you a more palatable option: Eat your own words. Open the Defense case with apologies to the Office of Public Prosecutions, Home Secretary Morrison, and the Portsmouth police and magistrates."*

Gathering courage for this odious task, Loseby inhaled visibly and stood tall. Turning to the gallery, addressing the press and public, the shame-faced barrister issued the required apology: "You may have heard, you may have seen—I cannot blind myself to the fact that you may have read the press—that in the lower court, merely on the initiation of this case, I did make a certain protest which was listened to with great courtesy by the local Bench. If there is a complaint of any kind in the matter, I agree it is a complaint not against the local Bench, nor against the police. I want to clear that up once and for all, as far as this trial is concerned."[38]

Loseby looked beseechingly at Chief Constable West, and West tilted his head in a gesture of magnanimous forgiveness. The Defense Counsel looked down, ruffled through his notes, and adjusted his wig, readying to advance the Defense case in earnest.

Chief Constable West surveyed the courtroom and found a nearly universal expression of befuddlement on the faces of jury and gallery. Loseby's audience had no clue what he had been prattling on about. From West's viewpoint, Loseby could not have launched his opening statement more perfectly.

Loseby, now freed from his fear of reprisal, faced the jury, motioned to the dock, and nearly sang, "Members of the jury, these four people are charged with conspiring together to pretend to exorcise."[39]

Prosecutor Maude leapt to his feet and shouted, "No—'exercise.'"[40]

Loseby grabbed his notes and muttered, "I thought it was a misprint. I have never been interested in that body of people called—possibly, ridiculously called—witches." Then, once again trying to recover his decorum, he did his best to bellow, "I am going to say, hotly if need be, that the Witchcraft Act of 1735 is completely obsolete, simply and completely ridiculous. The charge is that the defendants pretended that they were in a position to bring about the appearance of the spirits of deceased persons. Neither this, nor any other medium, would dream of making such a claim."[41]

Pausing to gaze respectfully at the talented Mrs. Duncan, Loseby caught sight of Mrs. Homer, or Mrs. Jones, or whatever the voluble mistress of the Master Temple called herself. Quite spontaneously, he confided to the jury, "Bye the bye, I do know that certain words are alleged to have been said by Mrs. Homer, the rather talkative Mrs. Homer, if I might respectfully call her 'Mrs. Homer,' that might possibly bring her in danger of that indictment."[42]

Having honestly dispensed with Mrs. Homer and her shamelessly boastful behavior, Loseby graced Mrs. Duncan with a toothy grin and continued: "I have never heard a medium claim that she could bring about the appearance of a spirit from the Other World. The medium has said, 'I am nothing; I am a person of no importance at all, but my body may be used.'"[43]

At the mention of Mrs. Duncan sacrificing her body to the will of her Spirit Control, Loseby touched his hand to his heart and moaned. "I cannot imagine that soldiers will fight less bravely because they are told that hope has become certainty, and that there is no such thing as death, and that continuity of life can be scientifically proven. It is, is it not, a large issue?"

Loseby closed his eyes reverently and nodded, affirming the answer to his own question. Lifting his lids, he motioned to the dock. "There are four persons standing there, but only one of them is a person of importance; there is one person there of great importance; that is the woman Helen Duncan."[44]

Swiveling to stare across the court, Loseby explained his purpose. "Members of the jury, it is my duty to watch you. I have to watch your minds, and I have to fight for your minds. I am struggling all the time to find out the workings of your minds. I am trying to prove in reality—why should I shrink from it?—it is scientifically proven that there is a Spirit World knocking at the door."[45]

For the next two hours, Loseby earnestly pleaded and preached to the jury. He begged them to set aside prejudice and consider objective evidence of the Afterlife. He previewed paranormally manifested details of Mrs. Duncan's séances. He instructed them in a bit of Spiritualist mythology. Mrs. Duncan, he said, suffered from spontaneous burn marks; sudden bursts of light had inflicted this stigmata-like injury on her. Loseby bemoaned the violent and sacrificial injustice of her arrest.[46]

Nearing his climax, Loseby sidestepped decorum, turned his back on the judge, and propositioned the jury. "Now I am going to pause, members of the jury, to make a digression. If it is true that Mrs. Duncan is a materialization medium, it means there is a spirit world near her at this moment. If she has got a guide, he will be with her now, probably waiting for an opportunity to help her. Under certain circumstances, she might materialize the spirits here in Central Criminal Court. Why not?"[47]

The thought of an evidentiary séance at the Old Bailey so excited Loseby that his tenor reached nearly an ecstatic pitch: "What would the difficulty be? Mrs. Duncan requires but a naked room, with a small bare portion curtained off, and a red light; that and no more! Members of the jury, I am going to ask you to ask my Lord if you might be allowed to see and hear Mrs. Duncan's guide, Albert."[48]

His Lordship Sir Gerald Dodson coughed.

Loseby stole a quick glance at the judge and reminded the jury of the necessary caveat: "Of course, on such conditions as my Lord thought right."[49]

Loseby bowed to the jury and turned to His Lordship. The Defense was prepared to call its first witness.

Chief Constable West braced himself. Helen Duncan was about to waddle to the stand and, in her guileless grandmother brogue,[50] humbly tell tales of self-sacrifice and blessed unions with angelic spirits. And His Lordship, with his tolerance for the entire pantheon of religious beliefs,[51] would patiently abide this heretical drivel.

*Helen and Henry Duncan, 1931*

*Chief Constable Arthur
Charles West*

*Harry Price*

*Byculla House, Police Headquarters, 1944*

Detective Sergeant
Fred Ford

Lieutenant Stanley Worth

*Holloway Prison, 1944*

*Helen Duncan, 1944*

*Charles Loseby,*
*Attorney for the Defense*

*Lead Prosecutor
John Maude*

*Henry Elam,
Assistant Prosecutor*

*Old Bailey, Central Criminal Court, 1944*

*His Lordship Sir Gerald Dodson, Recorder of London*

# 22

## Betrayal

THE PROSECUTION HAD RESTED, THE DEFENSE HAD BEGUN, AND HARRY
Price had not yet been called as an expert witness. To Price's admirers, the oversight was a shame. A few knew that the Chief Constable had implored him to testify and that Price had engineered his own escape.[1] The high-profile exposure might have backfired. Testifying in some backwater Sheriff's Court had presented little danger to his reputation, but being grilled by the likes of Charles Loseby at the Old Bailey could have conceivably exposed the embellishment of his autobiography.[2] Price had informed the Office of Public Prosecutions that due to ill health— "Angina, you know"—he could not endure the stress. The Assistant Director of Public Prosecutions had graciously passed Price's polite refusal onto the Chief Constable.[3]

But when Molly Goldney returned from the trial swooning over the witty young lieutenant, Price seethed with jealousy. He could have been the star witness who had basked in the limelight, with adoring fans retelling his stories and newspapers quoting him in headlines.[4] To this day, his colleagues delighted when he told the uproarious tale of the X-ray incident.[5]

Price's version began after Albert had mortified the psychic investigator with suggestions of sexual indiscretion.[6] Price had redoubled his efforts to depose the cheesecloth deity. The uneducated Mrs. Duncan, confusing a state-of-the-art X-ray machine with some kind of fearsome apparatus meant to probe her private parts, had slugged her husband and bolted from the room.[7]

On the sidewalk, as Henry Duncan knelt to mollify his wife, Price had convinced an overly sympathetic bobby that Mrs. Duncan was a hysteric and that Dr. Brown, a physician, and Mrs. Goldney, a midwife, could best soothe her tattered nerves. There was no need for that interfering police officer to know that just days earlier Mrs. Duncan had been subjected to, as Albert had called it, "a terrible time" and "had undergone such unspeakable things" at the hands of these same two people.[8]

Back in the laboratory, Price wrote a check. Mrs. Goldney kept watch over Mrs. Duncan, while Dr. Brown sidled up to Mr. Duncan, suggesting that the medium's "unfortunate disarrangement" might be partially remedied if the husband would allow himself to be thoroughly searched. An indignant Mr. Duncan refused the offer but did accept the check.[9]

At 11:20 PM, Price looked at his watch and said, "It's late, and we're getting nowhere. I'll call a private car to take Duncan and his wife away."[10]

Dr. Brown walked to the door, held it open, and told Henry Duncan, "Well, then, you've made your bed, haven't you?"

At that moment, Price assumed he had seen the last of Mr. and Mrs. Duncan. Most men would have taken irreparable offense had their integrity been so impugned and their wife's body so violated. Not Henry Duncan.

It was after midnight when the phone rang at Price's laboratory.

Mr. Duncan offered a sheepish, "Hello."

Irritated by the bothersome weasel, Price said, "Mr. Duncan, I'm certain you and I have no further business. You have served our purpose, and I am quite finished with you."

In response, Mr. Duncan mumbled pathetic excuses. "I just wanted to explain myself, sir . . . correct any negative assumptions about me . . . she handed me a sanitary napkin . . . in my pocket . . . an error in judgment . . . I trust you . . . not in cahoots with my wife . . . embarrassed by her commotion . . . next séance."[11]

At the mention of a next séance, Price realized he was in a very strong bargaining position; he cut a very good deal.

Exactly one week later, Mr. Duncan delivered his wife to Price's laboratory—
no strings attached. Once more, the two men shook hands, and Mr. Duncan left, off to the cinema.[12]

Price took Mrs. Duncan by the elbow and led her into his laboratory.

The medical exam table stood in the middle of the room. Five fashionably attired people, three men and two ladies, surrounded it. Two of the men, for reasons of deniability, introduced themselves as Dr. X and Dr. Z, a gynecologist and a physician. The men hoisted Mrs. Duncan onto the exam table. Noticing her wince, Dr. Z discovered a seriously infected abscess on her upper arm. By the time the full medical and gynecological exam was complete, the doctors had probed every orifice of the medium's body and come up with disturbing results. Mrs. Duncan was in a pitiful state. Her right eardrum had suffered multiple perforations, permanent injuries caused by slaving in thunderously loud textile mills. An infection of her left middle ear was oozing a purulent discharge. Her nasal passages were likewise seeping. And to Price's disappointment, her uterus was undersized and anteverted; her cervix small and scarred; her anus taut. There was no sign that Mrs. Duncan had hidden any foreign material in the recesses of her body.[13]

Exam complete, Mrs. Duncan sat up slowly. All the fight had gone out of her. As they had done many times before, the attending women sewed Mrs. Duncan into her séance garment and led the weary medium to the Cabinet.

An audience of fifteen sitters observed an uneventful séance punctuated by sharp moaning by the medium and carping by Albert about the investigators' cruelty. The lights were turned on to find Mrs. Duncan's eyes rolling back into her head and blood streaming from her nostrils. Price's assistants cut her out of her séance suit. She lifted her hand to wipe her nose, saw the abscess on her arm, and whimpered, "I am in an awful mess."[14]

Right then, Mr. Duncan came back to the laboratory. The miserable Mrs. Duncan looked at him adoringly. Mr. Duncan greeted Price with a handshake and a question, "Did you get what you needed?"

Dr. X and Dr. Z cut into the conversation and insisted that Mr. Duncan take his wife to the hospital for immediate medical care.

•

Mr. Duncan hesitated. "But I had really hoped to clear things up with Mr. Price."

"Not now," seethed Dr. X. "Now, Mr. Duncan, you will come with us and attend to your wife."[15]

Dr. X and Dr. Z had disappointed Harry Price. He had paid a generous purse and received nothing of value. Not only had they failed to find anything suspicious in Mrs. Duncan's anatomy, but they had exhibited unhelpful compassion and carted her off to St. Thomas's Hospital. With Mrs. Duncan recuperating under the watchful care of an infirmary staff, Price's research came to an untimely end. He had yet another theory of how the medium produced her phantoms. But without her body available for experimentation, Price resorted to Henry Duncan for confirmation.

Mr. Duncan arrived at Price's premises at 3:30 PM on June 11, 1931. A cohort of psychic investigators sat round the boardroom ready to have a heart-to-heart discussion with the medium's husband.[16]

Mr. Bois opened the meeting with a direct confrontation: "Mr. Duncan, we are rather suspicious as to the genuineness of the phenomena. It appears that the material extruded by the medium is butter muslin. How do you explain that?"[17]

"God only knows." Mr. Duncan shrugged. Then, in response to the skeptical facial expression of his interrogator, he struck a self-righteous note. "Do you think for one moment that I would get Mrs. Duncan to come here and produce fraud? The whole idea is preposterous."[18]

Clearly, the husband intended to save himself at his wife's expense.[19] The attitude pleased Price, and he observed, "The medium was searched thoroughly and led to the Cabinet. She must have secreted the muslin."[20]

Dumbfounded, Mr. Duncan asked, "How, in the name of anything and after you have examined her, could she secrete this substance?"[21]

Mr. Bois admitted, "I confess this is the puzzle. What is the explanation for all this?"[22]

"God knows. I do not. You know I am not a Spiritualist."[23] Mr. Duncan continued to plead his innocence. He confided that before two séances he had taken his wife into the bathroom and had forced his own pelvic exams on her. Attempting to elevate his status to that of an intelligent gentleman, he continued, "Here is my explanation: Some persons can easily go into hypnotic trance, and the idea of immortality is so much impressed within that mind that the subconscious will do anything to prove eternal life."[24]

Mr. Bois expressed interest. "So the medium is quite prone to take any steps to back up her belief? Is it to prove the existence of beings outside ourselves, and therefore the medium tries to back up her theory by producing something which she already arranged?"[25]

"Not consciously," explained Mr. Duncan. "All mediums have struck me as being of a very childish disposition. I would say that under trance conditions the child mind comes to the surface. That childish mind produces these things."[26]

Mr. Duncan then joined the other investigators in a lively discussion of how his wife might have hidden and produced her apparitions.

Another of Price's collaborators confronted the husband. "Do you swear that you do not know where the stuff is concealed?"[27]

"Of course, I do swear,"[28] Duncan reacted with indignation.

There it was: the husband's confession.

Mr. Bois summed up the husband's mealy-mouthed admission: "He thinks she is genuine sometimes, but that she is quite capable of humbugging."[29]

Harry Price savored Mr. Duncan's cowardly betrayal, and he intended to publish every word.[30]

As these memories receded from his mind, Price leafed through a stack of newspapers, all reporting on the most dramatic witch trial of the century. Even the society pages had taken up the controversy; fashion editors alternatively praised or berated Mrs. Duncan's sense of style. Once again, the bovine medium was upstaging him.[31] Price rang up Molly Goldney; he was determined to make his influence known at this trial after all.

## 23

## Surrender

THE MOMENT HAD COME FOR THE PRIMARY DEFENDANT TO TAKE THE witness stand. Head bowed, Nell wrestled with conflicting parts of her self. One part, the confident spirit buried within, had wanted to take the witness stand by storm and bellow her story.[1] Another part, the fear-stricken child, wanted to hide beneath a table, catatonic and ashamed.[2]

Mr. Loseby cleared his throat and addressed the bench. "My Lord, I hope, this case being of some difficulty to me, to be allowed to call Mr. Homer first."[3]

Nell folded her hands and squeezed them tight, the child praying for a reprieve. His Lordship mused, "I do not suppose there is any objection to who you call first, is there?"[4]

Nell's lungs filled with involuntary relief.

But before she could exhale, Prosecutor Maude objected. "My Lord, I should ask that the ordinary procedure of the Court be followed, as in every other case, and that Mrs. Duncan should be called now."[5]

Nell held her breath and gazed at her folded hands.

Mr. Loseby persisted. "All I ask is to be allowed to proffer Mrs. Duncan after my expert witnesses have been called. The real value of this proffering of Mrs. Duncan is really, to my mind, better, and more easily followed by the jury, if they know what to look out for and what to see."[6]

"I am anxious to help you personally, Mr. Loseby," His Lordship said sympathetically, but then hesitated. After a thoughtful moment, he added, "I do not think that is an adequate reason. Therefore, the ordinary procedure had better be followed. You should begin with Mrs. Duncan."[7]

Nell closed her eyes tight, praying harder.

Mr. Loseby resisted. "I hope your Lordship will forgive me, but that would be definitely embarrassing to me."[8]

There was irritation in every syllable of His Lordship's response. "Well, Mr. Loseby, I have asked for a reason and you have given it, but I do not think it is a sufficient reason. And, there, the matter must end."[9]

But Mr. Loseby did not yield. "May I say my Lord that Mrs. Duncan can give no evidence at all? She is in trance. I want to be allowed to offer her at a time which I think, watching her myself, would be a better time."[10]

Nell bit down on her lip as she heard scattered chuckles rise from the gallery below.

His Lordship barked at Mr. Loseby, "If Mrs. Duncan is not going to give evidence, call someone who is."

Nell heard the irritation in the judge's voice. His Lordship thought that Nell needed nothing more than a stiff jab to the midriff. Brits assumed defendants who didn't testify in their own defense had something to hide. The English found the American custom, "the right against self-incrimination," nothing more than naïve indulgence.[11] Despite the judge's disapproving snort, when Mr. Loseby called Mr. Homer to testify, Nell slumped more comfortably on her chair.

After Mr. Homer, more pallid than usual, bumbled through his softly spoken testimony,[12] Mr. Loseby informed his Lordship that Nell's other co-defendants, Elizabeth Homer and Francis Brown, would not testify in their own defense. Then Mr. Loseby had second thoughts and stumbled into a proposition.[13]

"I propose," Defense Counsel said, "to put Mrs. Duncan into the box in order that my friend can cross-examine her at a later stage, your Lordship."[14]

Sir Gerald Dodson responded to this breach of protocol through clenched teeth. "I thought we had dealt with that matter. If Mrs. Duncan was going in the witness box, she ought to have gone first. I made that plain." His Lordship paused to regulate his rising blood pressure and then broached Mr. Loseby's more irksome mutiny, his proposal that Courtroom #4 be transformed into a séance parlor and that Nell channel spirits of the dead for judge and jury. "I understand," fumed the judge, "that you would proffer Mrs. Duncan for some kind of experiment."[15]

Suddenly enlivened with possibility, Mr. Loseby chirped, "Yes, my Lord. Yes, my Lord. I make that offer."

"I shall not," snarled his Lordship, "allow the jury to be troubled with a matter of that sort. So that is the end of that."

The judge's pronouncement should have cut Defense Counsel down to size like a scythe slashing through winter wheat, but Mr. Loseby could not be so easily dismissed. He persisted, "I ought to draw your Lordship's attention to . . ."[16]

"You have made the offer," His Lordship growled. "I do not think there is much likelihood of my being inveigled into letting the jury witness some sort of demonstration or other. Now, we better go on with the evidence."[17]

When witnesses began testifying to her extraordinary gift, Nell lifted her chin. One sincere devotee after another spoke of lost loved ones who had returned bringing comfort and proof of eternal life. These believers told the jury what they had seen at the Master Temple: apparitions in different shapes—tall, wide, short, thin—had taken form. Often sitters recognized a family member and friend by a distinct physical feature: shining blond hair, a mole on the left cheek, an aquiline nose, a bronze complexion, rheumatoid knuckles, a handlebar mustache. All Nell's defenders glowed with reverent goodness. Every single one overflowed with gratitude for the gifts Nell had given them.[18]

Basking in their testimonials, Nell held her head high and realized that her husband had been right after all. Channeling the dead had been her destiny. But it wasn't actually Henry's words that brought her a Spirit Control; it was his breakdown.[19]

Nell had awoken, feeling Henry's ear resting on her bulging belly. The baby, her third pregnancy,[20] kicked, and Nell wanted to smack Henry straight across his big head. Her abdomen screamed in pain.[21] She gritted her teeth, held her temper, and managed to fake a grin.

Henry jumped from the bed and told her, "Don't get up, darling. I'll make the tea."

Nell glowered in his direction thinking: tea nothing. She needed a cigarette and a stiff shot of whiskey. She lifted her hands above her face and inspected her fingers. Even her fingers, the only delicate part of her entire body,[22] had ballooned. The outline of her hand blurred, and she closed her eyes. No matter what Nell did, she couldn't escape the throbbing and the pressure in her head. Neither Bella nor Nan had felt like a disease growing inside her. This baby was a parasite, and Nell needed to expel it before it killed her.[23]

The midwife arrived, and Nell braced herself for the familiar pain of childbirth. It did not come. Instead a foreign sensation like an invasion of an evil assaulted her body. Her face twitched. Her arms and legs flailed. The bed creaked in an involuntary rhythm. She saw lights flashing and heard the air buzzing. An unseen monster grabbed her, shook her, tortured her. Convulsions swept her away. In the violent shaking, she felt as possessed by demons as any epileptic.[24]

The baby was born and the seizures passed. Nell reached for baby Henrietta. The midwife handed her the infant bundled in a swaddling cloth. Wanting to touch her newborn's tiny hands and tickle her perfect wee toes, Nell unwrapped the baby blanket. Henrietta's arms and legs fell limply from her torso as though they were nothing more than cotton batten limbs. The little one screeched, and Nell's heart broke.

Eclampsia, a rare disease of pregnancy caused by high blood pressure and kidney disease, had caused Nell's convulsions, and those convulsions had dislocated her baby's arms and legs. The damage was permanent; Henrietta was a quadriplegic.

Little crippled Henrietta, petite and pretty, perfectly peaceful, melted hearts, especially Henry's heart. Henrietta was thirteen months old and still the happiest baby to ever grace a home, when the coughing started. Then came the wheezing, the high-pitched gasps, the trembling that brought no air to Henrietta's tiny lungs. Pneumonia. Nell rushed Henry's favorite child to the hospital, but the good care of Dundee Royal Infirmary worked no miracle. Henrietta died.[25]

Henry's spirit had been ripped from him as surely as Henrietta's soul had been torn out of her small body. Even Nell's swollen belly with its promise of a new baby brought him no solace. No light emanated from Henry's eyes. The sockets looked hollow, the pupils vacant. Ghostlike, he wandered off to his cabinet shop.[26]

As she scrubbed the dirt from another potato, Nell heard a voice command, "Nell. Hurry to Henry."[27]

Nell rushed through the city streets to Henry's shop. His door was locked. She rattled the handle, pounded the glass, and wailed out loud, "Please God, help me."[28]

A bobby touched her on the shoulder and asked, "What's the matter, Mrs. Duncan?"[29]

Nell heaved, "My husband's locked himself in."

The burly man put his shoulder to the door. "One." The door rattled. "Two." The lock crunched. "Three." The door flew open.

Nell pushed past the policeman and dashed to the back room. Henry lay slumped across his desk. Nell screamed, and with that scream, she entered the realm of sleepwalkers.

Later—it might have been minutes or it might have been hours—Nell watched an ambulance speed away with Henry inside. A doctor, with the demeanor of a pallbearer, summed up the situation: "A heart attack and a nervous breakdown. That baby in your tummy will be toddling around in diapers by the time they let your husband out of the veterans' hospital." Patting her on the shoulder, he added, "One thing's for sure, that child's lucky to be blessed with a powerhouse like you for a mum. You did yourself proud. You scared me up and dragged me here in the nick of time. A moment later and your husband would be gone for good, forever dead and buried."

Nell couldn't make heads or tails of what the doctor was talking about. Where had he come from? Who had found him? Who had dragged him around to the shop? Who was he talking about? Nell realized that a strong and friendly spirit had taken possession of her body and saved the man she loved.

The doctor left, and Nell stood alone in Henry's cabinet shop, surrounded by tables without legs and cupboards without doors. Contemplating her amnesia, she felt a strange serenity as though her mind had lost its memory the way the surface of a lake loses the rings made by raindrops. Refreshed, Nell attacked what needed to be done.

With the ducklike waddle of a woman nine months pregnant, Nell moved to Henry's desk. Bracing herself, one hand on either side of his ledger, she studied the figures, and then she opened the drawer and found stacks of unpaid bills. Henry was bankrupt. A fine fix she was in: one babe just buried, two wee ones at home, another about to pop, and a husband as useless as a cracked kettle.

Nell got on with her life.

While Nan and Bella danced about the shop playing hide and seek, she taped a paper banner across the window: EVERYTHING MUST GO. When every scrap of furniture was sold, she paid off creditors the best she could, declared herself bankrupt, closed the shop, walked away, and never looked back.[30]

Next, she scoured the back alleys of Dundee and found a cheap flat in a part of town where life was rough and neighbors were kind.[31]

On Nell's due date, she folded Bella's nightgown and bloomers into one cotton flour sack, and Nan's pajamas and nappies into another. A wave of pain washed over her.[32]

A knock sounded and Henry's aunt stepped in. The auntie smiled at Nan, and Nan toddled over to grasp her hand. Auntie gathered Nan's sack and Nan was gone.

Bella was left. Five years old and tall enough to reach Nell's tummy, Bella poked her mummy's bulging belly button and sang, "It's just me and you, Mummy." Bella screwed up her face and did a jig. The little show-off tried to bring a smile to her mummy's face.

"Bella, you have to be going as well," Nell explained.

All Henry's folk had refused to take Bella; she wasn't a Duncan by birth.[33] Nell's own kin had long since nailed the coffin shut on Nell and her bastard child.[34]

From the street, Nell heard the clippity-clop of the horses' hoofs and then footsteps on the stairs. A couple of traveling folk, Scots gypsies, burst in, smothered Bella in kisses and swooped her into their arms. In a flash, they were out the door and calling back, "Nellie, don't you give it a care. The midwife will be along soon, and your trials will be over."

Soon, the midwife was mopping Nell's brow and reassuring her, "Everything's normal. Now push."

Nell pushed and Lilian came out perfect.

Nan returned quickly from her auntie, but a full two weeks went by with no sign of Bella. Finally, Nell heard the sound of horses and the creaking of a wagon. Her Bella was home. Nell swung open the door. The faces of her traveler friends were ashen. The gypsy couple took turns speaking.

"Your wee Bella was napping in the caravan."

"Tucked in on the roller bed."

"We were outside."

"Not far from the caravan."

"Just doing our chores."

"Washing out the laundry."

"Shucking some peas."

"The wee one, she started hollering."

"Screaming at the top of her lungs."

"Something awful, it was to hear."

"We rushed in."

"So quick we did."

"Oh, Nellie, it was an awful sight."

"That it was."

"A ferret, a mad creature, had a hold of your wee one's face."

"Its teeth were all dug into her."

"Oh, there was so much blood."

"My man, he grabbed the stinking ferret, pried open its loathsome jaw, and pulled it off her."

"Oh, that I did. Flung the crazy stinker out. My wife grabbed Bella and wrapped her face in towels."

"We got to the hospital as quick as we could."

"Whipped the horses good, we did."

"But it was too late."

"Your little Bella lost an eye."

"She's in the hospital."

Bella returned home a changed child; it was as though the ferret's bite had infected her with an evil venom. Funny Bella, the little tike with the comic ways, who loved her mummy best of all, was gone. This poisoned Bella was a whiner, a child who seethed with resentment. This sour Bella, this small Isabella MacFarlane, resembled her grandmother; she loathed and judged Nell.[35]

Nell faced the damn facts: Bella was half blind; Henry was half dead; baby Henrietta was dead and buried; and she had three daughters to feed. To hell with self-pity—Nell had a needle and a few spools of thread, and she knew how to use them. With three little girls in tow, she knocked on doors. When the missus answered, she begged for honest work. "Do you have sheets in need of repair, socks for darning, shirt collars or cuffs for reversing. I'll give you a good deal. Just a penny per item."[36]

She went to door after door until she had a night's work. Back at the flat, she poured the older girls, Bella and Nan, a half-cup of warm milk with a spoonful of sugar and sent them off to bed. She nursed her newborn and then worked her needle into the wee hours. Each day, she earned her way.[37]

Nell could stretch a meal; she conjured up the most delicious soup. Whether fat and barley, or leeks and potatoes, or carrots and swedes, she set the largest pot out on the stove and the flavors came together. She added a few peas, just a few, just enough for a special treat. The little ones carefully spooned the broth into their mouths, being sure to leave each and every pea for the last precious bite. At the end, with only peas in the bowl, the girls counted. If Lilian or Nan had even one more pea than Bella, a spat broke out. "Unfair," Bella cried.[38]

Every meal, every day, Nell placed the plates on the table and told her children, "God is good. God takes care of us."[39]

God proved his goodness in another way. As life's challenges mounted, spirit visitors came to Nell more easily, and she began to get a reputation. Neighbors knocked on her door asking for messages from their dearly departed.[40]

But Nell was never more grateful than the day Henry came home from the veterans' hospital. She craved relief. No longer did she believe the dead were a dangerous lot. The spirit who had taken over when Henry lay at death's doorstep proved that spirit possession could be a blessed *gift*. She needed respite from her labor and her memories. If a Spirit Control could lighten her load, so be it. Nell allowed Henry to teach her to be a proper medium.[41]

As day three and day four of her 1944 witch trial turned into a parade of the faithful, Nell found self-respect. Realizing how much she had sacrificed to bring solace to the grieving multitude, she no longer plodded into the dock with her head hung low. Nell walked proud. As the *News of the World* reported on April 2, 1944: "She came up from the cells as if to a reception. After smiling at people in court, she sat down with as much elegance as a woman of her size could muster. Shortly afterwards, she took a wrap from her shoulders and, with the manner of a queen, handed it to the wardress behind her."[42] However, that reporter explained it all away by suggesting that Nell fell prey to a psychological disease, a multiple personality.[43]

# 24

# Sincerity Beyond Belief

DAYS INTO TESTIMONY, HIS LORDSHIP CONTINUED TO INDULGE THE infernal Spiritualists. Chief Constable West thought it was high time Sir Gerald put an end to the interminable tales from the crypt. But the judge bent over backward, contorting himself like an Indian fakir, just to prove his tolerance for all forms of religious quackery.[1] If only the witnesses had been made from one cloth—all gullible incompetents ready to believe in the boogey man—but many were intelligent men and women of considerable status.[2]

Mr. Gill, a gentlemanly sort, took the stand and confessed that he had thought Spiritualism was quite batty, until Chief Air Marshal Lord Hugh Dowding had convinced him otherwise. At the mention of Dowding's name, everyone in Courtroom #4, including His Lordship, registered respect bordering on reverence for the fatherly war hero who saved London from the Blitz.[3] To West's irritation, this religion of spook worshippers suddenly gained credibility as Mr. Gill described apparitions that appeared suddenly and then disappeared gradually, melting bit by bit into the floor.[4]

Unperturbed, Prosecutor Maude began his cross-examination, his every question cloaked in respectful curiosity. "Mr. Gill, you have been a convert to spiritualistic theory? You have seen ectoplasm. What does it look like?"[5]

"It looks like very white material, like a robe, like transparent sort of stuff,"[6] Mr. Gill mused.

As the witness searched for a precise description, Prosecutor Maude gradually pulled a swathe of finely woven muslin from some hidden recess beneath his black silk robe. Then, dangling the long thin transparent prop, he queried Mr. Gill's earlier testimony. "How much did you see going into the floor?"[7]

The witness answered, "I think about the size of a handkerchief."[8]

With irrepressible flare, Maude crushed the butter muslin into a ball and gripped it in the palm of one hand. Holding it out for the witness and the jury to see, he asked, "About that size?"[9]

Flustered, Mr. Gill objected, "Bigger than that."[10]

Prosecutor Maude flipped his hand and unfurled the cloth.

Mr. Gill carped, "Not as big as that."[11]

Delighting in his own theatrics, Maude continued manipulating his prop and toying with his witness. Despite Mr. Gill's protestations, the flimsy material appeared at one moment to be a crumpled handkerchief and at the next a transparent shroud.[12] Chief Constable West approved of Maude's intention to dangle this sheer white material before every remaining defense witness, not as evidence but merely for its demonstration value.

Next, Mr. Gill's wife, clad in quality fur[13] and reeking of sophistication, paraded past the jury and up the stairs to the witness box.[14] Needing little encouragement from Mr. Loseby, she described her memory of the police assault on Mrs. Duncan. Albert, according to Mrs. Gill's testimony, had materialized three spirit visitors. The first, a wrinkled crone, had grumbled, "I will speak but I cannot move. I am too tired," and then wilted to the floor and disappeared bit by bit. The second, a man, had materialized and spoken briefly with a friend. Then the third, the ghost of a boy who had died in battle, had stayed a short time, collapsed to the ground, and shrunken smaller and smaller, until only an ectoplasm patch the size of a handkerchief had remained.[15]

Then, in Mrs. Gill's embroidered account, Rupert Cross, Lieutenant Stan Worth's companion, had suddenly flown out of his second-row seat and dove for the last blotch of white. Sitters in the front row had crashed to the floor. Rupert had landed in front of them, grabbing at the evidentiary material. It had slipped though his fingers. He had scratched at the floor but had come up empty-handed.[16]

Mrs. Gill swore before judge and jury that she had believed that young Rupert must have been out of his mind with grief, and she had rushed to comfort him saying, "It's all right; it's all right. Don't worry."[17]

Rupert had continued to pursue the illusive phantom, crawling forward and clawing at the Cabinet curtains.[18]

Mrs. Gill explained that she had feared he might harm Helen Duncan and had shrieked, "Don't do it! Please! Oh, don't do it!"[19]

Undeterred, Rupert had scrambled to his feet and hurled himself through the drapes into the Cabinet. Mrs. Gill had charged in behind him and found Rupert Cross seated on Mrs. Duncan's lap, straddling the entranced medium. Mrs. Gill had wrapped her arms around Rupert's waist and tried to pull him off. Rupert, legs flailing, had held fast to the medium's neck. Then Mrs. Gill had lost her footing, and all three—Mrs. Gill, in her gray fur; Rupert, in his suit; and Mrs. Duncan, in her séance robe—had tumbled to the floor and through the Cabinet curtains.[20]

Mrs. Gill finished her testimony with a climactic flourish. "All the whistles were being blown and voices were shouting, 'You are all under arrest. You are all under arrest.'"[21]

Police officers rushed in with flashlights drawn. Pandemonium erupted. Horrified women squealed. Someone switched on the lights.[22]

In another memorable exchange, Wing Commander Mackie, one of Dowding's high-flying Royal Air Force fighter pilots took the stand and testified: "My own mother materialized. Our faces might have been three or four feet apart. The features were my mother. A man knows his mother." Then the Wing Commander, just by way of information, added, "I have the advantage of knowing my father."[23]

Chief Constable West took heart when His Lordship quipped, "Well, that's something."[24]

But fifteen witnesses later,[25] the judge's cranky tone turned disturbingly sympathetic to the Defense.

His Lordship asked Marine Horace Clayton, "Is it the ambition of a true Spiritualist to observe, if possible, some manifestation of spirit?"[26]

•

Clayton agreed, "I should say so my Lord."[27]

Sir Gerald pursued the question. "That is the purpose of Spiritualism, is it, to try and contact departed spirits?"[28]

Mr. Clayton explained, "Not necessarily; I should say the purpose of Spiritualism is to prove the Afterlife."[29]

His Lordship summed it all up. "In other words, Spiritualism is trying to prove the central feature of Christian belief?"[30]

With respectful enthusiasm, Mr. Clayton answered, "Yes."[31]

On yet another day, Mrs. Mary Jane Blackwell, a syrupy little old lady, came to the stand. Mrs. Blackwell swore, under oath, that she had personally seen fifteen or sixteen hundred materialized apparitions.[32]

With imagined ghosts scampering willy-nilly like sheep on a fretful night through Courtroom #4, His Lordship finally tried to herd in the unruly testimony. "What date are you going to speak of?"[33] barked Sir Gerald.

All sweetness and light, Mrs. Blackwell swooned, "Very many dates, my Lord. I have sat so many times. I cannot very well give you all those dates."[34]

In weariness, Sir Gerald pleaded for brevity. "I can't go on forever. We have got the numbers. Do you want to tell us about any particular one?"[35]

Mary Jane Blackwell struck a confused pose, and then her eyes widened with innocence as she recalled interactions with the spirits of her departed family members. "I will give you last year, if you like, my Lord. My father manifested. I saw him. I was his favorite daughter. The old man used to pat me on the hand. As I sat in the séance, the same pat came to my hand. My father touched me and I touched him.[36]

"Four months previous to that, I saw my husband. I was overjoyed. At another time, my mother and my aunt came back from the Afterlife and stood beside me. I recognized them by sight and by voice. I heard their manifestations speak Dutch, Welsh, Scotch, pure English, and Arabic."[37]

As His Lordship listened to this aging child of faith, a surge of paternal protectiveness seemed to wash all trace of irritation from his face.

Then the forebodingly gargantuan Mr. Elam stood to cross-examine.[38]

The naïve widow twinkled at her freakish interrogator.

Disarmed, Mr. Elam's voice turned gentle. "Mrs. Blackwell, you are frightfully keen on this, are you not?"[39]

"Yes, it is my religion,"[40] chirped the little lady.

"If it turned out—and I say 'if' again—that you had been tricked, you would be bitterly disappointed?"[41] Elam queried.

"You could not trick me,"[42] Mrs. Blackwell assured the Assistant Prosecutor.

"Suppose you found out afterwards that you had been tricked. Would you be very upset?"[43]

"I should, but I cannot imagine anyone tricking me on these things,"[44] Mrs. Blackwell confirmed without wavering.

Elam's square head bobbed sympathetically. "You are just so certain that you cannot think of it?"[45]

"No, I cannot,"[46] gleamed Mrs. Blackwell.

"And not only are you certain that nobody can trick you, but you cannot imagine it, and you would be very angry, would you not?"[47] Elam reasoned.

"The whole of my life would be at an end,"[48] Mrs. Blackwell confided.

"Everything about you would collapse like a pack of cards,"[49] Elam reflected.

"Because I know the truth and I have seen,"[50] Mrs. Blackwell finished Mr. Elam's thought.

Still locked in intimate dialogue, Mr. Elam asked, "You try to convert people to Spiritualism when you get a chance, I suppose?"[51]

"As it has brought happiness to me, I want to bring happiness to other people. Naturally,"[52] Mrs. Blackwell explained, her face radiating flawless faith.

His Lordship leaned forward and ventured into the conversation. Tentatively, he asked, "You need not answer this, unless you like. Are you a believer in the Christian religion?"[53]

"Yes, my Lord,"[54] said Mrs. Blackwell, flashing him a winning smile.

Expressing true curiosity, His Lordship inquired, "Why is Spiritualism necessary?"[55]

"Because those who profess the Christian religion have left out the part that pertains to Spiritualism, that pertains to spirit. They follow the letter of the law, instead of the spirit. The orthodox church teaches us that by faith alone we are saved, while we, as Spiritualistic people, believe that the Word of God is still living. God has not stopped talking. He reveals himself to his people daily; and therefore we cannot be bound by creed.[56]

"When my mother manifested, she told me she was exceedingly happy, and that life is worth it. Of course, everybody has troubles through life.[57]

"My aunt said that she had learned that the things of this world are ephemeral. She had been a connoisseur of silver and that sort of thing. Her whole life had been wrapped up in old silver; and when she materialized, she said, 'It was not worthwhile, it was absolutely silly.' I have learned that there is no person really dead. They are there waiting, and their love abides. That is a great consolation.[58]

"Mrs. Duncan's materializations prove the immortality of everybody. There is no death. Mrs. Duncan renews people's hope and trust in the power of God. It is a wonderful heritage."[59]

Beguilingly self-conscious, as though fearing she had talked too long, Mrs. Blackwell asked, "My Lord, shall I tell you what it gave me?"[60]

Sir Gerald Dodson, still spellbound by her openness, nodded his assent.

"Mrs. Duncan gave me courage. I felt I was giving up on life entirely. I was in trouble, both mentally and physically. I felt I could go on no longer; but when this glorious knowledge came along, it gave me courage to go along and face the difficulties of life."[61]

Sir Gerald, sensing her vulnerability, observed with empathy, "This is an enormous question. Some people may require Spiritualism, some people may not. You say you have been helped?"[62]

"Helped." Mrs. Blackwell's voice sounded a melancholy tone as she echoed His Lordship. "I would not be living now,"[63] she confessed and bit her lower lip, holding back sad details.

In that pause, even Chief Constable West worried for Mrs. Blackwell.

Cheerily, the witness turned to the question of her own Christian understanding: "We have learned the right meaning of the coming to earth of Jesus, who was the greatest incarnation of the Christ spirit. We understand his mission on earth, and we learn it from the spirit world."[64]

"And," Elam slipped in, "a fraudulent medium would be an absolute traitor to your cause."[65]

"Yes," said Mrs. Blackwell emphatically. Her eyes growing steely and her jaw brutally firm, she added, "Nothing could be too bad for a traitorous medium."[66]

Having given her consent to burn a wayward witch, the sweet little old lady, Mrs. Mary Jane Blackwell, left the witness stand.[67]

# 25

## Possessions

THE THIRD, FOURTH, AND FIFTH DAYS WERE PROVING TO BE SPLENDID for the Defense. With each witness, the appreciation of Nell's abilities swelled. Then Mr. Basil Kirby stepped up to testify. Mr. Kirby introduced himself as an expert witness, a man of private means who had devoted twenty years, full time, to psychic research. An educated and well-spoken member of the leisure class, Mr. Kirby proceeded to describe Nell's séances, including the appearances of spirit friends and relatives.[1]

With deferential curiosity, His Lordship asked about one such visitor, "Did your friend appear in what has been called ectoplasm?"[2]

Mr. Kirby answered, "Yes, with a shroud around the body."[3]

The judge wondered, "And the same as regards your mother? Does she appear in a shroud? They all appear in a shroud, do they?"[4]

Mr. Kirby said, "Yes, just a covering."[5]

His Lordship pressed further. "Is there any explanation for that?"[6]

Mr. Kirby offered his interpretation of the phenomenon.

"When the spirits enter the earth's atmosphere, they must have a covering for protection, like when you enter the stratosphere. I have worked side by side with Sir Oliver Lodge, the great physicist, and Sir Arthur Conan Doyle, creator of Sherlock Holmes, and they have observed the same thing."[7]

Sharing his personal experience with the judge, Mr. Kirby continued: "We all have many spirit guides. On one particular occasion, my first sitting with Mrs. Duncan in Portsmouth, a Chinaman known to me as Chang appeared. I have seen him often. He has a mustache eighteen inches long. His pigtail swings round. Chang helps anyone he can. Spirit guides are wonderful helpers. We all, everyone of us, have spirit guides."[8]

His Lordship admitted, "Well, I don't seem to have one."[9]

Undaunted, Mr. Kirby continued, "In all things, even on the earthly plane, you must have a master of ceremonies. Even in this court you must have someone to arrange things and organize. That's Albert's work. Albert is a kind of master of ceremonies."[10]

"That being so, why did your guide, the Chinaman Chang, interfere? Wasn't Albert doing a satisfactory job?"[11] His Lordship asked.

"Oh yes, quite all right. My Chinaman did not interfere; he just stepped in, and with Albert's permission."[12]

Mr. Kirby spoke the truth. Since Albert's first appearance, he'd done a fine job of controlling the souls who hovered around Nell, clamoring to cross the great divide. Before Albert took charge, other spirits had taken possession of Nell at will, and some had been the unruly sort.

Nell first channeled Dr. Williams, who came one stormy night when Nell had craved a bit of appreciation from her husband. Henry and his Spiritualist buddy Jim Murray huddled close around the kitchen table. Nell fetched the tumblers and the bottle. At first she sat quietly like a good wife, listening while the men talked about psychical matters. Telekinesis, ectoplasm, transfiguration, apports, materialization, levitation—the notions spewing from their mouths sounded like gibberish to Nell.[13]

Irritated by their exclusive club, Nell stood up and rattled around, slamming the kettle on the burner. Henry and Jim prattled on about the difference between Spiritualist faith and psychic investigation. The teakettle whistled. Nell poured water into the teapot, clunked it down on the table, and shoved teacups in front of the men. Henry pushed his cup aside.

Nell sat down again, cleared her throat, and asked, "Might you be wanting any biscuits?"

Jim shook his head without looking in Nell's direction. Nell stood again and opened and shut cupboards. Henry glowered at her, and she glowered right back at him.

"Sometimes my wife behaves like a toddler in need of attention,"[14] he whispered, and Nell heard every word.

Nell banged two candles on the table and set a box of matches between them. A flash of lightening lit the sky. Thunder rumbled, as if the gods in heaven were bowling. The lights went out.

With a begrudging, "Thank you, Nellie," Henry grabbed the matches, lit the candles, and leaned closer to Jim.

Suddenly rebellious, Nell blew out one candle.[15]

Like a stern father, Henry snapped, "Stop that Nell. We're trying to have a serious discussion."

The smoke floated from the wick and swirled about in an unnatural fashion. Jim pulled on Henry's shirtsleeve. Both men watched, mesmerized as the smoke spelled out the letters: WILLIAMS.[16]

As Nell felt herself float free, she heard an unfamiliar man's voice boom, "Good evening, gentlemen. My name is Dr. Williams."[17]

After Dr. Williams came on the scene, Henry was more loving toward Nell. But it wasn't enough that she gave Henry a son: Little Harry, a strapping ten-pound boy who suckled hard and grew strong like his mum.[18] And then another son arrived: Peter, a three-pound preemie who survived, swaddled in cotton wool and fed with an eyedropper.[19] Five children did not quell Henry's most heartfelt desire. Above all else, Henry wanted Nell to become a famous medium.[20]

Every Thursday, at six o'clock in the evening, Henry pushed his upholstered chair into a corner of the sitting room, between the pair of curtains he had rigged up to form a séance stage, a proper Cabinet. Nell tucked the children, five of them now, into bed. Returning to Henry, she helped him place seven kitchen chairs in a semicircle facing the Cabinet. When all was ready, Henry offered his chair to Nell. On séance nights, Nell took the place of honor. Henry knelt in front of her, speaking in soothing tones. For those few precious moments, Henry devoted himself solely to his wife. By the time the séance sitters arrived, Nell rocked serenely.[21]

But all Henry's promises, all the formal preparations, and even the polite spirit of Dr. Williams didn't keep the demonic side from preying on Nell's vulnerability. Not long after another labor plagued by convulsions and the birth of another child, baby Gena,[22] an irrepressible madness came over Nell. In the red glow of a séance lamp, a howling monster of extraordinary strength broke through the Cabinet curtains and ravaged the room. It toppled a sewing machine, flung the cast-iron fireplace grate across the room, and scattered furniture in all directions. The sitters fled in fear. Henry turned on the lights, and Nell sat in the middle of wreckage, weeping and disoriented.[23]

Then Henry decided to begin every séance with a prayer.[24] But even those sacred invocations didn't cleanse Nell's spirit guides of all their irreverent inclinations. For a time, Donald jumped into the driver's seat, and Thursday night séances took on a bawdy air. Henry and Nell still shared their special quiet time. The guests still arrived. Nell still fell into a trance. Henry still led the prayers, lit the red lamp, and closed the Cabinet curtain. As before, the atmosphere was charged with sublime calm. Then out of nowhere, the curtain flew open, and Donald hollered, "Hey, guys and gals! Look at this!"[25]

There, right next to Nell, stood Donald, looking like a traditional apparition, a white and gleaming ghost; but he didn't behave like an ethereal being. He barked, "See her? There's the fat lady, Nellie Duncan, just sitting there in her trance. She can't see me. She can't hear me. She's out there in the Blessed Beyond. Gone. I am the man in control, and I love being in control."

Donald swaggered clockwise, around and around Nell's chair, doing his dance, encircling her with this white otherworldly substance he called ectoplasm. When she was tightly bound, he shrieked, "I've got that girl all tied up." Then Donald pranced counterclockwise. His ectoplasm unwound and coiled up like a charmer's snake. Donald snapped the serpent in Nell's face and shouted, "Nellie! You hear me in there? Stand up, girl."

Nell followed Donald's orders like a mindless automaton.

Donald patted Nell on the head and strutted out through the drawn curtains into the circle. He pointed to a guest sitter and yapped, "You're new. I've got your number. I've got a spirit here for you, and she's chattering in my ear. She says her name is Margaret McMancus! She died from a liver condition. Hitting the bottle, was she? She died on October 30, 1910. Okay. Look here, this Margaret spirit says to tell you, 'All is forgiven, and she's having a jolly good time in the Nether World.'"

Henry hated Donald. Week after week, Henry's séance circle played host to Donald's obnoxious routine. Finally, Donald went too far.

Nell, pregnant yet again, sat between two curtains, hovering on the edge of a trance. Henry pulled the drapes shut. In the darkened room, Donald took control. Poking his ghostly face between the curtains, he bellowed, "Hello folks!" Then, waving his flaccid head from right to left, Donald caught sight of a gorgeous young lady. He dropped the curtain, popped straight out of the Cabinet, and roared, "Well, well, well! What do we have here?"

As Donald slithered toward the beautiful girl, he crooned, "Oooooo. What a delectable little dish for Donald. How about giving this old ghost a gander at those lovely tits? Woow. Baby, you're bringing me all back to life. I'll eat you up any time."

The poor budding child grabbed for a friend's hand and shrunk back out of fear and embarrassment.

Donald pressed closer and closer to the terror-stricken girl. His voice turned more threatening: "Going down, girl? Melting away under the spell of my ethereal charm? Oh God. Just let me have a cherry like this one more time."

Just as the flowing white of Donald's arms was about to envelop the shivering child, Henry bolted to his feet and shouted, "This will not happen in my home. Donald, behave yourself or get out!"

Donald whirled around and roared, "Shut up, Henry Duncan! You can't do a bloody thing to me. I don't need you. I'm not your damn wife." Twisting his head back toward the other sitters, he growled, "You. All of you. Watch!" He swept toward a cupboard, flung open its doors and grabbed a bottle of Nell's morphine pills. Twisting off the cap, he held the bottle high as if he was offering a toast. Donald glared at Henry vindictively, "I'll show you."

From within the Cabinet, a voice of authority sounded. "Stop! Donald, that is quite enough. Put down that bottle. You have gone entirely too far. Get back here at once. Now!"

Donald slammed down the bottle and rushed back to the Cabinet, yowling in ghostly rebellion.

Behind the curtain the heavenly rescuer held his ground. "I will hear none of that rubbish." The two spirits howled and growled at one another. As their angry voices receded into the Other Side, Donald folded in on himself, turned into a formless pile of white ectoplasm, and melted into the floor. There was merciful silence.

Henry breathed in the quiet and readied himself to end the séance, but the spirit world was not ready to call it quits.

The curtain snapped open, and a stately apparition stood next to Nell. Henry saw a tall man, some six feet in height, with a well-trimmed beard. Stepping forward, taking a courteous bow, the spirit visitor spoke. "Good Evening," he said in a voice that bespoke an effeminate gentility. "We must apologize for Donald's unseemly behavior. The man certainly was not doing his job properly, not up to snuff. We sent him back to the Other Side for retraining. Not to worry. I'll be in control now. May I introduce myself? Albert Stewart, at your service. Mr. Duncan, you have nothing more to fear. Together we will travel to increasing wisdom and more spectacular phenomena. We've had quite enough excitement for one night. I bid you adieu, until we meet again."[26]

Albert had come just in time. But Mr. Kirby, the man on the witness stand, didn't know the half of it. He thought Nell only channeled Albert at séances. Nell stared down into the gallery and caught sight of Henry, with his oldest daughter, Nan, by his side.[27] Poor sweet Nan.

What's a child to do when her Mum and Dad cry day and night? Nan had taken her younger sisters and brothers to the park, sat them down, and explained, "Mummy and Daddy are sad because little Alex went to heaven."[28]

Once upon a time, Nell and Henry had seven children, four daughters and three sons. She had scooped up her baby Alex into her arms, wrapped his shivering body in a blanket, and run through the streets of Edinburgh as fast as her legs would carry her. She had arrived at Edinburgh Royal Infirmary and sprinted across the white and black checkerboard tile to the reception desk. Right away, the nurse had heard her baby gasping for air. Pneumonia had stolen Alex's final breath.[29]

With Nell and Henry incapacitated by grief, the children—Bella, Nan, Lilian, Harry, Peter, and Gena—depended on Albert, and their Uncle Albert had visited regularly.[30]

Henry sat upright on a kitchen chair. Dressed in tie and starched collar, he peered toward the window.

In the living room, Nell sank into an overstuffed chair, her cheeks damp with tears. Nan lifted Gena and Peter onto sad Nell's lap. The two youngest snuggled into her soft body and poked at the loose flesh of her arms. The fat jiggled like jelly, and the little ones giggled.[31] Nell's eyes glazed, her head dropped to her chest. An instant later, her torso snapped up straight. All the children could see that Uncle Albert had jumped into their mother's body. Nell stood taller, moved faster, was stronger and loved to play.

Uncle Albert wiggled Mum's fingers in front of Gena's face and, in his BBC accent, announced, "Uncle Albert's in control now, and he's going to get you!" He tickled Gena, and she laughed and laughed.

Then Uncle Albert put his face, nose to nose with Peter, and asked, "Where is that brother of yours? Off lad. Go fetch Harry this very minute. It's time for a rousing game of Tarzan of the Apes."[32]

Peter ran to the garden, squealing with excitement. "Harry! Harry! Where are you? Come quick. Uncle Albert's here. Time to play Tarzan!"

Harry rushed into the room, shouting, "Here I am, Uncle Albert!"

Uncle Albert lifted Gena down to the floor, beat his chest like an ape, and bellowed, "Me not Uncle Albert. Me Tarzan." Pointing at Gena, he scratched his head as though he had never seen her before and asked, "You Jane?"

Gena snickered, "I'm Gena."

For just a minute, Uncle Albert switched back to Uncle Albert again. He bowed to Gena, took her stubby little hand, kissed it, and said, "Honored to make your acquaintance. Please excuse me. I need to be Tarzan right now."

Uncle Albert picked up a chair, held it over his head, and roared, "Me King of the Jungle." He put down the chair, made howling sounds, and chased Peter and Harry all around the living room and out to the garden.

Peter yelped, "Uncle Albert's Tarzan! Uncle Albert's Tarzan!"

The neighbors looked over the fence and shook their heads. The Duncans were looney—that's what the neighbors thought.

Other times Uncle Albert settled back into a soft chair; with all six children gathered at his feet, he preached a cryptic little sermon: "My dears, humans are like moths. Moths spread their wings at night and seek the light. So children, the moral of the fable is, Seek only the true light of the Savior."[33]

The children bobbed their heads up and down, up and down.

Whether he came to play or impart wisdom, Uncle Albert always ended his visits with the same words: "Au revoir, dear children. Until we meet again."

On that cue, Nell's head and her arms went as limp as a puppet when the puppeteer stops pulling the strings. After a minute, her head shook and her eyes opened. Sometimes, she'd look blankly into her children faces and mutter, "I don't know you." Then kindly Nan stroked her mum's hair.

At other times, other personalities took possession of Nell. Peggy Hazeldine, a naughty lass with a Scottish brogue, danced and sang.[34] Peggy entertained the children with her gay versions of "You Are My Sunshine,"[35] and "Loch Lomond."[36] But not all Nell's personalities lightened her children's load; Rosie, the orphan child, broke their hearts.

Rosie nestled into a corner, hugging her blanket. With teary eyes and a thumb held to her lips, she whimpered in a wee child's voice, "I don't know where my mummy is. I don't know where my mummy is. I don't know where my mummy is."[37]

Finally, Uncle Albert took charge, organizing the whole unruly crowd of refugees from the dead. Thursdays became the most dependable day of the week. That was the day that séances took place at the house.[38] More and more outsiders came knocking at the Duncans' door, and the séances

got bigger and bigger. Mr. James Souter wrote to the Spiritualist magazine, *The Light,* telling all the world: Albert had materialized fourteen
spirits, each of whom spoke clearly, gave their names, provided convincing particulars, and answered all questions.[39] Dr. Montague Rust, a doctor from Newport in Fife,[40] and Mr. Ernest Oaten, editor of *Two Worlds,*[41]
came by to meet Albert. Albert appeared in Glasgow, Edinburgh, and
Dundee.[42] An artist had sculpted a bust of Albert, and a treasured photo
of that sculpture hung in the Duncan home.[43] Albert became the patri-
arch of the Duncan family.

In October 1930, Nell had stood on the deck of a steamer, watching
the coast of Scotland grow smaller and smaller. She had expected only
good to come from her London séances.[44] Fourteen years later, sitting in
the dock of the Old Bailey, Nell knew better.

His Lordship didn't ask any more questions about spirit guides, but
Nell's lawyer, Mr. Loseby, had another question for Mr. Kirby. "Have you
seen Harry Price, the Honorable Director of the National Laboratory of
Psychic Research, anywhere in the vicinity of the court this morning?"[45]

Mr. Kirby pointed to the gallery and answered, "Yes, he is right in front
of me, sitting facing me."[46]

# 26

# An Extraordinary Rivalry

A S MR. KIRBY RAISED HIS HAND AND POINTED A FINGER AT HARRY Price,[1] heads swiveled to catch sight of the infamous investigator of psychic phenomena. With the haughty nod of a celebrity who relishes recognition, Price's lips parted, his bottom teeth showed, and the corners of his mouth twisted upward. Price did not smile; he expressed pleasure with a sneer.[2] Radiating power as hard and hot as a branding iron, he fixed his gaze on Henry Duncan. In response, the blood drained from Duncan's face. The weasel never had fulfilled his obligation to Price.[3]

So many years had passed since Mr. Duncan betrayed his wife. A shamed dog, his tail between his legs, Duncan had scurried out of Price's laboratory, clinging to one purpose: to save his own hide. He scampered two blocks due west to the white-columned premises of Price's Spiritualist rivals. Cornering Mr. Fielding-Ould, their venerated president, Duncan spouted his newly enlightened conviction: His wife was a bogus medium.[4]

Having scoured all possible soil from his own reputation, Mr. Duncan dropped by St. Thomas's Hospital. Helen Duncan did not take lightly the news of her husband's abandonment. The woman nearly killed herself by downing a half bottle of Eusol, a chlorinated lime and boric acid solution. The nurses wrestled the carafe from her grip. The medical staff pumped her stomach clean, and Mrs. Duncan survived.[5]

That portion of the tale brought Price only minimal pleasure.

The next installment—where Mrs. Duncan served Miss Mercy Philli-more, the venerated grande dame of Spiritualism, her just desserts—*that* gave Price unmitigated satisfaction.

Hearing of Mrs. Duncan's near demise, Miss Phillimore paid a visit to the recuperating patient, hoping to steal a confession straight from the medium's own lips.

A bouquet in hand, Miss Mercy tiptoed toward Mrs. Duncan: "Dear, dear lady. How are you?"

Seeing an ulterior motive plastered all over the genteel madame's face, the medium let loose an opinion that resonated with Price's estimation of the woman. Bolting upright, she shouted, "You're a bloody sod."

Undeterred, Miss Mercy clucked, "Why, Mrs. Duncan, we just want to express our sympathy."

Mrs. Duncan responded with rough eloquence: "Sympathy nothing. A bloody ass creeper is what you are. Get out of my sight you, before I bust your bloody head."

Miss Mercy scrambled out the door, as fast as her heeled shoes would carry her. With that indelicate threat reverberating, the Spiritualists' desire to further investigate Mrs. Duncan's phenomena came to an end.[6]

Price was not so easily deterred; he devised a fantastic finale.

Rumor reached Price that the Duncans had booked passage to Scotland for June 23, 1931. Price immediately dispatched his flame-haired acolyte, Mrs. Molly Goldney, to intercept the Duncans at their rented home. Mrs. Goldney found belongings boxed and six children ready to go, but Mr. and Mrs. Duncan were not at their residence. Undaunted, Mrs. Goldney tracked the couple down at a devotee's home on Eaton Terrace. Nearly pulling the wayward Mr. Duncan by his ear, the formidable Mrs. Goldney dragged the scallywag back to Price's laboratory.[7]

Scolded for his plan to bolt without notice, Mr. Duncan stammered implausible apologies.[8]

Price accepted Duncan's excuses with feigned benevolence and a magnanimous offer: "Mr. Duncan, if you can induce your wife to give us one final séance, and allow us to take a cinematographic film of the entire process, we will pay you 100 pounds sterling."[9]

Predictably, Mr. Duncan greeted news of the extravagant payment like a gambler with a winning lottery ticket in hand. The anticipated feel of a wad of bills in his pocket banished the nagging concern for his wife's degrading exposure and its potentially suicidal consequences. Once again, Mr. Duncan succumbed to Price's powers of persuasion and agreed to make every effort to deliver Mrs. Duncan to Price's laboratory.[10]

But this time, Helen Duncan rebelled against her husband's pimping.

As scheduled, the Duncans boarded the steamer and floated north to Scotland, where more credulous Spiritualists assured a modest but steady flow of cash.[11]

As Price revisited his regret over that lost opportunity, the clerk called out the name of the next witness: Hannen Swaffer.[12] Suddenly, all eyes turned from Price to focus on a crotchety geezer whose fame far outstripped Price's.

Hannen Swaffer was Britain's most celebrated theater critic. The power of his pen struck terror in the hearts of every thespian in the London area. The morning after premier performances, directors, actors, and producers gathered, and with trembling hands, praying Hannen Swaffer had treated them gently, one brave soul among them opened the newspaper. A kind word from Swaffer would propel a theater production skyward. A scathing remark would sink it.[13] All theater people, even an amateur thespian like His Lordship Sir Gerald Dodson, abhorred Hannen Swaffer.[14]

Swaffer—his white hair wild, uncombed, and unkempt, his shaggy eyebrows drooping over his lashless eyelids, his mouth in a scornful pout[15]—placed his hand disdainfully on the Bible.[16] In the Foreword to *Swaffer's Who's Who*, one of his dearest friends, Edgar Wallace, described the critic: "Swaffer accepts himself as one of God's gifts, just as he accepts sunlight and spring flowers, and other lesser creations of the Almighty."[17] Personifying this conceit, Swaffer glared over his tortoise-shell glasses[18] at the clerk of the court and mumbled, at double speed, some words meant to approximate the oath.[19]

But at this moment, Hannen Swaffer was not in the critic's box; he stood in the Court of the Recorder of London. His Lordship expected an audible and intelligible recitation of the oath.[20]

"Now, take the oath properly,"[21] Sir Gerald demanded with unflinching authority.

Showing more amusement than intimidation, Swaffer acquiesced.

Defense Attorney Charles Loseby, preening Swaffer's unruly feathers and making quite certain the members of the jury understood that the man in the box was THE HANNEN SWAFFER, asked, "Have you been a dramatic critic?"[22]

Swaffer groaned, "Unfortunately."[23]

His Lordship interceded, "For whom? You said, 'unfortunately,' Mr. Swaffer. 'Unfortunately,' for whom?"[24]

"Unfortunately, for this poor critic who has to sit through it all, my Lord,"[25] replied Swaffer, directing an acerbic smirk at His Lordship without realizing that the jurist's musical, *The Rebel Maid,* had recently made its debut.[26]

"Would you know most of the actors in London?"[27]

With an understatement that proved his pomposity, Swaffer chortled, "Some of *them* know me."[28]

Snickering along with the witness, Loseby posed the next question. "It has been suggested, Mr. Swaffer, that the phenomena exhibited by Mrs. Duncan could be simulated by a highly skilled actor. Is that your view? Could the greatest actor you have ever known simulate, with reasonable likeness, the phenomena?"[29]

Swaffer answered, "I could not do it; Albert is a separate entity."[30]

The Defense had no more questions.

Junior Prosecutor Elam rose to cross-examine, with the long swathe of cheesecloth dangling from his hand.

Swaffer leaned over the railing of the witness stand, his hand outstretched and asked, "May I have that cheesecloth, my Lord; I have heard about that ridiculous cheesecloth."[31]

"No," His Lordship stated firmly.[32]

Mr. Elam, all six feet six inches of him, clutched the cheesecloth, like a baby with a security blanket.

Swaffer grabbed wildly at thin air as though he could will his arm to lengthen across the courtroom well and snatch the barrister's prop.

His Lordship roared, "Don't be violent."

Suddenly smug, Mr. Elam made the material dance, twenty-five feet away from the old curmudgeon's reach.

His Lordship took a deep breath and glared at Office of Public Prosecutions representative Edward Robey. Everyone knew they were friends (Ed Robey and his famous father, George, lunched regularly with the insufferable Hannen Swaffer).[33] Couldn't the solicitor exert some influence over this unruly witness. The rows and the reconciliations between George Robey and Hannen Swaffer were legendary and endless. Feebly, Ed Robey shrugged his shoulders.

Left to his own authority, His Lordship lifted his head in serpentine fashion and hissed, "Mr. Swaffer, don't be violent. You shall not be bothered with the cheesecloth."[34]

Recovering his maturity, Swaffer straightened up in the witness box. With the excessive loudness of an elderly gentleman who has lost his hearing, he nearly shouted, "Butter muslin could not be used in an effective way. Mr. Harry Price invented this lunacy."[35]

Price had gone to print with his theory. His book *Regurgitation and the Duncan Mediumship* postulated that Helen Duncan possessed extraordinary powers of consumption and regurgitation. Price asserted that Mrs. Duncan swallowed cheesecloth (and on occasion, masks, rubber gloves, and pins), the paraphernalia needed to simulate apparitions, and that she retained these items in an anatomical abnormality, a second stomach, like a cow. Then the bovine Mrs. Duncan regurgitated this rubbish, like a cud, in silence. And finally, with the skill of a master puppeteer, she pulled cloth and other items from her mouth, manipulating these objects to resemble Albert along with other dead relatives and friends.[36]

Scanning the gallery and settling his glare on Price, Swaffer howled, "We wanted Harry Price to try eating cheesecloth."[37]

Swaffer slapped his knee and cackled gleefully at the idea of Price seated at a plate piled high with cheesecloth, munching and gagging. His derisive delight spread through Courtroom #4. All eyes turned on Harry Price; all the Spiritualists and all the reporters guffawed heartily.

Did Harry Price still believe that Helen Duncan vomited muslin apparitions? No, he did not. One clandestine trip to Edinburgh's bawdy burlesque house, the Royal Theater, had convinced him otherwise. There he had observed that even the famed regurgitator Kanichchka, the Human Ostrich, gagged loudly and only managed to emit unimpressive bits of material. Of course, Price had never acknowledged his blunder.[38] Now he clung to one last hope: that the arm of the law would strangle Albert and silence the insolent sheet for eternity.

# 27

## A Nemesis Returns

B Y DAY SIX OF NELL'S TRIAL, NEWSBOYS ON STREET CORNERS BELLOWED the headline: "PARALYSED GHOST APPEARS! Judge Wishes He Had a Spirit Guide."[1]

Nell, still glowing from Harry Price's humiliation, entered the dock with heady self-confidence. The Prosecution had faltered, and Nell's defenders, nearly forty witnesses thus far, had kept right on coming. Mr. Loseby announced that today would be the final day of testimony.[2] Sipping from her water glass, Nell settled in for another entertaining day of battle and looked forward to this evening's celebratory banquet at the Bonnington Hotel.[3]

The day's events began with Mr. Alfred Dodd placing his manicured hands on the Bible,[4] looking every bit like a nineteenth-century poet. Every feature of the frail, gray-haired, elderly gentleman came to a point.[5] The tops of his ears, the widow's peak of his hairline, the end of his nose, the profile of his mustached lips, the sweep of his chin—all were pointed. He wore a suit with thin lapels and sported a bow tie that fluffed out like a satin ribbon on a girl's braid. His round spectacles balanced unsteadily on the bridge of his nose.[6] A man of letters, Alfred Dodd was famous—or notorious, depending on one's viewpoint—for proposing the controversial theory that William Shakespeare had signed his name to works actually written by Francis Bacon.[7] As expected, Dodd related his séance experiences with refinement and clarity.

"In 1932," Dodd began, "I unexpectedly had a séance with Mrs. Duncan. The curtains went to one side and out came the living form of my grandfather. I knew him because he was very big, a very tall man, about six feet one, at least, very corpulent. My grandfather looked round the room very quizzically until his eyes met mine. He then strode across the room from the séance Cabinet to me and put out his hand. As he grasped my hand, he said, 'I am very pleased to see you, Alfred.'

"I said to him, 'Why, you look just the same.'

"My grandfather had on his smoking jacket. He had his hair cut in the donkey fringe. His face was brown and bronzed, just the same way; the same look in his eye; the same expression that I knew so well.

"He next said, 'I am so sorry you are having a rough go of it.'

"I was losing a lot of money on property at that time. Grandfather seemed to know all about it; he said, 'Keep your pecker up, old boy. Never say die while there is still a shot in the locker.'

"That was one of his favorite expressions. Grandfather turned round, walked back to the Cabinet, lifted his leg, and slapped his thigh three times, three loud resounding smacks. He went right into the curtain and smote himself on the breast three times and said, 'It is solid Alfred; it is solid.'

"That was just one personal experience of Albert bringing the dead back to life."

Then Dodd testified, "I saw before me the living form—the living form of my wife! I knew her absolutely. She stood there and waved in exactly the same way that she waved when I took her to her last social. She stood there dressed in a white flowing robe, and over that white flowing robe was a fine curtain of net. I was so astonished that I stood up and called out to my wife, 'Why, it's Nell; it's Nell.' My sweetheart came out and stood before me, a living, palpitating woman. The same hair I knew so well, dark and ruddy; the same eyes, hazel; they shone with animation; her face, the same ivory pallor on her cheeks.

"Then I heard her speak, and she spoke with the same soft Scotch accent that I knew so well. It was cultured Scotch, not harsh Glasgow Scotch, nothing like that, not harsh at all, a soft cultured voice, mixed, of course, with her educational training in England. I put my hand out to touch her, but she backed away and dissolved into nothing."[8]

It was Junior Prosecutor Elam's turn to cross-examine. Just then, Lead Prosecutor Maude rushed in, and the two put their heads together and conferred briefly. Finally, Mr. Elam rose up and posed his question. "Have you followed Mrs. Duncan's career since 1931?"[9]

Dodd answered, "I know what has gone on."[10]

Mr. Elam raised his eyebrows, "You do?"[11]

"Yes,"[12] replied the witness.

Mr. Elam faced the judge and announced, "At this point, I would like to argue something in the absence of the jury."[13]

The jury filed out of court. Nell, sensing a dangerous turn in events, leaned forward, her ears primed to hear every word.

Mr. Elam told the judge, "The tenor of evidence is that Mrs. Duncan is a genuine medium and has been from 1931. That being so, I should like to put questions to Mr. Dodd as to whether he knows what happened at a séance in Edinburgh on the 4th of January, 1933."[14]

With the mention of that date, Nell struggled to hold back her emotion but failed. Her muffled sobs were her first show of emotion during the trial.[15]

Mr. Loseby had assured Nell that the ugliness of that séance would not be resurrected in this court.[16]

On January 4, 1933, Nell had arrived at 24 Stafford Street,[17] a decaying Victorian house just around the corner from the majestic spires of Melville Street and the newly established site of the Edinburgh College of Parapsychology.[18] Miss Snowden, the picture of femininity in frilly shawl and rose brooch,[19] had greeted Nell and introduced herself as Miss Esson Maule's personal secretary.[20] As Nell, weary from a long day of work, plodded behind the young woman, every floorboard creaked.[21] In the musty office, Nell met Miss Maule, a hefty suffragette who had traded in frilly starched collars for suits and ties.[22] Nell admired that fashion statement. In her youth, she too had preferred her brothers' clothes to her own.[23]

This muscular mistress slammed a pile of ten-shilling notes, four pounds worth,[24] on the desk and growled, "You're late. There are eight sitters waiting on you."

With that unceremonious welcome, Miss Maule stomped out of the office.[25]

Alone, Nell took a moment to soothe her frayed nerves, lit a cigarette, eyed the payment, but did not pocket the cash. Snuffing out her fag and tossing the butt into her purse,[26] Nell decided to forgo changing from her brown frock into her séance costume. Hurrying, she trundled her way up a flight of stairs into the séance parlor and deposited herself inside the flimsy chintz-curtained Cabinet. With candlelight flickering and red light glowing, the sitters launched into a jaunty tune, and Nell fell into a trance, arms limp at her side.[27]

Some indeterminate amount of time passed. All of a sudden, a flash of light blinded Nell, and Miss Maule seethed with accusation: "Mrs. Duncan, I'm not going to stand for this; it's disgusting."[28]

Nell roared, "You're a dirty rotten swine."[29]

The sitters started clamoring at Nell: "Take off your clothes! Take off your clothes!"

Nell shouted back, "I'll not be showing my knickers to any men."[30]

Like a drill sergeant, Miss Maule bellowed above the racket, "Mrs. Duncan, you will strip this instant."

That order was over the top, too much like past indignities forced upon Nell. She picked up the closest chair, lifted it above her head like a caveman's club, and screeched, "I'll brain you, you bloody bugger. I'll kill you, I swear I will."[31]

A man jumped up and grabbed the leg of the chair, averting it away from Miss Maule's skull. As a reward for his chivalry, Nell cracked the chair over *his* head. He was spurting blood, but Nell wasn't finished. She took off her shoe and whacked him with it. Then with a savage yell, she whirled her arm and let fly the other shoe. Miss Maule ducked as it whisked by her head.[32] Satisfied that she had made her point clear, Nell recovered her dignity, stood tall, and informed Miss Maule, "I'll gladly lift my skirt, if the men leave the room."[33]

The four men filed out.

But Nell saw them peeping through a crack in the door, like lads thirsting for a glimpse of frilly under-things. What the hell, she thought. Give 'em a thrill. She stooped down, took a firm hold of her hem and petticoat, and with a flourish, pulled her frock off in one sweep of her arms. There she stood proudly in her bright blue knickers. Even those she took off and then turned them inside out for all to see.[34]

Miss Maule pointed at the floor. In triumphant self-righteousness, she snarled, "That's Peggy. You can't deny that is Peggy."[35]

Nell looked at the clump of cloth at her feet. She picked up the cloth and shook it out. It was a torn undershirt. Nell wasn't about to deny a thing. Instead, she told her the truth; she screeched, "Miss Maule. You're a dirty swine."[36]

Miss Maule spat, "I want that vest."

Nell came back at her with, "Why don't you keep all my clothes, why don't you? I'll just go out into the winter's night and run on home naked."[37]

Miss Maule laughed at her and then, steely-eyed, repeated, "I want the vest."

Nell threw the damn thing in Miss Maule's ugly face and slipped back into her knickers and frock. Then, turning away in disgust, she noticed the chair and thought, "I really do want to throw that chair at that bloody bitch." And so she did. And then Miss Maule flung it back at Nell.

Nell stomped down the rickety stairs and, for all her trouble, snatched the stack of ten-shilling notes from Miss Maule's nasty den, and walked out the door.[38]

After that, Miss Maule called in the coppers, Nell landed in front of the sheriff, Harry Price showed up in court, and the whole ugly mess got splashed all over Edinburgh's newspapers.[39]

Miss Esson Maule, who looked and sounded like Nell's high-society twin,[40] took the stand.

The Prosecutor asked, "What did the voice of Albert first say?"[41]

Miss Maude reported that in the middle of a song, Albert, a beanpole swathe of white, popped out from between the curtains and declared, "That is an awful singing voice you have, Miss Maule. If you heard what it sounds like you would not sing again."[42]

Everyone in the sheriff's court giggled, just as everyone at the séance had chortled at her expense. But Esson Maule had the skin of a rhinoceros and the wit of satirist. She had replied, "Happy New Year to you, Albert."[43]

Miss Maule tromped off the witness stand and was replaced by her comely assistant.[44] According to the lovely Hilda Snowden, Albert disappeared and transformed into a slimy gentleman caller who sidled up to her. Hilda patted the spirit visitor on the chest and was impressed by his voluptuous bosom. For the next hour, ghostly refugees gave evidence that Everlasting Life provided an endless supply of tobacco. Each and every apparition reeked of stale cigarette smoke.[45]

Next, little Miss Peggy, a sprightly scamp from Nether Nether Land peeped out from behind a vase on Miss Maule's sideboard and lisped an annoying tune. Watching Mrs. Duncan kneel behind her cupboard, manipulating some white cloth in the manner of a sock puppet and droning on with irritating nursery rhymes, strained Miss Maule's patience to the breaking point. Overcome by a desire to strangle Peggy, she grabbed the scallywag and pulled. Mrs. Duncan also pulled, and a tug of war ensued. Mrs. Duncan won that round.

However, truth prevailed, according to the prosecution witnesses. A dutiful sitter aimed a beam from a handheld lamp at Mrs. Duncan. Flooded with light, the medium doubled over, stuffed Peggy up her skirts, presumably the shortest route back to the Other Side. That's how Miss Maule and her cohort had told their side of the story.[46]

Eleven years later, in the highest criminal court in England, the monster lawyer Mr. Elam argued for telling the jury about the whole embarrassing incident.[47]

His Lordship ruled, "If the Prosecution wishes to ask this question, it is admissible."[48]

The jury filed back into the court, their ears burning.

Mr. Elam, a hungry glint in his eye, questioned the elderly gentleman. "Mr. Dodd, did you know that as a result of a séance at Edinburgh in 1933, Mrs. Duncan was convicted of fraudulent mediumship? Did you know Mrs. Duncan was fined ten pounds? Did you read that the child's spirit was a woman's stockinet undervest manipulated by Mrs. Duncan?"[49]

With those questions, Nell wilted, but Mr. Dodd remained rock solid. "Yes," he replied, "I have read it, but I did not accept it."[50]

Mr. Elam's square brow furrowed in disbelief. "You did not accept the finding of the Court?"

With unfaltering faith, Dodd turned to the jury, lifted his spectacles from his nose, and explained. "It has made no difference to me whatsoever. Not at all. Not one bit. I have spoken with Albert about this matter."[51]

# 28

# Coffee and Clairvoyance

A FTER COURT ADJOURNED FOR THE DAY, NELL, HENRY, AND MR.
Loseby headed to the Bonnington Hotel.[1] On Southampton Row,
they joined walkers rushing shoulder-to-shoulder toward double-decker
buses and the Holborn tube station.[2] These late-day pedestrians had
spent their day cheering a gargantuan display of firepower. March 30,
1944, had been United States Armed Forces Day. A parade—one and a
half miles of American soldiers, tanks, howitzers, cavalry, anti-aircraft
guns, bands, and aircraft—had snaked its way through downtown London.[3] Brits had turned out in droves to gawk at the rosy-cheeked foreign-
ers and their spanking-new equipment. Most spectators walked away
shaking their heads, thinking exactly what the government wanted them
to think: The coming invasion would eventually be mammoth, but the
Yanks were still too soft for battle. It would take six months to toughen up
those farm boys.[4]

In the meantime, the Little Blitz raged on. By late afternoon, the celebration was over, and the spectators were in retreat, scuttling home for
an evening meal before air raid sirens blared, bombs dropped, and neighborhoods burned.[5]

Charles Loseby wiggled through the crowd, cutting a too slender path
for Nell and Henry. Leaving the crowd outside, Nell, Henry, and Mr.
Loseby walked into the carpeted and chandeliered dining room of the

174

Bonnington Hotel.[6] From a private corner, a small gathering of the most supportive Spiritualists—the President of the Spiritualist National Union among them—greeted the threesome with wine glasses held high.

For the next few hours, ghost stories, good food, and wine flowed freely. The hotel took on an ethereal glow.

As waiters cleared dinner plates, Mr. Loseby removed a silver cigarette case from his breast pocket and, with a toothy grin, offered Nell a cigarette.[7] As Nell delicately extricated a fag, the others praised Loseby's courtroom performance and decried the judge's small-minded prejudice.

"A séance in court! Brilliant!"

"Stroke of genius."

"That would have gotten our dear Mrs. Duncan off the hook."

"And proved the continuance of life, beyond all doubt."

"Too bad that Christian judge, the dupe of the Archbishop, foiled your plan."[8]

To this last remark, Mr. Loseby responded with a veiled comment, "It's not over yet. You never know. You never know."[9]

All eyebrows raised, but Mr. Loseby deflected interest with a bright idea. Leaning toward Nell, he gave a flick of his cigarette lighter and asked, "Mrs. Duncan, how about a demonstration of clairvoyance?"

As Nell bent toward the flame, Loseby continued, "Direct writing. Let us invite the spirits to predict the verdict."

"Jolly good idea." Murmurings of satisfaction circulated about the table.

"Then it's settled: clairvoyance with coffee," chimed Loseby.[10]

Pleased, Nell inhaled, as a wave of confident nostalgia washed over her. Ever since her last year at Callander Primary School, she had trusted the written messages that spontaneously appeared beneath her hand.

By age eleven, Nell lived in a world of daydreams and took her sweet time walking to class.[11] Her skirt swaying gently, her black hair pinned up neatly, she drifted right on Main Street, passed the Gothic church in Anacaster Square, turned north on Church Street, and east on Cragard Road.[12] To Nell, the sounds of younger children playing, shouting, singing, and cheering blended together like the soundtrack to another girl's life.

The brass bell clanged, the hubbub died out, but Nell didn't mind being last. Lingering at the end of the girls' column, she floated through the arched doorway, across the foyer, up the stairs, and into the classroom. Rows of desks were mounted on cast-iron pedestals and bolted to the hardwood floor. Arriving at her assigned seat, she slipped into her straight-backed chair[13] and stared out the tall triple windows at the sky,[14] the heavenly backdrop for her visions.

Mr. Cummings, the headmaster, a gaunt gentleman who took meticulous care to camouflage his hairless dome by plastering an eight-inch lock across his crown,[15] stood in front of Nell's class.[16] This teacher had power over their futures. The students he passed could go on to secondary school. The students he failed would be forced to labor for a living.[17] Nell expected to go to work. Hard work never scared Nell. Mr. Cummings, however, scared the wits out of her.[18]

The stern headmaster began this day like every other. He lifted his palm ceremoniously, and his pupils stood. He intoned a single note, and his class sang "God Save the Queen." He said, "Our Father," and his students prayed. At the "Amen," he nodded, and all the girls and boys lowered themselves into their chairs.[19] For Nell, the morning ritual cast a spell, and her mind wandered off to otherworldly realms.[20]

Midmorning, Mr. Cummings interrupted her reverie. His thin shadow crossed her desk. He laid an eight-by-twelve inch, exam-sized chalkboard[21] in front of her and instructed the class, "I've written your history exam on the blackboard. Kindly, write the answers to those questions on your slates."[22]

Nell stared at the slate and remembered the preacher's words, "Ask and ye shall be given." She picked up the small black chalkboard, held it to her chest, prayed for answers, and fell into a deep calm, a sweet nothingness beyond time and memory.

When Nell returned from her prayerful state, the slate lay on her desk with answers written on it. Pleased and proud, she crossed her arms over her puffed-up chest, and watched other students puzzle over the questions.

Taking long, silent steps, Mr. Cummings came to Nell's side. Studying her answers, his brow furrowed and his face flushed. His jaw stiffened and his mouth moved. "Victoria Helen MacFarlane, I expect better of you. Where's the cribbing book?"[23]

Nell felt the hard beat of her heart and stammered, "What book? I haven't got a book."[24]

Mr. Cummings bellowed, "Young lady. This is not your work. I do not tolerate cheating."[25]

Nell whimpered, "Mr. Cummings, sir, I don't know what happened. Really. I don't know. I didn't do anything. I didn't."[26]

Mr. Cummings turned around and marched straight-legged to the cane hanging next to his desk. He grabbed his weapon and whirled round. The greasy strand of hair that normally clung to his bald head spun free. Brandishing his rod, with his naked skull shining brightly and his hair flapping over one ear,[27] Mr. Cummings lunged at Nell.

Triggered by the rush of this madman, Nell leapt into action. Faster than the speed of thought, she grabbed the inkwell from her desk and flung it with full force at her attacker. Mr. Cummings saw it coming, turned, and ducked, but Nell scored a direct hit. Black ink splattered all down the back of the schoolmaster's white shirt.

Nell ran—down the stairs, through the foyer, out the entryway, west on Cragard Road, left on Church Street, right on Main. Gasping for breath, she doubled over at the corner of Main and Bridge Street. She ran to Bridgend, flung open the door of Cherry Cottage and screamed, "Mummy!"[28]

Next day, Nell's inkwell attack on Mr. Cummings won her an unexpected burst of popularity. One boy even wrote a poem:

> *Tiger Cummings in a rage,*
> *Like a monkey in a cage.*
> *When the inkwell went down his back*
> *He was like a jumping jack.*[29]

For Nell, that case of the magic slate had ended happily. Now, at the swank Bonnington Hotel, she poised herself for an easier test.[30]

As the waiter poured out cups of coffee, Loseby tucked a pad of paper and pencil under the tablecloth in front of Nell.

Nell placed her right hand on top of the cloth. With her left hand, she held her cigarette. Fueled by caffeine, the conversation traveled merrily from one topic to another. Then Mr. Loseby tapped his crystal goblet with a silver demitasse spoon. The gentle ring silenced conversation, and he asked, "Should we unveil the message?"

As those around him murmured agreement, Loseby retrieved the paper and read, "Two will be convicted and two will go free."

Everyone shared one opinion: Nell and Mr. Homer would go free. Francis Brown and Elizabeth Jones (alias Mrs. Homer) would reap the consequences of their tendency to oversell and overcharge.

Nell took another self-satisfied drag on her cigarette.

# 29

## Judgment Day

Finally, closing arguments. On Friday, March 31, 1944, Chief Constable Arthur Charles West made his way through the packed corridor outside Courtroom #4. West had been held hostage at the Old Bailey for nearly a fortnight while this witch trial, one of the longest criminal trials of the war,[1] droned on and on. Forty-nine defense witnesses had told their ghost stories,[2] too many of them too well educated, too famous, and too well bred for the Chief Constable's liking.[3] As far as he was concerned, the host of cheesecloth worshippers just proved that in wartime rational intelligence is in short supply. West only hoped the jury possessed enough common sense to find Helen Duncan guilty beyond reasonable doubt. He stationed himself at his all too familiar post behind Prosecutor Maude.

As happened every day, all stood for the grand entrance of His Lordship Sir Gerald Dodson. Once seated, His Lordship inspected the rows and rows of spectators. Then veering from his usual course, he turned to the jury and said, "Members of the jury, if you think any kind of demonstration is likely to assist you, I will consider the matter."[4]

The Chief Constable scowled disapprovingly. Loseby smirked, his fanged smile dripping with anticipation. In the pews to the right and the left of the dock, faithful Spiritualists clasped their hands in prayerful expectation. Reporters, committed to their role as scribes of the preposterous, pulled out their notepads and scribbled wildly.

Evidently, cries of religious persecution had intimidated Sir Gerald,[5] and he was now willing to turn his court into a charade. The jurors huddled together. For a tense three minutes, they mumbled. At last, their spokesman announced, "The general opinion, my Lord, is 'No.'"[6]

His Lordship responded crisply, "Thank you."[7]

Emotions suddenly reversed: Chief Constable West smirked and Charles Loseby pouted.

There could be no more delays. The time had come for Mr. Loseby of the Defense and Mr. Maude of the Prosecution to go head to head.

Closing statements began with the Defense. Loseby stood and laid a sheaf of paper on his rostrum. More a sermon than a legal argument, Loseby's feverish pitch ebbed and flowed; Chief Constable West's attention waxed and waned. Finally, in seeming culmination, Loseby's voice reached a crackling crescendo:[8] "That is the essence of my case: Through Mrs. Duncan, God shows Himself in an unexpected way, in humble surroundings."[9]

But Loseby did not rest at this reverential height for more than a breath. Instead, he dove straight into the muck. "Mrs. Duncan," he explained with condescension and prejudice, "is a Scot, with a Scottish accent, a canny Scot, being apt to take a rather Scotch view of things who, though it may be totally wrong, charged a fee and opened herself to charges of fraud by any busybody or any duffer."[10]

Defense Counsel paused to indulge in a sigh of regret, before rallying to impugn his three remaining clients. "Mr. and Mrs. Homer are incompetent and foolish," he said. "Mrs. Homer is a person who gets up for shows; she talks about ectoplasm in ways that sound ridiculous. But Mrs. Homer is not charged with saying foolish things; if she were, I should have pleaded guilty immediately. Mrs. Brown is puffing Mrs. Duncan. If Mrs. Brown had minded her own business, it would have been a very good thing, but she did not. Yet, Mrs. Brown is not charged with being over-garrulous; if she were, I would have pleaded guilty immediately."[11]

Rotating his head to bestow a sympathy-evoking gaze on His Lordship, Loseby caught the judge tapping his long fingers impatiently. With rare self-reflection Loseby observed, "Perhaps I am beating a dead horse."[12]

A moment later, the Defense rested.

Prosecutor Maude rose wearily, shook his head as though awakening from a stupor, and then resumed his characteristic pose. Hands on his hips, he leaned toward the jury[13] and told them: "If this is the sort of thing we are coming to, it is time we began to pull ourselves together and exercise a little common sense."[14]

Maude's brevity was genius. A grateful judge and jury retreated for a bite to eat and jolt of strong tea.[15]

That afternoon, His Lordship made his summary and issued his final instructions.

"Now, members of the jury, these four persons are charged with pretending, through the agency of the accused Mrs. Duncan, that spirits of deceased persons appeared and communicated. That is a kind of conjuration, an unlawful act, made unlawful by an Act of Parliament. It is the duty of the Prosecution to prove beyond a reasonable doubt the truth of that charge. You are the judges of fact in this case."[16]

His Lordship put both hands on his bench signaling his intention to rise, but Mr. Loseby called out, "Might I ask your Lordship, if your Lordship might think it right to remind the jury that I offered Mrs. Duncan for cross-examination only."[17]

Patience worn to a frazzle and not recalling any such offer, Sir Gerald articulated his response with derisive clarity: "Mrs. Duncan was not called. You did not call her. I did not stop you from calling her, Mr. Loseby."[18]

The jury retired to deliberate.[19]

Chief Constable West watched the jury leave and his control over Helen Duncan vanish. Courtroom #4 emptied, but the most dutiful spectators stayed within earshot of the clerk's call. The optimistic spook worshippers lined the narrow hallway outside the courtroom. Propped against the cold beige tile, they buzzed happily, sure of acquittal. Others retreated to the grubby benches of the dingy waiting room. There a crowd gathered around Mr. Duncan and his daughter Nan. The willowy girl, less hopeful than her mother's acolytes, sobbed, "My mum's a sick woman. If they imprison her, she'll die."[20]

The time ticked slowly.

Chief Constable West studied the face of his wristwatch: 4:55, the last Friday in March.[21] Any minute, Londoners, anxious for one final weekend at the shore, would pack themselves on trains and head for Portsmouth.[22] Next week, the travel ban would be in place, and West's city would finally be off limits to outsiders.[23]

Suddenly the call rang out.[24] The jury had returned.[25]

Everyone rushed to reclaim their seats.

The jurors filed past Mrs. Duncan,[26] who continued in her role as confident diva: black eyes sparkling, head thrown back, shoulders squared, lips pursed beatifically.[27]

The clerk of the court posed the preliminary question. "Members of the jury, are you agreed upon your verdict?"[28]

The jury foreman answered, "Yes, sir."[29]

The clerk asked the pivotal question. "Do you find the prisoner Helen Duncan guilty or not guilty of conspiracy to contravene the Witchcraft Act?"[30]

"Guilty, sir."[31]

The effervescent Mrs. Brown clasped her hands to her face and erupted in a flourish of, "No. No. No."[32]

The other defendants stood immobilized.[33]

# 30

# A Slip of the Tongue

THE SENTENCING PHASE HAD ARRIVED. CHIEF CONSTABLE WEST locked eyes with Prosecutor Maude. Only these two men fully understood: The conviction had been foreplay; the climax was yet to come. For the sake of merry old England, Helen Duncan, the cheesecloth saint along with her loose-lipped alter ego had to be thrown in a dungeon and gagged until Hitler screamed "Uncle." There could be no bleeding-heart half-measures: no fines or suspended sentences, no slaps on the wrist or probation. Anything less than nine months in Holloway and this whole game of witches and spooks would have been for naught.[1]

With long sure strides, West left his post, crossed the court, and ascended to the witness box.[2] In dress uniform, standing above the fray, he focused on finishing his mission.

Prosecutor Maude asked West to introduce himself. "What is your full name."[3]

"Arthur Charles West, Chief Constable, Portsmouth,"[4] he said with dignity. Everyone in the courtroom recognized the importance of his position.

Maude then issued an open invitation to his clandestine partner. "Tell my Lord what you know about the prisoners."[5]

West studied the four criminals in the dock, all of them standing in a row. Three—Mr. Homer, the henpecked old joker; Mrs. Homer, the gabby, lard-laden con artist;[6] and Mrs. Brown, the chirpy would-be conjurer[7]—cowered in fear and contrition.[8] Not Mrs. Duncan. The waddling goddess of goblins conducted herself with confident aloofness,[9] as though providence had assured her freedom.[10]

With the thoughtful articulation of a man who had risen above his station, West made his assessment: "Mr. Homer has a good character; I know nothing against him."[11]

"What about Mrs. Homer?"[12] Maude inquired.

"Mrs. Homer's correct name is Elizabeth Anne Jones. She was married at nineteen and has one daughter, Christine. During the last war she toured France, entertaining troops."[13]

"Now tell me about Mrs. Brown,"[14] His Lordship interjected.

"In 1929, Mrs. Brown was charged with larceny from Selfridges; she served ten weeks imprisonment. That same year, she was charged with shoplifting at Sunderland and sentenced to three months imprisonment. She has been traveling the country with Mrs. Duncan acting as an agent and prompter."[15]

Sir Gerald scribbled a quick note and peered over his spectacles at the dock. "Mrs. Duncan,"[16] he said, curtly indicating the primary defendant.

Straightening his body and stiffening his tone, West reported: "My Lord, the defendant's name is Victoria Helen Duncan. She was born on November 25, 1898, at Callander, Perthshire, Scotland. She was educated in Callander public school. She married Edward Henry Duncan, who apparently does no work but travels with the defendant. She has six children."

Having quickly dispensed with those regrettably sympathetic details, the Chief Constable launched into the less appealing portion of his rehearsed portrait. "Mrs. Duncan has been a so-called Spiritualist for many years past and is well known as such. She spends much time traveling about the country to carry out engagements as a medium. Neither Mrs. Duncan nor her husband pay income tax. She was convicted at Edinburgh Sheriff's Court of fraud on the 11th of May, 1933, when she used blasphemy. She said, 'I will brain you, you bloody bugger.'"[17]

At the mention of her foul mouth, Helen Duncan shook her fist and exploded, "I never did! I never heard so many lies in all my life!"[18]

West's eyes gave a little twinkle, delighted that he had so successfully triggered Mrs. Duncan's fuse.

His Lordship pounded the gavel and coolly commented, "From the noise Mrs. Duncan is now making, I gather she disputes what has been said. It is not much use her emitting noises now."[19]

Order restored, the Chief Constable summed up his appraisal of the volatile shrew. "I cannot find any redeeming feature in her character."[20]

Out of the blue, His Lordship interjected, "Except that she has not been in any trouble since."[21]

Unaccustomed to such impertinence, not even from a man dressed in shoulder-length wig and silk robes, West barked, "No, that is not true."[22]

Silenced, His Lordship lifted his gray eyebrows dubiously and waited for an explanation.

West had no trouble setting Sir Gerald straight.

"Mrs. Duncan has been in trouble. This is a case where she attempted and succeeded in deluding confirmed believers in Spiritualism. She has tricked, defrauded, and preyed upon minds of a certain credulous section of the public who, in sorrow and grief, have gone to meetings in search of comfort. Many left with a firm conviction that the memory of the dead had been besmirched. She thought fit to come to Portsmouth, the first naval port in the world, where she would have found many bereaved families, and there practiced her trickery."[23]

The Chief Constable's words came to a full stop; he had told the tale of Mrs. Duncan's heartless sins and told it well.

His Lordship quipped, "Mrs. Duncan might have been invited there by the Homers."[24]

"Possibly," West hissed slowly, trying to quell his impatience. But despite that long breath his irritation escaped. The Chief Constable shot daggers at His Lordship and snarled, "Can I finish this, my Lord?"[25]

"Yes,"[26] teased His Lordship, and there was a mischievous glint in the judge's eye, like a juvenile delinquent who gets a thrill from goading a bobby. Sir Gerald Dodson wasn't considering this matter with proper seriousness. This judge, with his naïve respect for civil liberties and his tolerance for religious crackpots, was about to levy a ten-pound fine and send Mrs. Duncan back on the séance circuit.

West saw the writing on the wall and he blurted out the truth. "In 1941, Mrs. Duncan transgressed the security laws."[27] Then he glared at

Sir Gerald Dodson, inspecting the judge's face to see if his message had registered. Had Dodson really thought this ridiculous seven-day charade had been about witchcraft?

His Lordship recovered his maturity and said nothing.

As a conspicuous hush descended on Courtroom #4, the Chief Constable caught sight of Lieutenant Worth. Stan's eyes blinked involuntarily. Security laws. That didn't mesh with what Stan had been thinking. Stan really had believed that the Home Office and Office of Public Prosecutions had gone to all this trouble to prosecute the plump Mrs. Duncan for playing boogey-boogey with a sheet.[28]

West now fastened his gaze on Mrs. Duncan. Panic and confusion caused her to grimace.

Maintaining the demeanor of a stern taskmaster, Chief Constable West refocused his full attention on His Lordship. This was West's opportunity to wipe out any last trace of insubordination. In that crucial moment, the Chief Constable measured his words and delivered them for maximum effect. "In a naval connection, Mrs. Duncan foretold the loss of one of His Majesty's ships long before the fact was made public."[29]

The shock that struck the gallery dumb immediately gave way to a buzz of whispering voices throughout the court. West's carefully guarded secret (Albert might be cheesecloth, but Mrs. Duncan had an unfortunate gift for accurately gleaning and distributing classified information) had escaped, and it had escaped through the Chief Constable's lips. West wanted to suck the truth back in. Trying to erase his gaffe, he addressed the gallery and, in a voice as loud as a clanging bell, declared: "This woman is an unmitigated humbug who can only be regarded as a pest."[30]

His Lordship neither agreed or disagreed; he curtly announced, "I shall consider what is the proper course to take here. I will deal with it on Monday morning."[31]

## 31

# Two Shall Be Set Free

On Monday, April 3, 1944, Nell entered Courtroom #4 one last
time. Despite her weekend sojourn in Holloway Prison,[1] her appearance was most regal. Head held high, her Sunday-best hat upon her
head, her fur draped over shoulders, she promenaded between the pews,
making her way through the well of the court to face His Lordship. Her
three acolytes—Ernest Homer, Elizabeth Homer, and Francis Brown—
meandered to her rear, heads bowed. This was not the usual procession of
the guilty[2] but more a beautification.[3] For her persecution, Nell was about
to be crowned Saint Helen of Spiritualism. She smiled sanctimoniously at
the devotees assembled to her right and to her left. Women flung their
arms around her, kissed her cheeks and hands, and wept over her.[4]

The true believers murmured, in chorus, "Bless you, Mrs. Duncan.
Bless you."[5]

Others whispered, "Where's her husband?"

"Gone back to Edinburgh."

"Poor dear Mrs. Duncan. Poor dear."

"Alone at her day of reckoning."

"Rats always abandon a sinking ship."[6]

Nell didn't judge Henry so harshly, however. Her husband didn't have
the constitution to bear disgrace. The guilty verdict had been too much
for him. This final appearance was but a formality. Nell believed the

Bonnington Hotel prophecy: *Two will be set free.*[7] She looked forward to leaving the Old Bailey within the hour and returning to her family on the next train. She felt sorry for poor Mrs. Homer, the secret mistress, and Mrs. Brown, the common thief;[8] they were about to be imprisoned. The queenly Nell gazed across the courtroom directly into the eyes of Sir Gerald Dodson.

His Lordship's elongated face grew longer as he stared back at Nell. Finally, he addressed the defendants.

"Helen Duncan, Ernest Homer, Elizabeth Jones, and Francis Brown you have been convicted of pretending to recall spirits of deceased persons in a visible and tangible form. There are many people, especially in wartime, searching for loved ones. There is a great danger of their suscepti-bilities being exploited, out of a yearning for comfort and assurance. There are those, unfortunately, who are ready to profit. Many of these persons who seek solace are trusting by nature, and in poor circumstances. The law endeavors to protect such persons against themselves. I have considered very anxiously the course I should take and have come to the conclusion that Mrs. Duncan has made the most of this. The sentence of the Court upon her is that she be imprisoned for nine months."[9]

Those words were so unforeseen that Nell did not immediately catch their meaning. Horrified gasps spread through the courtroom. A moment later, Nell moaned, then groaned, then sobbed, and then her eyes rolled back, as she toppled to the floor. Her hat flew from her head. Her fur coat flapped open.[10] Nell, a mound of silk polka-dots,[11] lay in a dead faint.[12]

As the other defendants and guards knelt to revive her, Mr. Loseby jumped up to his feet and begged, "Your Lordship, would your Lordship allow me to make an application for a Certificate of Appeal?"[13]

Making no effort to disguise his weariness, Sir Gerald sighed, "Mr. Loseby, you have said all you could possibly say. I am unable to see that this case deserves an Appeal."[14]

Part III

RESOLUTIONS

# 32

## Loose Lips

S ATISFACTION SURGED THROUGH THE CHIEF CONSTABLE'S VEINS. HIS Lordship Sir Gerald Dodson had done exactly as West had intended. Of course, his cause was helped along by Mrs. Duncan's diva-like performance. Those who perch on pedestals assure their own downfall. As for the rest of her hapless crew, they got their just desserts. Mrs. Francis Brown, the chirpy charlatan-in-training, was sentenced to four months imprisonment. Mr. Homer and his "wife," properly down in the mouth, displayed enough contrition to escape the jailor.[1]

As the two defendants registered as official residents of Holloway Prison and the other two walked free, Chief Constable Arthur Charles West sped back to Portsmouth, a city preparing for total lock down. Two days earlier, a travel ban to all coastal areas from north of Edinburgh to west of Portsmouth had come into force.[2] From his mahogany desk, West now focused on putting teeth into the restrictions. Within the week, he oversaw the issuing of identity cards to all residents. His men patrolled railway stations and roads, checking all would-be visitors.[3] Over the next month, barbed wire encircled the city, and security regulations hung like a noose over the heads of would-be violators.[4] By mid-May of 1944, Portsmouth Police Headquarters, the flamboyantly ornate Byculla House,[5] bustled with the activity of constant vigilance,[6] while neighboring Edwardian mansions stood empty.[7] Those with no wartime status were evacuated from Southsea. A few hoteliers were required to stay on.[8]

By month's end, the neighborhood re-awakened. A stealthy flow of men in uniform, Americans and Brits, trickled through checkpoints into Southsea, an unlikely fortress replete with seaside elegance. Foot soldiers and top brass occupied hotels cushioned in velvet and estates ringed by gardens. Helmeted soldiers marched, weapons in hand, on the boulevards along Clarence Pier, Southsea Common, and South Parade Pier. On the beach and along the seawall, Allied landing craft practiced their attacks.

Chief Constable West should have insisted that Malcolm and Ursula, the charming grandchildren of a most respectable hotel mistress, leave the area. But Arthur didn't have the heart to send them away. Instead, he revoked their access to the world outside Southsea. No longer did Malcolm and Ursula attend school. They had more important work: The children bolstered troop morale. Each day, the two urchins walked a few blocks and watched war games. The little ones saluted the men, cheered for their simulated victories, and mingled at the military canteen. No pep talk of any kind could have given those soldiers more will to fight.

By June, the beach exercises stopped. The soldiers unrolled barbed wire along the seawall and planted land mines in the sand. Transport craft packed so tight into Portsmouth harbor that a child could have jumped from deck to deck. Curious, Ursula climbed through the spirals of barbed wire to get a better glimpse. Tearing her dress, she yelped. At the sound of her voice, fusiliers surrounded her, screaming, "Don't move." She froze, and a courageous young man extricated her from a field of land mines.

Chief Constable West heard the story with relief, but the happy ending only allayed his anxiety for a moment. The ships in the harbor and the troops in the hotels made Southsea a prime target for the *Luftwaffe*. He took some solace in his secret knowledge that from the air, the Thames estuary—a more predictable staging area, with Patton, the fiercest of Allied generals, in command—looked even more like a staging area than Portsmouth. Of course, those tanks and ships were built of plywood and cast from cement. One item above all gnawed at the Chief Constable: The pavilion at South Pier was packed with every manner of ammunition imaginable. One direct hit by an adventurous German pilot and that inferno would make the attack on Guildhall look like a Boy Scout campfire.[9]

West heard the bomb drop. From the sound, the incendiary had hit the neighborhood. He waited for a second, more disastrous, explosion. Five quiet minutes elapsed before he breathed a sigh of relief. Then he rushed to the site of the bombing. When he arrived, his heart sank. The hotel where little Ursula and her brother Malcolm lived had been reduced to a mountain of rumble. The fire brigade poured water on the flames, and his men screamed above the roar of the fire, "The children, grandmother, and family are buried inside."

Word of the children's fate spread faster than the fire. Within minutes, troops carrying shovels descended on the scene. All night, hordes of soldiers dug. By morning, the spontaneous rescue crew found the family alive and freed them to live another day.[10] The blessing of their survival only increased the Chief Constable's concern. Arthur Charles West's family—his wife, Ida, and son, Michael—lived in Southsea.[11]

Two months and two days after Helen Duncan was tossed in jail, Arthur West made an unusual decision. He took time off from his work to stop by his home in the late afternoon[12] for tea. On June 5, 1944, the Chief Constable wanted to linger in the company of his gentle and comforting wife.[13]

The windshield wipers of his cruiser clicked to and fro like a ticking clock.[14] As he pulled up to the curb in front of his cottage, he spied Lieutenant Stan Worth's motorcycle on the pavement and the young officer's Airedale on the doorstep. He stepped from his car and gave the dog's mop an affectionate pat. This was not the perfect day to take a spin around Portsmouth and drop in on friends. But the rain had let up a tad,[15] and Stan Worth had no way of knowing.

Ida greeted her husband with a kiss and sparkled as she spoke. "Stan Worth came by. I was so happy to see him that I invited him for tea. Can you stay?"[16]

The Chief Constable felt some ambivalence about the situation. He thoroughly enjoyed Stan Worth's company, but he craved his wife's full attention. Of course, everyone craved Ida's full attention, and she gave it freely. West's wife was the pleasantly plump, kindly mother every soldier and sailor wanted to hug before leaving home.[17] Arthur followed Ida into the dining room. Cucumber sandwiches and slices of sweet cake lay arranged on a platter in the middle of the table.

Ida set out three cups, plates, teaspoons, and napkins. In the background, the kettle whistled. The Chief Constable extended his hand, and the Lieutenant shook it firmly. Ida returned with the teapot, set it down, and covered it with the cozy.[18] Squeezing the Chief Constable's hand, she gushed, "Arthur, it's so good you're home."

As the three sat down, Ida turned to Stan and explained, "Arthur's so busy these days. I hardly ever see him."

Stan smiled at Ida's intimacy; very few people in Portsmouth called the Chief Constable by his first name.[19]

Eventually, the conversation wound its way to the sensational trial that had taken place two months earlier. Already nostalgic for his Old Bailey victory, West enthused, "Ida, you should have seen Stan on the witness stand. Brilliant. Stan here made mincemeat of the Defense."

"Loseby's a one-eyed fool. Mrs. Homer, she talks a good game, and Mr. Homer, he's just an old duffer." Stan offered his brusque assessment and followed with a story. "At the first Spiritualist meeting I went to, Elizabeth Homer was prattling on about the spooks. Suddenly she stops and stares at Mr. Homer. She says, 'Oooo. Look everyone. Mr. Homer has gone into a trance.' So everyone focuses on Mr. Homer. The mealymouthed husband sits there like a limp of lead and mumbles, 'I'm not Mr. Homer. My name is Abdul.' Someone asks, 'Abdul, do you have a message from the spirit world?' Mr. Homer—excuse me, I mean 'Abdul'—moans 'I have a message, but I'm not going to tell you what it is.'"[20]

Arthur laughed, Ida giggled.

"Actually, Helen Duncan did have the ability to go into a trance," Stan conceded. But then he quickly corrected his misstatement. "At least, she *looked* like she was in a trance."[21]

"That story isn't over yet," the Chief Constable volunteered with a scowl. "The Supreme Court has agreed to hear an appeal of her sentence."

Stan, surprised, responded, "The Supreme Court? At the Royal Courts of Justice? Unbelievable! When?"

"Two days after tomorrow," West answered without disclosing his secret assessment: *much too soon.*[22]

The subject changed. The three talked about this and that, until the conversation settled on the West's sixteen-year-old son, Michael.

In passing, Ida mentioned, "By the way, Michael's going to bike along the coast to Southampton tomorrow."

"In a flash, West's eyes blazed with dictatorial authority. In a voice of steel, he shot back, "No, he's not. Michael's not going anywhere tomorrow."

The Chief Constable's tone sent a shiver from Stan Worth's head to his toes. He excused himself, hopped on his motorcycle, and dashed off.

West had dropped a hint, and Stan Worth became privy to World War II's most dearly guarded secret. Stan went to his apartment, locked himself inside his room, and didn't breathe a word. Tomorrow was D-Day.[23]

Back on duty at Byculla House, West peered into the darkness. No stars twinkled through the drizzle of the still night air. Without warning, a deafening noise shook the calm, as hundreds of British and American bombers filled the heavens. The battle was on.[24]

Toward morning, as the black sky lightened to gray,[25] Chief Constable West walked along Clarence Pier. There soldiers pulled ammunition from the pavilion and loaded it onto barges. Three figures, a woman with two children, stood on the beach. Little Ursula had come with her cousin and aunt to wave goodbye to her buddies. As the soldiers marched by the children, some broke ranks and hugged them. No officers had the heart to deprive them of a child's final embrace. Other young men pressed money into the children's hands. Pounds were worthless where they were headed. All the Chief Constable's guilt about allowing that little girl and boy to stay in Southsea lifted.[26]

By daylight, no ships or barges remained in Portsmouth harbor. The Invasion of Normandy, the largest seaborne expedition in history, had been launched without a hitch.[27]

Alone in the solarium of Byculla House, overlooking the lotus pond, Chief Constable Arthur Charles West gave a gentle snort. How many civilians had known the exact date and location of D-Day? A precious few. No doubt, Lieutenant Stan Worth's respect for the Chief Constable had reached the stratosphere.[28]

# 33

## The Supreme Court

ON JUNE 8, 1944, THE SUN ROSE ON A DAY FILLED WITH PROMISE. Two million Allied troops flooded into France. The Fuehrer's fall appeared imminent.[1]

And Nell had an appointment at the Royal Courts of Justice.[2] Packed into the back of a steamy prison lorry,[3] she fingered the two hankies in her dress pocket.[4] One she reserved for tears; hopefully today's tears would be tears of relief. The other she needed now; she took it out and dabbed the perspiration from her brow.

Today, more than two months after her imprisonment, the Supreme Court would hear an appeal of her conviction.[5]

The van paused, then bumped along cobblestone for less than a half minute before coming to a full stop. The doors swung open. With prison guards pressing in on both sides of her, Nell stepped onto stone slabs. Looking back, she stared through the swirling wrought-iron gridwork of a bolted gate and saw pedestrians scurrying toward Fleet Street. This courtyard—the Bell Courtyard, an enclosure of brick, concrete, and granite—was reserved for the arrival of prisoners and their wardens.[6]

Prodded by her guards, Nell lumbered toward a tarnished cellar door and entered the retaining cells of the Royal Courts of Justice. No one greeted her. After a solitary moment that smacked of eternity, a guard pointed to a narrow archway and ordered her to walk. Without enthusiasm, Nell inched forward.

Beyond the graceful arch, the walls of a staircase pressed in on Nell. Hundreds of years and thousands of criminals had worn the stone steps smooth and left the wooden handrail coated in grime.[7] Heart pounding, Nell reached the top of this haunted passage and caught her breath behind weighty curtains, not unlike those of a Spiritualist Cabinet. A jailor, acting like a courtier, pulled the curtain open and motioned for Nell to walk through. Pressing forward, her body forced the lavish velvet to spread wide.[8]

There Helen Duncan stood, on display at the Court of the Chief Justice, scarlet drapes at her back and iron bars, elegantly wrought, boxing her in. Light streamed down through a glass-paneled ceiling onto rows of hardwood pews. To her right, three Supreme Court Justices—bewigged, bespectacled, and robed—roosted on straight-backed thrones:[9] in the center, Lord Chief Justice Viscount Caldecote, Britain's supreme jurist, flanked by Mr. Justice Oliver and Mr. Justice Birkett.[10] This court reeked of unimpeachable power, and Nell's knees trembled. Mercifully, she was allowed to sit.[11]

The gavel sounded, and without a ceremonial pause, the arguments began.

Defense Counsel Charles Loseby stood at a rostrum and faced the Justices. To his right and to his left, stacks of legal texts lay at the ready. At the Court of Appeals, these crusty calf-hide volumes served as witnesses. No people, with surprising opinions and hidden pasts, faced questioning here. Only the printed word, constant and predictable, was to be examined.[12] Loseby had spent two months in the law library at the Inns of Court. He had dug out parchment manuscripts dating back to the reigns of Henry the VIII and Queen Elizabeth. He had placed bookmarks and made notes in relevant passages. He had taken his meals in the dining hall and slumbered in his chambers. Day after day, night after night, he had returned to the dusty stacks and unearthed legal gems. With these irrefutable arguments as his ammunition, he planned to make history in the world of jurisprudence.[13]

Loseby cleared his throat and read his finely crafted Grounds for Appeal: "The indictment under the Witchcraft Act of 1735 should be quashed. Sir Gerald Dodson, the Recorder of the Old Bailey, wrongly directed the jury. The Recorder exhibited bias throughout. The verdict of the jury was unreasonable and perverse. The trial was unsatisfactory and there was a miscarriage of justice."[14]

Loseby stretched his neck, stuck out his chin, and glared across the aisle at his honorable adversary, King's Counsel John Maude.

Maude, lounging next to his own piles of worn leather volumes, smiled back, his eyes alight with a maddening twinkle.[15]

Lord Chief Justice Caldecote, an aging cherub-faced man,[16] studied the papers before him and read in a mumbled voice: "Section 4 of the Witchcraft Act of 1735: passed for the more effectual preventing and punishing of any pretenses to use any kind of witchcraft, sorcery, enchantment or conjuration whereby ignorant persons are frequently deluded and defrauded." Then, settling back in his chair, the Chief Justice stroked his pudgy chin and mused: "Conjuration. Conjuration. The charge against Mrs. Duncan and her three associates was that they pretended to exercise a kind of conjuration. Mr. Loseby, what do you suppose is the meaning of the word conjuration?"[17]

Loseby perked up at this line of inquiry and answered: "The Witchcraft Act of 1735 repealed a statute passed in 1603. Under the reign of King James I, Parliament had passed a law entitled, *An Act against Conjuration, Witchcraft and Dealing with Evil and Wicked Spirits.*" Loseby paused for effect and made his point, "The Witchcraft Act of 1735 updated a law against trafficking in evil and wicked spirits. Evil and wicked spirits. Conjuration refers to calling up the forces of evil. Mrs. Duncan was wrongly convicted of intercourse with the Devil."[18]

Nell sobbed loudly and trumpeted into her handkerchief. "Intercourse with the Devil": That was exactly what her mother had accused her of,[19] exactly what the preacher and the villagers had cursed her for.[20]

Dr. Todd had to be one of the first men in Callander to own a horseless carriage. God knows a parish doctor needed a car. All that running around from house to house and out to the country to save the sick. Even if it was a luxury, Dr. Todd deserved a little luxury in his life.[21]

By then Nell was finished with school, she was nearly a woman, and she didn't want to be a prophet. She dreamt of love and marriage—marching down the aisle of the Presbyterian Church, settling down in a cottage surrounded by her married sisters and brothers, and giving birth to bonnie babies. Nell kept her ghostly visitations to herself and won her mom's approval.[22]

But with winter came a temptation too great to ignore. Nell had never had a premonition like the one about Dr. Todd. She didn't want to see it. She didn't want to know, but the vision had come to her. Nell had no choice; she had to tell.[23]

Pulling her wool coat tight around her body, Nell walked up the hill against the wind.[24] Once on level ground, she moved faster, resolved to do the right thing. At Dr. Todd's office, taking a deep breath, hesitating for no more than an instant, she tapped on his door.

Dr. Todd cracked it a tad, looked into Nell's worried brown eyes, and asked, "Nell, what's wrong? Is it your mum or dad? One of your sisters or brothers? I'll come right along."

Without waiting for an answer, he turned and grabbed his black leather bag, ready to follow Nell back to Cherry Cottage[25] and care for an ailing MacFarlane.

Nell shook her head from side to side. "No. No. My family's all fine."

The doctor stopped, faced her, let his shoulders drop, and smiled. "Then come in. Come in, out of the cold. Don't be so glum. Nellie, what can I do for you?"

Dr. Todd had no idea. None. How could she tell him? She just had to blurt it out. "You can't go away in your car today. You've got to stay here."

The good doctor's eyes adopted a mocking glint, and he teased, "Nellie MacFarlane, you're an odd one, you are."

Nell pleaded, "Hear me, please. If you drive to Strathyre, you'll fall on a terrible fate."

For an instant, almost too quick to catch, Dr. Todd's face turned serious. Maybe it wasn't fear; maybe it was confusion. Either way, he blurted out, "How on God's good earth did you know I'd be making a trip to Strathyre, child?"

Nell shrugged her shoulders.

Late that night the falling snow did not soften the sound of the howling wind. Under the bed covers, Nell struggled to put her fears to rest. A frantic knocking echoed through Cherry Cottage, and the sound of men's boots tramped into the house. Nell strained to hear. A man's worried voice told her dad, "Dr. Todd's missing."

In her linen nightgown, Nell scurried from her bed, ran in, and blurted out, "You'll find him through the forest, on the curve by Loch Lubnaig, buried in a snowdrift."[26]

Mum glowered at Nell, but Dad's friends took Nell seriously; Nell had a reputation.

Men on horseback carrying torches gathered at the corner of Bridgend and Main Streets. Bracing themselves against the whipping storm, the search party began the slow trek toward the Pass of Leny. Nearing Loch Lubnaig, they strained to see through the swirling snow. No doubt, the rescuers would have missed Dr. Todd's car, if not for Nell's directions. The men shoveled furiously. Forcing the car door open, they pulled the doctor's frozen body out. Dr. Todd was dead.

From that day forward, all Callander dubbed that curve in the road between Callander and Strathyre "the Doctor's Corner."[27]

On Sunday, the whole MacFarlane clan—Isabella, Archie, and all eight children—lined up on their pew. From his pulpit, the minister fixed his eyes on Nell and issued a public chastisement: "Nellie MacFarlane is consorting with the Devil, falling into a godless hole where evil entities wait to possess her."[28]

Hellish Nell—that's what Johnnie Drummond, the postman; Robert McLaren, the butcher; Willie Henderson, the smithy; and all God-fearing folk of Callander christened her.[29]

Nearly twenty-five years had passed since Nell's mother had slammed the door of Cherry Cottage and exiled her forever.[30]

As Nell tried to squelch her sniveling,[31] Mr. Loseby told the Chief Justice, "The Witchcraft Act of 1735 never intended to punish those gifted with psychic powers."[32]

Bewildered, Chief Justice Caldecote demanded, "Psychic powers, whatever does that mean?"[33]

Nell's defender patiently put down his sheaf of notes and attempted an answer. "The gifted commune with virtuous entities."

"Who's to define what's virtuous and what's malevolent?" Justice Birkett interjected with another question.

"What's the nature of good and evil?"[34] Justice Oliver echoed.

"Are these questions for the Court of Appeal?" an incredulous Justice Birkett wondered aloud.

Taking a deep breath, Mr. Loseby attempted to reply. "Spiritualists define psychics as . . . "

As though having a sudden epiphany, His Lordship the Chief Justice, bellowed, "'Psychic' comes from the Greek. 'Spiritualist' comes from the Latin."[35]

The heads of all three Supreme Court Justices bobbed in self-satisfied agreement.

Justice Oliver wondered, "Might it not be useful to discern the legal difference between conjuration and witchcraft."[36]

That suggestion sent Mr. Loseby frantically leafing through the brittle pages of the volumes stacked in front of him.[37]

King's Counsel Maude, irritatingly competent, suggested that an errand boy run off to the law library and return with some antiquated dictionary or other. The Justices thought that was a fine option and agreed to take up the question when an authoritative definition was introduced.

The Lord Chief Justice continued to scrutinize the exact wording of the Witchcraft Act of 1735. "Pretend," he muttered. Then, more assertively, he shouted, "What does 'pretend' mean?"[38]

King's Counsel Maude mused, "A cat, a rabbit, and a parrot materialized at the Portsmouth séance, but I don't think members of the animal kingdom are capable of giving testimony."

Childish giggles erupted from the newspaper reporters in the gallery.

Maude waited for the chuckling to subside before adding, "Excuse me. What was I saying? The parrot might have been able to speak on such matters."[39]

Ignoring the witticism, Chief Justice Caldecote loudly queried, "Whatever does 'materialization' mean?"[40]

In answering this question, Mr. Loseby rested on solid ground. No barrister in all of Britain understood the intricacies of psychic science better than Charles Loseby. After explaining the ethereal nature of ectoplasm, he reminded the Justices that neither a sheet nor any other means of humbuggery had been discovered at the Portsmouth séances. He bemoaned the Recorder's failure to emphasize the lack of material evidence and posed the essential dilemma: "How could Mrs. Duncan simulate a child? How could she speak in foreign languages and dialects? How could she produce the likenesses of deceased relatives and friends?"[41]

The errand boy rushed back into court with a crumpled volume of parchment. Bowing, he laid it open in front of the Justices. The three legal arbiters read and whispered among themselves.

The heads of court officials nodded in slumber, and to their sonorous chorus, the legal haggling continued.

After lengthy discussion, Chief Justice Caldecote proudly announced the judges' findings. "We have discovered the difference between conjuration and witchcraft. Conjuration means using the name of God to summon the Devil and then employing the Devil to do your will. Witchcraft is an established pact with the Devil whereby the witch exacts favors in exchange for some ungodly price. Clearly witches rely on incantations."

Mr. Loseby found no reason to quibble; instead he fumed, "The Recorder exhibited bias throughout."[42]

The Lord Chief Justice removed his spectacles, leaned forward, glared at Mr. Loseby, and spoke icily: "Are you accusing the Recorder of London of a crooked motive? Do you assert that Sir Gerald Dodson is twisted and prejudiced?"[43]

"No!" Loseby nearly shouted. He had not intended to impugn the Recorder's ethics.[44]

"Do you wish to withdraw your complaint?"[45] the Chief Justice asked.

Attempting to eat his implication, Mr. Loseby explained: "The learned Recorder seemed unable to get from his mind a certain distaste for the whole subject. From beginning to end, not a question was put by him to assist me."[46]

Justice Birkett then took up Sir Gerald Dodson's defense. "Assuming the judge takes the view that human credulity could go no further, surely that is not bias. Must the judge be mealymouthed? If the Recorder had been disposed to rule in your favor, would you complain of bias, Mr. Loseby?"[47]

Even Mr. Loseby had to laugh. "If the Recorder has been sympathetic to my cause, we should not be here today,"[48] he admitted. The Defense Counsel then itemized his complaints: The Recorder had implied that Spiritualism was a valueless anti-Christian religion designed for ignorant persons with wavering faith; His Lordship Sir Gerald Dodson had belittled defense witnesses and called Lieutenant Stan Worth "a wonderful witness"; and most grievously, His Lordship had refused to allow Mrs. Duncan to materialize spirits in court, depriving Mrs. Duncan of the opportunity to produce irrefutable proof of her innocence.

Justice Birkett listened attentively and then asked, "Could the jury have handled the parrot and rabbit when they materialized?"[49]

The reporters guffawed.

Loseby's voice rose indignantly. "All advances in human knowledge have initially been received with skepticism."[50]

All three justices conceded Loseby's point, and Nell's first day at the Royal Courts of Justice came to a close.

On the second day, Loseby reminded the Justices of the facts: Forty-four witnesses testified in defense of Helen Duncan and the Prosecution produced not a shred of incriminating material.

King Counsel John Maude relaxed on his wooden bench, said nearly nothing, and occasionally grinned like Alice's Cheshire cat.

Chief Justice Caldecote thanked his learned friends, Loseby and Maude, for their arguments. Then he told everyone present that the Court of Appeals would issue its ruling eleven days hence, on June 19, 1944.[51]

Nell never again appeared in the Court of the Chief Justice. On June 15, 1944, exactly one week after her appeal, an entirely new type of bomb appeared above the Royal Courts.[52]

As the three Supreme Court Justices considered the wisdom of the Witchcraft Act of 1735, they heard a distant rumble, reminiscent of a badly tuned motorcycle. Within moments, the engine noise reached a deafening pitch.[53] On Fleet Street, pedestrians looked toward the sky and saw, just above the rooftops, a low-flying plane.[54] Its dark silhouette shone like an enormous black cross spewing flames from its rear. Mysteriously, the clattering stopped. The plane took a nosedive, but oddly, it did not speed to earth.[55] The enormous projectile floated down on the Royal Courts of Justice and disappeared behind its gothic spires. The explosion shook the earth. Smoke rose from the Inns of the Court.[56]

In the next days, hundreds of the flaming monsters pummeled London. Hitler had unleashed his Vengeance Weapons, his V-bombs, robotic planes powered by burning petrol. The flying bombs reached speeds of up to 400 miles per hour. Their noses were packed with warheads containing a ton of explosives. When their engines cut out, they headed to earth. The descent took fifteen seconds.[57] The blasts destroyed, killed, and maimed. Appearing like ominous buzzing insects, the V-bombs attacked by day and by night. With typical understatement, Londoners took to calling the missiles "doodlebugs." In one week, the swarming doodlebugs killed 765 people, injured 2,697, and destroyed 12 hospitals, 12 schools, and 4 churches in and around the British capitol.[58]

With the Inns of the Court still smoldering and London bracing for more, Chief Justice Caldecote had no intention of issuing the witchcraft ruling in the usual splendor of the Royal Courts. On Monday, June 19, the Court of Appeals convened underground, in a crypt deep in the bowels of Lincoln's Inn Chapel.[59]

Crammed onto a wooden bench with prison guards pressing in on her, Nell waited. Reporters jostled for seats.[60] The three Chief Justices, stubbornly attired in silk robes and horsehair wigs, kicked up dust as they tramped over the cement floor.[61]

Lord Chief Justice Caldecote read the Court's judgment at double-speed. Even with that quickened pace, it took him a good twenty minutes to reach the punch line:[62] "Nine months in prison was in no way excessive."[63]

It was over. The guards heaved Nell to her feet.[64]

# 34

# Freedom in Deception

C ONSIGNED TO A CELL IN THE JAIL'S INFIRMARY,[1] NELL LANGUISHED ON a cot, staring blankly through a barred window into the dark. Sixteen days after Chief Justice Caldecote nailed her coffin shut,[2] all the fight had gone out of her. Nothing was good. Nothing was bad. Everything was bleak.[3]

From beyond the prison's ramparts, Nell registered the now familiar rattling of a distant doodlebug. This time the rumble gradually grew to a deafening roar. Suddenly, there was silence, and in that silence, fear of disastrous inevitability:[4] Her mother's third and final prophecy had finally caught up with her: "You'll be burned alive in a hell fire."[5]

Mobilized by terror, Nell bolted to her cell's barred window. The nose of the plane-sized missile, carrying a ton of explosives, pointed down, directly at Holloway Prison. Within seconds, it struck its target: Cell Block B. Bricks and shingles flew sky high. Flames, red, black, brown, and blue, swirled and engulfed, devouring their quarry, until finally, with a thunderous roar, Cell Block B caved in.[6] The floor beneath Nell's feet quaked, and she scurried to a corner of her cell. There she collapsed, cowering on the brink of hell's fiery pit. The brick walls grew hot, and she screamed.[7] Smoke and fumes crawled in and surrounded her. In that choking fog came a vision of her mother, laughing.[8]

Fate cheated her mother's prophecy. Nell lived; in that victory, she pondered her childhood with revived curiosity and resurrected a forgotten memory of her mother's laughter.[9] There had been a time, before Nell's banishment, before her marriage to Henry, before the spirit of Albert possessed her, when her mum had taken secret delight in Nell's rebellious nature.

One restless summer night long ago, Nellie had lain in bed, smarting from another bedtime scolding. "Gone swimming again. How many times does your Mummy have to punish you? It's dangerous and it's not ladylike. Can't you control yourself? Won't you ever learn how to behave?"

Just as she was about to fall asleep, Nellie heard Mummy giggle, and the incorrigible tomboy slipped out of bed, tiptoed toward the lamplight, and crouched on the floor by the kitchen door.

Mummy sipped her tea.

Dad nursed his Scotch whiskey and chuckled about the wayward antics of his brood: "'The Wild Slaters.' That's what the village folk call the Archie MacFarlanes,[10] but our little Nellie proved her worth when she scaled the schoolhouse."[11]

From her listening post, Nell took pride in her victorious moment. At Callander Primary School, children were taught their place.[12] Even on the playground, girls played like girls and boys like boys. The lads kicked the football; the lasses cheered.

Nell had stood alone, away from the others. She wanted to be in the middle of the fray, heading the ball with the best of the boys,[13] but school clothes and school rules got in her way.[14] One bragger of a lad had missed the goal by miles, and the ball had landed on the schoolhouse roof. Nellie had not hesitated; she scurried up the side of the building,[15] with her petticoat and bloomers in shameless view.[16] As her hands and feet moved surely and swiftly up the stone wall, the jaws of bickering boys and silly girls had fallen open. Nell had snagged the ball and held it high. There above the admiring crowd, a triumphant rebel in pinafore and starched blouse, she had savored her first taste of public adoration.[17]

Mummy snickered. "Nellie, she's a MacFarlane through and through. Can't keep that girl off a roof or away from water. She sneaks off to swim. Tries to get away with it, you know, but I catch her every time. The little urchin thinks I'm a mind reader."[18]

Daddy chuckled. "So how do you know? What's the secret?"

Leaning forward, speaking softly, Mummy revealed the source of her powers: "When I dress Nellie in the morning, I button her petticoat down the back. When she goes swimming, she buttons it up the front."

Dad laughed, a loud belly laugh, and Mummy joined in.

To that joyful chorus, Nellie had snuck back to bed and snuggled up with her sisters.[19]

In that recollection, many years after her mother's death, the stern veneer fell away from her mother's image. Beneath the façade, Nell could finally see the protective intention of a concerned mum. The damning prophecies ("You'll be thrown in a dungeon, tried as a witch, and burn alive in a hell fire") sprang not from a well of clairvoyance and loathing but from a mother's fear for her child's fate. Nell had raised six children of her own. Now she understood that motherly impulse.[20] Nell had been a devil of a child.[21]

Comforted by recalling that her mother had secretly enjoyed her shenanigans, Nell took new delight in the end of that episode.

Wee Nellie MacFarlane had been emboldened by her mummy's giggly confession. Next day, after the dishes had been washed and the chickens fed, Nellie had grabbed Pate and pulled him out the cottage door. Stealing a fast look toward home, the pair had run down the muddy street toward the bridge. All clear. They had veered to the left and run to the water. Nell had tossed her clothes over a bush and dove straight into the Lena. She had swam free, until Pate had yelled, "Enough now, Nellie. Time's up. We need to get home, before Mum gets suspicious."

On the shore, Nellie had scurried to the shelter of the bush and ordered Pate to button her petticoat up the back.

For the very first time, Nellie manipulated her clothing in service of deception. Mummy had never again caught Nell swimming, and Nellie took pride in her trickery.[22]

Trapped within the fortress walls of Holloway Prison, Nell recalled that secretive delight and felt a resurgence of freedom. No longer would she allow fear to paralyze her or scruples to drive her to madness. Instead, she would take fresh joy in the art of deception.[23]

On visitors' day, Nell swung a shoddy vampire-style cloak over her prison uniform and followed a prison guard.[24]

"Over there. Take a seat at that table,"[25] the wardress ordered.

Nell smiled as she followed directions. Nothing could dampen her anticipation. Jean Beatson visited regularly and ministered to Nell's spiritual needs. The door at the end of the room opened wide, and Jean walked toward Nell carrying the loveliest bouquet of posies. Nell swallowed Jean up in a grateful hug.[26]

The wardress stepped forward. "That's quite enough contact,"[27] she snapped.

Jean took one step back, handed Nell the flowers, and said, "I hope these bring some joy to you."

Nell studied each blossom and exclaimed, "I've never been so thankful for a bouquet in all my days."[28]

The guard returned to her watching post.[29]

Jean caught Nell up on all the family news. Henry was bedridden. Gena had gone to collect a living stipend from the haughty Spiritualists on Harriot Row. The secretary had thrown the dole at her and sneered, "Don't you think your mother has kept your father for long enough?" Gena had run into the street crying.[30] Lilian was seeing to Henry's needs.[31] The granddaughters, Dawn and Joan, were keeping the family entertained. Nan was recovering from jaundice and rheumatic fever.[32] None of them really knew how to get along without Nell.

Jean folded her hands, and Nell did the same. Jean spoke a little prayer, asking for the spirits to bring good news and better times.[33]

Time was up. Cradling her flowers, Nell followed the guard back to her hospital cell. Carefully, with her back to the door, she placed the bouquet in a jug of water by her bed.[34]

Sitting on her bed, sipping her afternoon tea and chewing on a stale crust of bread, Nell didn't even think about whether tomorrow's noon-day meal was to be potatoes, vegetables, or haricot beans with roast mutton, or boiled beef, or Irish stew, or cottage pie, or shepherd's pie.[35] It was all slop meted out from vats. Instead, for the first time in her life, Nell craved the solace she found in solitude.

Night fell. Her warders dozed off at the nursing station.[36] With quiet stealth, Nell shuffled through Jean's lovely bouquet. Feeling the slippery surface of shiny paper, she pulled out a pack of cigarettes and then a box of matches. Triumphant, Nell held back her laugher.

Prison was, for sure, reforming Nell. She was learning a lost skill; she was learning to lie. Freed of shame,[37] she inhaled the loveliest taste on earth, the smoke of tobacco, made even lovelier by the recognition of her power. Neither Harry Price nor the Chief Constable of Portsmouth had caught her with one scrap of muslin. Too bad Miss Maule had blemished Albert's perfect record. Nell snuffed out her cigarette and tucked it back among the posies. Still, staring up at the bars of her cell window, Nell could not escape the consequences of her chosen profession. Reluctantly, she admitted the wisdom of her mother's warnings.

## 35

## Released

THROUGH AUGUST 1944, THE FLYING BOMBS BLASTED LONDON TO BITS. That summer, while Nell resided at Holloway Prison Infirmary, 2,300 V-bombs exploded in and around London, killing 5,475 people. The dead were nothing compared to the injured; 16,000 were bloodied and maimed. And 25,000 houses had been burnt to rubbish.[1]

By September, Nell no longer kept herself confined to her infirmary cell. Instead, by her own request, she often lumbered off to the workroom.[2] There she sat with other inmates, mending sheets and darning socks[3]—and gathering the latest gossip. On September 7, Churchill's son-in-law, Duncan Sandys started a comforting rumor: "The attack of the doodlebugs was over."[4] That night, Nell retired to her cell in blessed relief. The next morning, at 6:40 AM,[5] as she settled in front of the workbench, a double clap of thunder sounded.[6] Nell held her breath, and all the fourteen-inch-thick walls of the entire prison trembled.[7]

Wild speculations began circulating in whispers. Hitler's never-ending, ever-escalating monster bombs had turned into rockets, the stuff of science fiction.[8] The government tacitly made reference to gas mains exploding, but no one believed that bit of fiction. The guards and nurses took to calling the mighty two-stroke rumble "the flying gas main."[9] Eventually, the truth leaked out: The Germans had unleashed their final weapon, the V-2 bomb, a missile weighing 13 tons and traveling 3,000 miles per hour.[10] The double clap was a result of it breaking the sound barrier. Its explosion had left a crater thirty feet wide, obliterated six houses, killed three people, and injured seventeen,[11] all within earshot of Holloway Prison. Nell wanted out.[12]

With the bombardment, her mother's protective prophecies once again echoed through her troubled mind. What had her psychic powers brought her? Insult, injury, and heartbreak compounded by imprisonment. Everybody had been grabbing for a piece of her, tearing her to bits. To Spiritualists, she was nothing more than a convenient martyr. To grieving folk, she was just a vehicle for getting through their mourning. To Albert, Peggy, "Rosie," and a host of other spirits, she was an easy body to use and abuse. Even Henry had a bit of the parasite in him. No more. Nell intended to throw her damn *gift* out the window and let it burn in hell with the rest of London.[13]

On Friday, September 22, 1944, Nell pulled her dotted dress over her head and stepped into her own shoes.[14] Her nine-month sentence had miraculously been reduced to six months, presumably for good behavior. Twenty-five pounds lighter, stronger and healthier, she walked more briskly than when she had entered Holloway Prison.[15] Out an exit door and through the courtyard, she passed prisoners in capes and striped frocks.[16] Her heeled pumps clicked along the cobblestone. She hurried through the fortress gate, and the bars of Holloway Prison clanged shut behind her.[17] A few diehard journalists and devoted Spiritualists cheered her release. Henry, along with her daughters Gena and Nan, rushed to encircle her. After much hugging and tears of joy, Helen Duncan announced her decision: "I will never work as a medium again, not for anyone or anything."[18]

The Spiritualists skulked off to lament their loss.[19] Henry hailed a cab.[20]

Whisked away and deposited on the pavement in front of King's Cross Station, Nell joined a small crowd gathering around a lamppost. A city worker in overalls climbed a ladder and replaced a long extinguished globe. The crowd cheered. The Blackout was over. The night lights of London were about to glow once more.[21] Victory was just around the corner.

In Portsmouth, even the ever-cautious Chief Constable Arthur Charles West had no objection to Helen Duncan's release. No V-bombs had fallen on his city for more than two months.[22] The Royal Air Force fighter boys had bombed the Reich's remaining oil reserves,[23] and *Luftwaffe* squadrons no longer had enough fuel to visit nighttime terror on Portsmouth. Allied Bomber Command had sunk Germany's last seaworthy battleship,[24] and all possibility of Nazi troops setting foot on British soil had been eradicated. Signaling his confidence, West ordered the dark covers removed from the police cruiser headlights. All over town, citizens scraped black paint off windows.[25]

Four months earlier, in the buildup to Normandy, Eisenhower had secretly taken up residence in Portsmouth's Southwick House.[26] Any day now, the Allied Commander-in-Chief intended to move his headquarters to Versailles. Since D-Day, Hitler had lost one million fighting men on the western front. Allied Forces now controlled an unbroken line from the English Channel to Switzerland.[27] With that safe buffer zone secured, the British government lifted the travel ban.[28]

Once again hourly trains chugged into Portsmouth harbor. Hordes of weekend visitors wanted to do more than make up for lost fun; they wanted to pay their respects. South Pier, the Pavilion, and the boardwalk marked the spot where the course of civilization had changed, where the world's greatest seaborne invasion had been launched and the demise of history's most demonic dictator had been secured. West's men welcomed their fellow Brits with pride and without checking identity cards.[29] As young ladies who worked in Byculla House played tennis on its private courts,[30] a newly minted American military helicopter alighted on its grounds. Chief Constable Arthur Charles West ducked beneath its whirling propellers, climbed into the insect-like craft, and took a complimentary spin around Portsmouth harbor. And his son, Michael, was now free to bike along the coast to Southampton.[31]

Inside King's Cross Station, a throng of pushy passengers jostled Nell, clamoring to get on trains destined for Edinburgh. The coast of Scotland had been off limits the whole time Nell had been in prison. Now Londoners were anxious to visit neglected relatives and meander through the charmed streets of Scotland's fairest city.[32]

Finally home, Nell sank into an overstuffed chair. Comforted by her resolve to never again practice as a medium, she drifted into a well-earned sleep.

Henry sat at her feet and sobbed softly.[33]

In Pulborough, Harry Price no longer sat with one hand on a loaded Colt automatic.[34] Instead, he gnawed on the stem of a Sherlock Holmes–style pipe[35] as he read the current issue of *Psychic News*. Mrs. Duncan had announced her retirement.[36]

Price scoffed. The medium wasn't any more capable of forsaking her talent than he was of renouncing his ambition. Secretly, Price believed that he and Mrs. Duncan shared an enormous capacity for showing people what they wanted to see. Begrudgingly, he respected her for that.

Picking up a fountain pen and pulling out a piece of stationary, Price composed a note to his one-time protégé, the flame-haired Mrs. Molly Goldney: "There is one last certainty; Mrs. Duncan will be back at her old game."[37]

# Epilogue

WORLD WAR II ENDED IN ALLIED VICTORY AND A MIRACULOUS transformation occurred: Helen Duncan turned into a jolly old lady, overflowing with the confident wisdom and generosity of a triumphant survivor.[1]

Her two sons returned from battle: Harry, raring to get on with life, and Peter, emotionally scarred by a kamikaze attack.[2] Reunited, the expanded Duncan family—grown children, in-laws and grandchildren—crammed into Nell's cottage. Between the bouts of joyous laughter, Nell found her voice. Without any intrusions from Uncle Albert, she advised her brood to live a responsible life, listen for inner guidance,[3] not speak in anger, give freely,[4] and above all, forgive without reservation.[5]

In the aftermath of war, neighbors came knocking at Nell's door, begging for some comforting communication from beyond the grave. Their pain awakened Nell's pity and melted her resolve. She welcomed the grief-stricken into her home and delivered personal greetings from the dearly departed. Believers left with a reassuring message: Death is only a brief parting between two worlds.[6]

Nell saw the needy everywhere, and she wanted to open her home, her heart, and her handbag to the less fortunate.[7] The more Nell wanted to give, the more she faced the facts: Henry wasn't about to earn the family's daily bread, and he certainly wasn't going to provide an extra crust to feed the poor.[8]

When invitations came from Edinburgh and Glasgow, Nell agreed to once again enter the Cabinet and allow Albert a little time in the limelight.[9] Now more respectful of his mistress, Albert served Nell's needs. When she eyed a stately brownstone on Rankeiler Street, she was able to buy it.[10] While Henry moved his collection of Spiritualist literature into the oak-trimmed library, Nell opened her freshly polished door to a motley assortment of fun-loving survivors.[11]

Homeless wayfarers signaled Nell's soft touch by marking her stoop with chalk.[12] A steady stream of the torn and tattered, smelling of booze, tramped down their lovely cobblestone street, sure of a handout. Uppity neighbors looked down their noses, while Nell enjoyed issuing a Christian reminder: "There but for the grace of God . . . "[13]

One day, Nell happened on a pregnant teenager, alone and rejected by her family. Remembering her own similar plight, she bundled the girl off to Rankeiler Street. There, surrounded by nonjudgmental love, the young lady became a mother. When the lucky girl—babe in arms—managed to reconcile with her parents, Nell befriended another waif.[14]

On market day, Nell looked up from pondering produce and saw a sorry sight: a ragged girl disfigured by ringworm, her hair falling out. Nell took the child home for tea. Four years and many hospital treatments later, Maggie left the Rankeiler house with a smartly coifed wig on her head and another one in her hatbox.[15]

By 1948, Harry Price was gloating. His prediction had proved true: Helen Duncan was back at her old game. Except now, his guinea pig had enough sense to stay in Scotland and play to small audiences where unrestrained credulity abounded. Finally, Price's audiences outstripped Mrs. Duncan's. With sales of his creative autobiography, *Search for Truth,* and his entertainingly spooky *Most Haunted House* books piercing the stratosphere, the public clamored to get a glimpse of him. Queues formed outside lecture halls and standing-room-only audiences applauded his presentations.[16]

On the afternoon of March 27, 1948,[17] still motivated by undaunted enthusiasm for increasing fame and royalties,[18] Price retreated to his ground-floor office[19] and mulled over his next manuscript, a third book about the lively ghosts of Borley.[20] At the lifting of his pen, his breath grew short and his chest tight.[21]

When Price did not emerge for tea,[22] his matronly wife went to his office at the back of the house. Standing next to her husband's most prized relic, the Borley Bell from England's most haunted house, Mrs. Price tapped on the stall-like door to his workroom.[23] When he did not respond, she pushed open the entry and tiptoed over the threshold. There she found his body, collapsed at the foot of his desk.[24]

By the following day, Constance Knight Price, the perfumery heiress who had indulged and financially supported her husband's dabbling in psychic research,[25] had reported his death to the appropriate media.[26]

In 1951, another piece of liberating news reached the Duncan household. Parliament revoked the Witchcraft Act of 1735 and replaced it with a modern bit of legislation, the Fraudulent Mediums Act.[27]

Freed from the specter of witchcraft accusations and assured that Harry Price could never again torment her, Nell put the "Albert Show" back on the road.[28] Hell-bent on enjoying life and making the most of her *gift*, she traveled with a twinkle in her eye,[29] a flask in her pocket,[30] and a crusty philosophy on her lips: "I've got to die sometime from something."[31] Her family and her disciples agreed: Helen Duncan glowed; she lit up the room with sunshine born of serenity.[32]

Her detractors asked a more damning question—"Dear Madam, What are your spirits—whisky, gin, or rum?"[33] With a hearty laugh, Helen toasted their wit and dismissed their accusations.

On Sunday, November 16, 1952, Chief Constable Arthur Charles West presided over a solemn ceremony. He did not escort the Queen Mother or Winston Churchill to this event; his city no longer garnered such officious attention. Instead West stood in the opulent ballroom of Byculla House, flanked by men of local stature.[34] Behind him, three floor-to-ceiling leaded glass windows glowed with the muted light of an English autumn. In front of him, his men and their families sat in rows of wooden chairs. Other loyal citizens of Portsmouth gathered around the carved banisters of the mezzanine, looking down at the proceedings. The glass-paneled ceiling bathed the majestic room in pale luminosity.[35] Here was a police station fit to honor the men who died in war. As Chief Constable West unveiled a wooden plaque engraved with the names of Portsmouth constabulary officers who had died in World War I and World War II, the soothing voices of the Police Choir filled the hall with a comforting hymn:

> *I saw a new heaven and a new earth . . .*
> *I saw the holy city coming down from God . . .*
> *I saw the dead, small and great, stand before God.*
> *And God shall wipe away all tears . . .*
> *and there shall be no more death.*[36]

On October 26, 1956, Nell stood naked as three women dressed her in her black séance robe, knickers, and tennis shoes. She lumbered to her place behind the curtain and took comfort in the words of the 23rd Psalm: "Though I walk through the valley of the shadow of death, I fear no evil." Finally content with her calling, her spirit lifted and Albert appeared.

Lights flashed. Men shouted, "Police. This is a raid."

Nell fell off her chair, broke into a sweat, and lost consciousness.[37]

Driven home to Rankeiler Street, Nell crept to her first-floor bedroom and steadied herself on the bedpost. Gena, her youngest child, untied her mother's corset and loosened the bra. Nell shrieked. The Spiritualist stigmata, three burn marks the size of saucers, angry and inflamed, were seared into her breasts and abdomen.

Her doctor rushed to her bedside but could give no medical explanation.

Henry asked, "Could all this have been self-inflicted?"[38]

Six weeks later, as Nell lay dying, a scent of roses flooded her room. Welcoming a vision, she sighed, "It's my mother." Opening her eyes, she told her children, "Please, all of you, forgive."

Then, after whispering "I love you" to her daughters, Nell let go of untold hurt and made a final request. "Take care of your father for me."[39]

# Notes

Years have passed since I unearthed Winston Churchill's note in that file stamped CLOSED UNTIL 2046. Britain loosened its security laws, and more documents were declassified. In England, other books about Helen Duncan were published, one by Mary Armour, a medium with close ties to Helen Duncan's niece, and another by Malcolm Gaskill, a historian with a particular interest in witchcraft. I continued researching, following new leads. As I pieced together the ever-accumulating bits and pieces of information, the plot and subplot of an untold story emerged. The plot: an officially documented, sometimes comic, cautionary tale of a witch trial and of a woman swept up by historical events, targeted and elevated to prominence by wartime paranoia. The subplot: a richly chronicled personal drama of betrayal, rivalry, and forgiveness.

As narrator, I have called upon verbatim transcripts, eyewitness accounts, interviews, archives, site visits, contemporaneous newspapers, and books to construct scenes and present characters. Each scene communicates specific factual information in the context of typical, rigorously sourced routines, behaviors, thoughts, conversations, and opinions. Chapter-by-chapter explanations and endnotes are provided to make this scene-building process transparent to interested readers.

## Prologue

1. Imperial War Museum, *The War Cabinet Rooms* (London: Imperial War Museum Publication, 1996), 29.

2. "Bombs Start London Fires," *Daily Herald*, March 25, 1944.

3. "Government Defeated on Equal Pay," *Daily Express*, March 29, 1944.

4. *World War II: Day by Day* (London: Dorling Kindersley, 2001), 502.

5. "2,000 Ton Blitz Hits Nuremberg," *Evening News* (Portsmouth), March 29, 1944; "600 Bombers Warn Berlin, 'We're Coming,'" *Daily Herald*, March 23, 1944; "Air War Gigantic—4 German Cities Ablaze," *Sunday Pictorial*, March 26, 1944.

6. *World War II: Day by Day*, 502–506.

7. "Longest Raid in a Year," *Daily Express*, March 25, 1944; "Bombs Start London Fires," *Daily Herald*, March 25, 1944.

8. "Special Cabinet Summoned: One Vote Defeat for Government on Equal Pay," *Daily Herald,* March 29, 1944; "Premier Challenges Equal Pay Rebels," *Evening News* (Portsmouth), March 29, 1944; "Prime Minister Issues Ultimatum—Rose to Cheers from House of Commons," *Daily Herald,* March 30, 1944; "Reversal of Equal Pay: MP's Cancel Vote," *Daily Herald,* March 31, 1944; "MP's Queue to Vote for Churchill, Undid Equal Pay," *Daily Express,* March 31, 1944.

9. Michael Howard, *British Intelligence in the Second World War,* vol. 5 (New York: Cambridge University Press, 1990), 112.

10. Ibid., 115–116.

11. Ibid., 123–124.

12. *The War Cabinet Rooms,* 29.

13. "Medium Weeps and Shouts at Verdict," *New Chronicle,* April 1, 1944; "Witchcraft Act Offences," *Times,* April 1, 1944; "Police Revelations Do Not Shake Followers," *News of the World,* March 30, 1944; "Medium Defied Handcuffs and Sashcord," *New Chronicle,* March 30, 1944; "'All Lies' Cries Medium," *Daily Express,* April 1, 1944.

14. Maurice Barbanell, *The Case of Helen Duncan* (London: Psychic Press, 1945), 102.

15. Winston Churchill, letter to Home Secretary, April 3, 1944, HO 144/22172, Public Records Office, Kew, England.

16. Ibid.

17. Ibid.

18. "Weekend Edition with Scott Simon," National Public Radio, Washington, D.C., January 31, 1998.

19. Ibid.

20. C. E. Bechhofer Roberts, ed., *The Trial of Helen Duncan* (London: Jarrolds, 1945).

21. Gena Brealey, *The Two Worlds of Helen Duncan* (London: Regency Press, 1985).

22. Manfred Cassirer, *Medium on Trial* (Essex: PN Publishing, 1996).

23. Barbanell, *The Case of Helen Duncan.*

24. Harry Price, *Regurgitation and the Duncan Mediumship* (London: National Laboratory of Psychical Research, 1931).

25. Gerald Dodson, *Consider Your Verdict* (London: Hutchinson and Company, 1967).

26. Winston Churchill, letter to Home Secretary, April 3, 1944, HO 144/22172.

## Chapter 1

This chapter depicts formative scenes from Helen Duncan's childhood. Vignettes from earlier biographers are enriched by scenic detail from my visit to her home village of Callander and by insights obtained through personal interviews and correspondence with the townfolk.

1. Dorothy Mahoney, letter to author, October 28, 1999; Mr. and Mrs. J. K. Dunn, personal interview, Callander, Scotland, December 18, 1999; Mr. and Mrs. Harvey MacNaughton, personal interview, Callander, Scotland, December 19, 1999.

2. Gena Brealey, *The Two Worlds of Helen Duncan* (London: Regency Press, 1985), 15–16; "The Last Witch in England," interview with Shelia Downey and Ann Pooey, Helen Duncan's granddaughters, BBC Radio, London, August 13, 1998.

3. Site visit, Callander, Scotland, December 17–19, 1999.

4. Dorothy Mahoney, personal interview, Callander, Scotland, December 18, 1999.

5. Ibid.

6. A. M. Campbell, *Let's See Callander and the Trossachs* (Fort William, 1951).

7. David Ross, *The Story of Rob Roy* (New Lanark: Corbie, 1998), 20–28.

8. Dorothy Mahoney, letter to author, November 2, 1999.

9. Brealey, *Two Worlds*, 15. Quote is typical of young Nell's personality.

10. Harvey Duncan, contemporaneous journal describing Callander and its townfolk in the early 1900s, Harvey MacNaughton's private collection, Callander, Scotland.

11. Malcolm Gaskill, *Hellish Nell* (London: Fourth Estate, 2001), 33–34.

12. Mahoney, letter to author, October 28, 1999.

13. Mahoney, letter to author, November 2, 1999.

14. Duncan, journal describing Callander.

15. Anonymous, personal interview, Callander, Scotland, December 18, 1999.

16. Brealey, *Two Worlds*, 17; Mahoney, personal interview, December 18, 1999.

17. Photograph, Bridgend in the early 1900s, Harvey MacNaughton's private collection, Callander, Scotland.

18. Gaskill, *Hellish Nell*, 32–33.

19. Anonymous, personal interview, Callander, Scotland, December 19, 1999.

20. Childhood photograph of Helen Duncan, *People's Journal*, undated. My impressions in this portion of the vignette are derived from this photograph.

21. Mahoney, letter to author, October 28, 1999. Dialogue is typical of Callander.

22. Brealey, *Two Worlds*, 15; Victoria Duncan, "Secrets of My Second Sight," *People's Journal*, October 7—December 16, 1933; Gaskill, *Hellish Nell*, 17 (childhood photograph).

23. Anonymous, personal interview, December 19, 1999.

24. Brealey, *Two Worlds*, 15–16.

25. "Last Witch," interview with Downey and Pooey, BBC Radio, August 13, 1998; Gaskill, *Hellish Nell*, 35.

26. Brealey, *Two Worlds*, 15–16; "Last Witch," interview with Downey and Pooey, BBC Radio, August 13, 1998.

## Chapter 2

This scene assumes that the séance attended by Marion Gray in the summer of 1940 conformed to Helen Duncan's séance routine as sourced below.

1. Gena Brealey, *The Two Worlds of Helen Duncan* (London: Regency Press, 1985), 48, 60, 84; Harry Price, *Regurgitation and the Duncan Mediumship* (London: National Laboratory of Psychical Research, 1931), 79.

2. "The Hex Files," *Daily Mail*, December 6, 1997, photograph; Brealey, *Two Worlds*, 30; C. E. Bechhofer Roberts, ed., *The Trial of Helen Duncan* (London: Jarrolds, 1945), 40.

3. Manfred Cassirer, *Medium on Trial* (Essex: PN Publishing, 1996), 151; "Witch Hunt," interview with Margaret Pratt, Channel 4, London, July 13, 1999.

4. Price, *The Duncan Mediumship*, 79–80; Paul Tabori, *Harry Price: Biography of a Ghost Hunter* (London: Athenaeum Press, 1950), 136.

5. Brealey, *Two Worlds*, 60.

6. Cassirer, *Medium on Trial*, 151; "Witch Hunt," interview with Margaret Pratt, Channel 4, London, July 13, 1999.

7. Price, *The Duncan Mediumship*, 11; "Witch Hunt," interview with Margaret Pratt, Channel 4, London, July 13, 1999.

8. Brealey, *Two Worlds*, 32–60; Alan Crossley, *The Story of Helen Duncan* (Greenford: Psychic World Classic, 1999), 23–38; Malcolm Gaskill, *Hellish Nell* (London: Fourth Estate, 2001), 58–69.

9. Price, *The Duncan Mediumship*, 13; Roberts, ed., *Trial of Helen Duncan*, 39–41; "Witch Hunt," interview with Margaret Pratt, Channel 4, London, July 13, 1999.

10. Brealey, *Two Worlds*, 22–26.

11. Price, *The Duncan Mediumship*, 11–83; Brealey, *Two Worlds*, 55–9; Gaskill, *Hellish Nell*, 124–146.

12. Crossley, *The Story of Helen Duncan*, 57; "The Last Witch in England," interview with Shelia Downey and Ann Pooey, Helen Duncan's granddaughters, BBC Radio, London, August 13, 1998.

13. Cassirer, *Medium on Trial*, 151; Gaskill, *Hellish Nell*, 186–187.

14. Brealey, *Two Worlds*, 70, 74–75, 85; Cassirer, *Medium on Trial*, 16, 38, 222; Gaskill, *Hellish Nell*, 113.

15. Roberts, ed., *Trial of Helen Duncan*, 39; *Rex v. Duncan*, hearing transcript, February 1944, CRIM 1/1581, Public Records Office, Kew, England.

16. Crossley, *The Story of Helen Duncan*, 57; Cassirer, *Medium on Trial*, 126; Gaskill, *Hellish Nell*, 257.

17. Brealey, *Two Worlds*, 50–51; Cassirer, *Medium on Trial*, 18; Roberts, ed., *Trial of Helen Duncan*, 119.

18. Cassirer, *Medium on Trial*, 57; Gaskill, *Hellish Nell*, 81.

19. Brealey, *Two Worlds*, 86–88; Gaskill, *Hellish Nell*, 168, 176.

20. Maurice Barbanell, *The Case of Helen Duncan* (London: Psychic Press, 1945), 151.

21. Brealey, *Two Worlds*, 86–88; Gaskill, *Hellish Nell*, 175–176.

22. Brealey, *Two Worlds*, 30–32; Crossley, *The Story of Helen Duncan*, 57; Gaskill, *Hellish Nell*, 80–81; "Last Witch," interview with Downey and Pooey, BBC Radio, London, August 13, 1998.

23. Brealey, *Two Worlds*, 50; *Rex v. Duncan*, hearing transcript, CRIM 1/1581.

24. Brealey, *Two Worlds*, 30–32; Crossley, *The Story of Helen Duncan*, 57; Gaskill, *Hellish Nell*, 80–81; "Last Witch," interview with Downey and Pooey, BBC Radio, London, August 13, 1998.

25. Cassirer, *Medium on Trial*, 18, 163.

26. Chris Isaak, "South of the Border."

27. "Materialization Medium," *The Scotsman*, May 5, 1933.

28. Cassirer, *Medium on Trial*, 16, 38, 222.; Crossley, *The Story of Helen Duncan*, 57; "Last Witch," interview with Downey and Pooey, BBC Radio, London, August 13, 1998.

29. Chris Isaak, "South of the Border."

30. Cassirer, *Medium on Trial*, 223; Gaskill, *Hellish Nell*, 253.

31. Brealey, *Two Worlds*, 32; Victoria Duncan, "Secrets of My Second Sight," *People's Journal*, October 7, 1933; Gaskill, *Hellish Nell*, 78.

32. Brealey, *Two Worlds*, 34, 39, 60.

33. Gaskill, *Hellish Nell*, 120–121.

34. *Rex v. Duncan*, hearing transcript, CRIM 1/1581.

35. Cassirer, *Medium on Trial*, 151; Gaskill, *Hellish Nell*, 186–87.

36. Cassirer, *Medium on Trial*, 62.

37. Crossley, *The Story of Helen Duncan*, 57–63; Cassirer, *Medium on Trial*, 121–141. These sources confirm typically high praise for Helen Duncan's séances, here presented as dialogue.

38. Price, *The Duncan Mediumship*, 9–65; Crossley, *The Story of Helen Duncan*, 63; Cassirer, *Medium on Trial*, 160–167.
39. Crossley, *The Story of Helen Duncan*, 57–63; Cassirer, *Medium on Trial*, 121–141.
40. Brealey, *Two Worlds*, 87; Gaskill, *Hellish Nell*, 174–176.
41. Brealey, *Two Worlds*, 89.
42. Brealey, *Two Worlds*, 86; Cassirer, *Medium on Trial*, 224.

## Chapter 3

This chapter introduces Harry Price, investigator of psychic phenomena and Helen Duncan's longtime tormentor. Price, his personality, his relationships, and his initial encounter with the medium are depicted to reflect his autobiography, *Search for Truth*, along with other sources given below.

1. Harry Price, *Search for Truth* (London: Collins, 1942), 111.
2. Manfred Cassirer, *Medium on Trial* (Essex: PN Publishing, 1996), 39–40; Trevor Hall, *The Search for Harry Price* (London: Duckworth, 1978), 1, 11; Paul Tabori, *Harry Price: Biography of a Ghost Hunter* (London: Athenaeum Press, 1950), 1–19.
3. Price, *Search for Truth*, 163.
4. Ibid., 111–163.
5. Cassirer, *Medium on Trial*, 40; Tabori, *Harry Price*, 65–75.
6. Price, *Search for Truth*, 180–182; Harry Price, *Regurgitation and the Duncan Mediumship* (London: National Laboratory of Psychical Research, 1931), 79–103; Tabori, *Harry Price*, 134–140.
7. Cassirer, *Medium on Trial*, 151; Malcolm Gaskill, *Hellish Nell* (London: Fourth Estate, 2001), 126–127.
8. Price, *Duncan Mediumship*, i.
9. Tabori, *Harry Price*, 76.
10. Hall, *The Search for Harry Price*, 22, photographs; Tabori, *Harry Price*, 3–4.
11. Marion Gray, letter to Harry Price, in Cassirer, *Medium on Trial*, 151; Gaskill, *Hellish Nell*, 126–127.
12. Ibid.
13. Hall, *The Search for Harry Price*, photograph.
14. Cassirer, *Medium on Trial*, 39–48; Price, *Search for Truth*, 180–182; Price, *Duncan Mediumship*. These sources give evidence of Price's obsession.
15. Site visit to 16 Queensbury Street, London, still in existence as the College of Psychic Studies.
16. Cassirer, *Medium on Trial*, 40; Tabori, *Harry Price*, 65–75.
17. Gena Brealey, *The Two Worlds of Helen Duncan* (London: Regency Press, 1985), 57–58; Cassirer, *Medium on Trial*, 40. Helen Duncan's daughter reports her first meeting with Harry Price from her viewpoint; Cassirer quotes Price on the subject. Here I assume Harry Price's viewpoint on this event.
18. Photograph of Helen and Henry, College of Psychic Studies Archive, London, England.
19. Logan Lewis-Proudlock, personal interview, April 7, 2005. Typically, Miss Phillimore received celebrity mediums.
20. Cassirer, *Medium on Trial*, 40; Hall, *The Search for Harry Price*, 65–76. Miss Phillimore's attitude toward Price is based on these sources.

21. Brealey, *Two Worlds,* 57–58; Price, *Duncan Mediumship,* 13, 79–80. Henry Duncan's attitude toward Price is evidenced throughout Price's exposé.

22. Hall, *The Search for Harry Price,* 65–75.

23. Brealey, *Two Worlds,* 57–58.

24. Cassirer, *Medium on Trial,* 40; Gaskill, *Hellish Nell,* 126; Tabori, *Harry Price,* 134.

25. Tabori, *Harry Price,* 63–74.

26. Kevin Jones, *Conan Doyle and the Spirits* (Wellingborough, England: Aquarian, 1998), Appendix.

27. Cassirer, *Medium on Trial,* 42.

28. Tabori, *Harry Price,* 63–74. My impression is based on reported animosity.

29. Cassirer, *Medium on Trial,* 40; *The Light,* April 28, 1931.

30. Brealey, *Two Worlds,* 57–58; "The Last Witch in England," interview with Shelia Downey and Ann Pooey, Helen Duncan's granddaughters, BBC Radio, August 13, 1998. I conclude, from subsequent events, that Price intended to take advantage of Helen Duncan's subservience to her husband.

31. Cassirer, *Medium on Trial,* 45.

32. Gaskill, *Hellish Nell,* 126; Price, *Duncan Mediumship,* 13.

33. Hall, *The Search for Harry Price,* 3–13, 18; Tabori, *Harry Price,* 2–4.

34. Hall, *The Search for Harry Price,* 2, 188–208; Tabori, *Harry Price,* 2–4.

35. Maurice Barbanell, *The Case of Helen Duncan* (London: Psychic Press, 1945), 58.

36. Hugh Dowding, *Many Mansions* (London: Rider & Co., 1943); Gaskill, *Hellish Nell,* 175; C. E. Bechhofer Roberts, ed., *The Trial of Helen Duncan* (London: Jarrolds, 1945), 149.

37. Arthur West, letter to E. G. Robey, February 15, 1944, DPP 2/1204. My assumption is based on this source and Price's subsequent involvement.

## Chapter 4

This chapter introduces Chief Constable Arthur Charles West, Mayor Denis Daley, and Detective Sergeant Fred Ford. The scenes within the chapter, including locations and dialogue, conform to their duties, personalities, and historical events as documented below.

1. Paul Jenkins, *Battle Over Portsmouth* (Midhurst, England: Middleton, 1998), 23–40.

2. Jenkins, *Battle Over Portsmouth,* 15; Terry Swetnam, personal interview, Portsmouth, England, November 3, 1999.

3. Terry Swetnam, letter to author, "Arthur Charles West, service record," February 16, 2000.

4. Swetnam, personal interview, November 3, 1999.

5. "Chief Constables: Arthur West," *History of British Transportation Police,* available at www.btp.co.uk; Jim Cramer, conversation with author, May 2005; John Mainwaring, personal interview, April 13, 2005; Swetnam, letter to author, February 16, 2000; "The Last Witch in England," interview with Arthur West, BBC Radio, August 13, 1998. My impression of Chief Constable Arthur West is based on these sources.

6. Jenkins, *Battle Over Portsmouth,* 40.

7. Hampshire Constabulary Historical Society, "Transport," available at www.hants.gov.uk; Nick Walker, *Those Were The Days: British Police Cars* (London: Velco, 2001), photograph.

8. Jenkins, *Battle Over Portsmouth,* 5–13.

9. *World War II: Day by Day* (London: Dorling Kindersley, 2001), 101.

10. Jenkins, *Battle Over Portsmouth,* 41–42, photographs.

11. Swetnam, personal interview, November 3, 1999; Stanley Worth, personal interview, October 16, 2001. Based on these interviews, I depict the scope of the Chief Constable's responsibility.

12. Jenkins, *Battle Over Portsmouth*, 64.

13. Worth, personal interview, October 16, 2001.

14. Jenkins, *Battle Over Portsmouth*, 39–67.

15. *World War II: Day by Day*, 123.

16. Ibid., 132.

17. Ibid., 140.

18. Ibid., 145.

19. Ibid., 107.

20. Worth, personal interview, October 16, 2001.

21. "Portsmouth Guildhall," available at www.portsmouth-guide.co.uk.

22. "LD. Mayor at Palace," *Evening News* (Portsmouth), July 10, 1941, photograph.

23. Swetnam, letter to author, February 16, 2000, photograph; "Chief Constables: Arthur West," available at www.btp.co.uk (photograph).

24. "Chief Constables: Arthur West," available at www.btp.co.uk; Cramer, conversation with author, May 2005; Mainwaring, personal interview, April 13, 2005; Swetnam, letter to author, February 16, 2000; "Last Witch," interview with Arthur West, BBC Radio, August 13, 1998. Again, my impression of West is based on these sources and subsequent events.

25. F. H. Hinsley and C.A.G. Simkins, *British Intelligence in the Second World War*, vol. 4 (New York: Cambridge University Press, 1990), 22–23, 25, 29; *World War II: Day by Day*, 88.

26. Malcolm Gaskill, *Hellish Nell* (London: Fourth Estate, 2001), 184. I assume the Mayor and Chief Constable discussed this report.

27. Maurice Barbanell, *The Case of Helen Duncan* (London: Psychic Press, 1945), 23; "Portsmouth Guildhall," available at www.portmouth-guide.co.uk.

28. Manfred Cassirer, *Medium on Trial* (Essex: PN Publishing, 1996), 52; C. E. Bechhofer Roberts, ed., *The Trial of Helen Duncan* (London: Jarrolds, 1945), 28.

29. "Last Witch," interview with Arthur West, BBC Radio, August 18, 1998; Worth, personal interview, October 16, 2001.

30. Swetnam, personal interview, November 3, 1999; Worth, personal interview, October 16, 2001. My assumptions are evidenced by these sources and proved by subsequent events.

31. Frederick Ford, report to the Undersecretary of State, February 12, 1944, HO 144/22172, Public Records Office, Kew, England; Frederick Ford, report to the Undersecretary of State, April 5, 1944, HO 144/22172, Public Records Office, Kew, England; *Rex v. Duncan*, hearing transcript, February 1944, CRIM 1/1581, Public Records Office, Kew, England; Roberts, ed., *The Trial of Helen Duncan*, 108–111; Swetnam, personal interview, November 3, 1999. My description and presentation of Ford's behavior reflects these sources.

32. Cramer, conversation with author, May 2005; Swetnam, personal interview, November 3, 1999. My impression of West's attitude toward Ford is assumed, based on these interviews.

33. Jenkins, *Battle Over Portsmouth*, 4–5.

34. Jim and Olive Cramer, telephone interview, May 12, 2005; Worth, personal interview, October 16, 2001. My description of Ida West is based on these conversations.

35. Worth, personal interview, October 16, 2001.

36. "January 10, 1941," *Evening News* (Portsmouth), D-Day Supplement, January 1991.

37. "Blitz of Portsmouth: Lack of Water Killed Guildhall," *Evening News* (Portsmouth), D-Day Supplement, January 1991; "January 10, 1941," *Evening News* (Portsmouth), D-Day Supplement, January 1991; Jenkins, *Battle Over Portsmouth*, 15; *World War II: Day by Day*, 153.

## Chapter 5

This chapter brings together specific dates and historical events, placing them in the context of Helen Duncan's typical routines and activities.

1. Alan Crossley, *The Story of Helen Duncan* (Greenford: Psychic World Classic, 1999), 66; Malcolm Gaskill, *Hellish Nell* (London: Fourth Estate, 2001), 184; "Witch Hunt," interview with Margaret Pratt, Channel 4, London, July 13, 1999.
2. Gena Brealey, *The Two Worlds of Helen Duncan* (London: Regency Press, 1985), 89–90; Gaskill, *Hellish Nell*, 176.
3. Brealey, *Two Worlds*, 39. Helen Duncan's daughter describes her mother's specialty, "mealy pudding."
4. Ibid., 39.
5. Brealey, *Two Worlds*, 89–90; Gaskill, *Hellish Nell*, 176.
6. Brealey, *Two Worlds*, 36; Gaskill, *Hellish Nell*, 166.
7. Gaskill, *Hellish Nell*, 117.
8. Manfred Cassirer, *Medium on Trial* (Essex: PN Publishing, 1996), 126; Crossley, *The Story of Helen Duncan*, 63.
9. "Witch Hunt," interview with Margot Walker, Firebrace's daughter, Channel 4, London, July 13, 1999.
10. "Brigadier R. C. Firebrace," *The Light*, 1975, 34–36.
11. Ibid. Here I've constructed dialogue and behavior consistent with Firebrace's personality, as described in this source.
12. Crossley, *The Story of Helen Duncan*, 57; Cassirer, *Medium on Trial*, 126; Gaskill, *Hellish Nell*, 257.
13. Crossley, *The Story of Helen Duncan*, 66; Gaskill, *Hellish Nell*, 184; "Witch Hunt," Channel 4, London, July 13, 1999.

## Chapter 6

This chapter introduces security concerns shared by Chief Constable West and Military Intelligence about revelations made during Helen Duncan's séances. In 1941, such a meeting would have been typical of regular briefings between the head of law enforcement in Portsmouth and one of twelve Regional Liaison Officers, upper-class men recruited for their pedigree. The setting and information communicated in the scene are based on the following sources.

1. F. H. Hinsley and C.A.G. Simkins, *British Intelligence in the Second World War*, vol. 4. (New York, Cambridge University Press, 1990) 66, 73–74, 175; Nigel West, *MI 5: British Security Operations, 1909–1945* (London: Triad Granada, 1983), 147–148, 171.
2. Maurice Barbanell, *The Case of Helen Duncan* (London: Psychic Press, 1945), 86; Gena Brealey, *The Two Worlds of Helen Duncan* (London: Regency Press, 1985), 91–92; Alan Crossley, *The Story of Helen Duncan* (Greenford: Psychic World Classic, 1999), 66–68; Malcolm Gaskill, *Hellish Nell* (London: Fourth Estate, 2001), 230; C. E. Bechhofer Roberts, ed., *The Trial of Helen Duncan* (London: Jarrolds, 1945), 337.
3. Site visit to Byculla House, Portsmouth, April 13, 2005.
4. Kelvin Shipp, e-mail to author, August 15, 2005; Terry Swetnam, personal interview, Portsmouth, England, November 3, 1999; Stanley Worth, personal interview, October 16, 2001.
5. Shipp, e-mail to author, August 15, 2005.

6. Site visit to Byculla House, Portsmouth, April 13, 2005.

7. Shipp, e-mail to author, August 15, 2005; Swetnam, personal interview, November 3, 1999.

8. Shipp, e-mail to author, August 15, 2005; Swetnam, personal interview, November 3, 1999.

9. Worth, personal interview, October 16, 2001.

10. Hinsley and Simkins, *British Intelligence*, vol. 4, 66; West, *MI 5*, 21, 147–148, 171.

11. Gaskill, *Hellish Nell*, 185–186; Hinsley and Simkins, *British Intelligence*, vol. 4, 66, 73–74; West, *MI 5*, 21, 147–148, 171.

12. Hinsley and Simkins, *British Intelligence*, vol. 4, 66, 73–74.

13. Jim Cramer, conversation with author, May 2005; John Mainwaring, personal interview, April 13, 2005; Terry Swetnam, letter to author, February 16, 2000; "The Last Witch in England," interview with Arthur West, BBC Radio, August 13, 1998. My impression of Chief Constable Arthur West is based on these sources.

14. Jason Stevenson, "The *Barham* Conspiracy," *World War II Magazine*, December 2, 2004, 62–68.

15. "Most Secret: Loss of *Barham*—Board of Inquiry," April 28, 1942, ADM. 1/11948. Public Records Office, Kew, England; Stephen Roskill, *The Navy at War* (London: Collins, 1960), 172, 387.

16. Stevenson, "The *Barham* Conspiracy," 62–68.

17. Brealey, *Two Worlds*, 91–92; Crossley, *The Story of Helen Duncan*, 66–68; Gaskill, *Hellish Nell*, 181–183, 230; Stevenson, "The *Barham* Conspiracy," 68–69; "Witch Hunt," interview with Margot Walker, Firebrace's daughter, Channel 4, London, July 13, 1999.

18. Relatives of sailors lost on the *Barham* did not receive notification until January 1942, two months after the ship sank. After the British released the information, Hitler decorated the U-boat crew.

19. Brealey, *Two Worlds*, 91–92; Crossley, *The Story of Helen Duncan*, 66–68; Gaskill, *Hellish Nell*, 181–183, 230; Stevenson, "The *Barham* Conspiracy," 68–69; "Witch Hunt," interview with Margot Walker, Firebrace's daughter, Channel 4, July 13, 1999.

20. Hinsley and Simkins, *British Intelligence*, vol. 4, 34, 178–179.

21. "Brigadier R. C. Firebrace," *The Light*, 1975, 34–36.

22. "Witch Hunt," interview with Margot Walker, Firebrace's daughter, Channel 4, July 13, 1999.

23. *World War II: Day by Day* (London: Dorling Kindersley, 2001), 125.

24. Ibid., 186.

25. Ibid., 104.

26. Gaskill, *Hellish Nell*, 184.

27. Hinsley and Simkins, *British Intelligence*, vol. 4, 25.

28. Gaskill, *Hellish Nell*, 184.

29. Crossley, *The Story of Helen Duncan*, 67; "Witch Hunt," interview with Margot Walker, Firebrace's daughter, Channel 4, July 13, 1999.

30. *World War II: Day by Day*, 179.

31. Crossley, *The Story of Helen Duncan*, 67; "Witch Hunt," interview with Margot Walker, Firebrace's daughter, Channel 4, July 13, 1999.

32. *World War II: Day by Day*, 190.

33. Paul Bevand and Frank Allen, "The Pursuit of the *Bismarck* and Sinking of the *Hood*," www.hmshood.com, 22–31; Patrick Beesley, *Very Special Intelligence* (London: Sphere Books, 1977), 110–115; Roskill, *The Navy at War*, 127–132.

34. Bevand and Allen, "The Pursuit of the *Bismarck* and Sinking of the *Hood*," 31–32.

35. Crossley, *The Story of Helen Duncan*, 67; "Witch Hunt," interview with Margot Walker, Firebrace's daughter, Channel 4, July 13, 1999.

36. Crossley, *The Story of Helen Duncan*, 67; "Witch Hunt," interview with Margot Walker, Firebrace's daughter, Channel 4, July 13, 1999.

37. Crossley, *The Story of Helen Duncan*, 67; Gaskill, *Hellish Nell*, 183–184.

38. "Witch Hunt," interview with Margot Walker, Firebrace's daughter, Channel 4, July 13, 1999.

39. "Most Secret: Loss of *Barham*—Board of Inquiry," April 28, 1942, ADM. 1/11948.

40. Gaskill, *Hellish Nell*, 175.

41. "We Will Fight for Her to the End," *Sunday Pictorial*, April 2, 1944.

42. Barbanell, *The Case of Helen Duncan*, 147; Arthur West, letter to Francis Graham-Harrison, HO 144/22172, February 14, 1944, Public Records Office, Kew, England.

43. This is my assumption, given subsequent events.

## Chapter 7

This chapter—a goodbye scene, train ride, flashbacks, and arrival in Portsmouth—introduces Mrs. Brown, Helen Duncan's traveling companion, and Mr. and Mrs. Homer, the proprietors of the Master Temple. Dialogue and details are constructed based on documentation below.

1. Site visit, Helen Duncan's home at 19 Kirkhill Drive, Edinburgh, December 16, 1999.

2. Gena Brealey, *The Two Worlds of Helen Duncan* (London: Regency Press, 1985), 89–91.

3. Malcolm Gaskill, *Hellish Nell* (London: Fourth Estate, 2001), 174.

4. Brealey, *Two Worlds*, 90.

5. Ibid., 89.

6. Brealey, *Two Worlds*, 89–90; Gaskill, *Hellish Nell*, 176.

7. Brealey, *Two Worlds*, 90–91.

8. Ibid., 90. Poor health was Gena Duncan Brealey's explanation for her father not traveling.

9. Manfred Cassirer, *Medium on Trial* (Essex: PN Publishing, 1996), 21; Harry Price, *Regurgitation and the Duncan Mediumship* (London: National Laboratory of Psychical Research, 1931), 17–18, 33. I suspect Albert's verbal abuse had a chilling effect on Henry's traveling with his wife.

10. "Helen Duncan's Wealth," *Daily Herald*, April 4, 1944; "Lies," *Daily Herald*, April 1, 1944; "Woman Medium's Trance," *Daily Herald*, March 28, 1944, photograph.

11. Brealey, *Two Worlds*, 90–91.

12. "Helen Duncan's Wealth," *Daily Herald*, April 4, 1944.

13. Site visit, Helen Duncan's home at 19 Kirkhill Drive, Edinburgh December 16, 1999.

14. Brealey, *Two Worlds*, 91.

15. Price, *The Duncan Mediumship*, 58.

16. Gaskill, *Hellish Nell*, 105.

17. "Says He Heard Row Between Ghost and Medium," *Daily Mirror*, March 24, 1944; *Rex v. Helen Duncan*, hearing transcript, February 29, 1944, CRIM 1/1581, Public Records Office, Kew, England.

18. Gaskill, *Hellish Nell*, 166.

19. "The Last Witch in England," interview with Shelia Downey and Ann Pooey, Helen Duncan's granddaughters, BBC Radio, August 13, 1998; Brealey, *Two Worlds*, 48–55, 75–82.

20. Gaskill, *Hellish Nell*, 66.

21. Ibid., 338.

22. Ibid., 62–63.

23. Brealey, *Two Worlds*, 38–44; Alan Crossley, *The Story of Helen Duncan* (Greenford: Psychic World Classic, 1999), 20–22.

24. Brealey, *Two Worlds*, 86–87.

25. Brealey, *Two Worlds*, 38–39; Crossley, *The Story of Helen Duncan*, 20–21.

26. Crossley, *The Story of Helen Duncan*, 21–22; Gaskill, *Hellish Nell*, 6–67.

27. Brealey, *Two Worlds*, 37; Crossley, *The Story of Helen Duncan*, 21.

28. C. E. Bechhofer Roberts, ed., *The Trial of Helen Duncan* (London: Jarrolds, 1945), 15.

29. Cassirer, *Medium on Trial*, 111; Roberts, ed., *Trial of Helen Duncan*, 13. These references report Mrs. Brown's attempt at being a medium, providing evidence of her ambition.

30. Anonymous, personal interview, December 19, 1999; Dorothy Mahoney, letter to author, October 28, 1999.

31. Roberts, ed., *Trial of Helen Duncan*, 13; *Rex v. Duncan*, hearing transcript, CRIM 1/1581. Mrs. Brown later displayed these photographs to Stanley Worth and to the police.

32. Site visit, Churchill's Britain, at War Experience Museum, London, poster.

33. Brealey, *Two Worlds*, 89.

34. Site visit, 301 Copnor Road, Portsmouth, England, October 18, 1999.

35. Cassirer, *Medium on Trial*, photograph; Roberts, ed., *Trial of Helen Duncan*, photograph; "Story of Mrs. Duncan's 100 Pounds a Week," *Evening News* (Portsmouth), April 4, 1944, photograph.

36. Paul Jenkins, *Battle Over Portsmouth* (Midhurst, England: Middleton, 1998), 4–5.

37. Roberts, ed., *Trial of Helen Duncan*, 29–30. In this reference, Prosecutor Maude expresses a similar reaction to "The Master Temple."

38. Brealey, *Two Worlds*, 89.

39. Roberts, ed., *Trial of Helen Duncan*, 18–19, photograph.

40. "Helen Duncan's Wealth," *Daily Herald*, April 4, 1944. This article describes Mrs. Homer.

41. *Rex v. Duncan*, hearing transcript, CRIM 1/1581; Roberts, ed., *Trial of Helen Duncan*, photograph; Stanley Worth, personal interview, October 16, 2001.

42. Roberts, ed., *Trial of Helen Duncan*, 337. In this reference, Chief Constable West assesses Portsmouth similarly.

43. Cassirer, *Medium on Trial*, 52–53.

44. *Rex v. Helen Duncan*, hearing transcript, CRIM 1/1581.

## Chapter 8

This chapter introduces Lieutenant Stanley Worth along with his complaint to the police. Setting, dialogue, and details are constructed based on sources below.

1. Frederick Ford, "Report to Undersecretary of State," February 12, 1944, HO 144/22172, Public Records Office, Kew, England; Roberts, 49.

2. F. H. Hinsley and C.A.G. Simkins, *British Intelligence in the Second World War*, vol. 4 (New York: Cambridge University Press, 1990), 175.

3. Site visit, Byculla House, Portsmouth, England, April 13, 2005; Olive Cramer, telephone interview, October 26, 2005.

4. Michael Howard, *British Intelligence in the Second World War*, vol. 5 (New York: Cambridge University Press, 1990), 112–113, 154.

5. Stanley Worth, personal interview, October 16, 2001.

6. Ibid.

7. "Witch Hunt," Channel 4, London, July 13, 1999, photograph of Stanley Worth.

8. Maurice Barbanell, *The Case of Helen Duncan* (London: Psychic Press, 1945), 37–41; Roberts, ed., *Trial of Helen Duncan*, 36–67; Worth, personal interview, October 10 and 16, 2001; "Witch Hunt," interview with Stanley Worth, Channel 4, London, July 13, 1999. My impressions of Stanley Worth are based on these sources, including our conversations.

9. "Helen Duncan's Wealth," *Daily Herald*, April 4, 1944; "Mrs. Duncan's 100 pounds," *Evening News* (Portsmouth), April 4, 1944.

10. Stanley Worth, letter to author, January 13, 2006.

11. Worth, personal interview, October 16, 2001.

12. Roberts, ed., *Trial of Helen Duncan*, 149.

13. *World War II: Day by Day* (London: Dorling Kindersley, 2001), 117, 121,139, 582, 681.

14. Basil Collier, *Leader of the Few* (London: Jarrolds, 1957), 182–183; *World War II: Day by Day*, 139.

15. Hugh Dowding, *Many Mansions* (London: Rider, 1943), 16.

16. Muriel Dowding, *Beauty, Not the Beast* (London: Rider, 1968), 88.

17. Hugh Dowding, *Many Mansions*, 12–13.

18. Roberts, ed., *Trial of Helen Duncan*, 149.

19. Roberts, ed., *Trial of Helen Duncan*, 337; "The Last Witch in England," interview with Arthur West, BBC Radio, August 13, 1998.

20. Worth, personal interview, October 16, 2001. This is based on my experience of speaking with Stanley Worth.

21. Site visit, Byculla House, Portsmouth, England, April 13, 2005.

22. "Frederick David Ford," service record, private collection, Terry Swetnam, Portsmouth, England.

23. Jim Cramer, conversation with author, May 2005; Terry Swetnam, personal interview, Portsmouth, England, November 3, 1999.

24. *Rex v. Duncan*, hearing transcript, February 1944, CRIM 1/1581, Public Records Office, Kew, England; Roberts, ed., *Trial of Helen Duncan*, 51.

25. Worth, personal interview, October 16, 2001.

26. Gena Brealey, *The Two Worlds of Helen Duncan* (London: Regency Press, 1985), 93; "Last Witch," interview with Arthur West, BBC Radio, August 13, 1998.

27. *Rex v. Duncan*, hearing transcript, CRIM 1/1581; Roberts, ed., *Trial of Helen Duncan*, 110.

## Chapter 9

This chapter, depicting Helen Duncan's arrest, is based primarily on eyewitness testimony in *Rex v. Duncan* (hearing transcript, CRIM 1/1581, and trial transcript, DPP 2/1234, Public Records Office, Kew, England). Trial testimony is also reproduced verbatim in C. E. Bechhofer Roberts, editor, *The Trial of Helen Duncan* (London: Jarrolds, 1945).

1. *Rex v. Duncan*, hearing transcript, February 1944, CRIM 1/1581, Public Records Office, Kew, England; C. E. Bechhofer Roberts, ed., *The Trial of Helen Duncan* (London: Jarrolds, 1945), 39.

2. Roberts, ed., *The Trial of Helen Duncan*, 120.

3. Harry Price, *Regurgitation and the Duncan Mediumship* (London: National Laboratory of Psychical Research, 1931), 44, 71.

4. *Rex v. Duncan*, trial transcript, DPP 2/1234; Roberts, ed., *The Trial of Helen Duncan*, 38–39. Stanley Worth's testimony.

5. *Rex v. Duncan*, trial transcript, DPP 2/1234; Roberts, ed., *The Trial of Helen Duncan*, 91, 169. Bessie Lock's and Jane Rust's testimony.

6. *Rex v. Duncan*, trial transcript, DPP 2/1234; Roberts, ed., *The Trial of Helen Duncan*, 40–41. Worth's testimony.

7. *Rex v. Duncan*, trial transcript, DPP 2/1234; Roberts, ed., *The Trial of Helen Duncan*, 160. Bertha Alabaster's testimony.

8. *Rex v. Duncan*, trial transcript, DPP 2/1234; Roberts, ed., *The Trial of Helen Duncan*, 89. William Lock's testimony.

9. *Rex v. Duncan*, trial transcript, DPP 2/1234; Roberts, ed., *The Trial of Helen Duncan*, 53, 131. Stanley Worth's and Ernest Homer's testimony.

10. *Rex v. Duncan*, trial transcript, DPP 2/1234; Roberts, ed., *The Trial of Helen Duncan*, 131. Ernest Homer's testimony.

11. *Rex v. Duncan*, trial transcript, DPP 2/1234; Roberts, ed., *The Trial of Helen Duncan*, 170. Jane Rust's testimony.

12. *Rex v. Duncan*, trial transcript, DPP 2/1234; Roberts, ed., *The Trial of Helen Duncan*, 53. Stanley Worth's testimony.

13. *Rex v. Duncan*, trial transcript, DPP 2/1234; Roberts, ed., *The Trial of Helen Duncan*, 167. Christine Homer's testimony.

14. *Rex v. Duncan*, hearing transcript, CRIM 1/1581, photograph.

15. *Rex v. Duncan*, trial transcript, DPP 2/1234; Roberts, ed., *The Trial of Helen Duncan*, 167. Christine Homer's testimony.

16. *Rex v. Duncan*, trial transcript, DPP 2/1234; Roberts, ed., *The Trial of Helen Duncan*, 131–132. Ernest Homer's testimony.

17. *Rex v. Duncan*, trial transcript, DPP 2/1234; Roberts, ed., *The Trial of Helen Duncan*, 167. Christine Homer's testimony.

18. Terry Swetnam, letter to author, February 16, 2000, photograph.

19. *Rex v. Duncan*, trial transcript, DPP 2/1234; Roberts, ed., *The Trial of Helen Duncan*, 131. Ernest Homer's testimony.

## Chapter 10

In this chapter, my abridged depiction of Helen Duncan's 1930 séances—as incredible and outrageous as they may seem—adhere closely to eyewitness accounts found in archives and Spiritualist publications. In the interest of scientific investigation, conversational details were recorded, making it possible to accurately reconstruct dialogue. I assume Price's motivation, based on these events and my understanding of his personality as sourced below.

1. Harry Price, *Search for Truth* (London: Collins, 1942).

2. Trevor Hall, *The Search for Harry Price* (London: Duckworth, 1978), 1–2; Price, *Search for Truth*, dust-jacket flap; Paul Tabori, *Harry Price: Biography of a Ghost Hunter* (London: Athenaeum Press, 1950), 17.

3. Hall, *Search for Harry Price*, 20, 22, 25–40.

4. Ibid., 50, 52–53.

5. Hall, *Search for Harry Price*, 3–13, 18, 50; Tabori, *Harry Price*, 2–4.

6. Hall, *Search for Harry Price*, 184.

7. Harry Price, *The Most Haunted House in England*, (London: Longmans, 1940); Tabori, *Harry Price*, 254–263; "Borley Rectory," www.occultopedia.com.

8. Hall, *Search for Harry Price*, 184; Tabori, *Harry Price*, 254.

9. Maurice Barbanell, *The Case of Helen Duncan* (London: Psychic Press, 1945), 22, 93, 143; Maurice Barbanell, "Editorial," *Psychic News*, September 21, 1940; Malcolm Gaskill, *Hellish Nell* (London: Fourth Estate, 2001), 188; Ernest Oaten, "Law Relating to Mediumship," *Manual of Who's Who of Spiritualism and Psychic Research* (London: Spiritualist National Union, no date), 249.

10. Gena Brealey, *The Two Worlds of Helen Duncan* (London: Regency Press, 1985), 55–71; Manfred Cassirer, *Medium on Trial* (Essex: PN Publishing, 1996), 17–50; Harry Price, *Regurgitation and the Duncan Mediumship* (London: National Laboratory of Psychical Research, 1931); Tabori, *Harry Price*, 133–140. These sources provide evidence of Price's long-standing campaign to discredit Helen Duncan.

11. "Constable Grabs 'Spirit': Shocking Things Divulged," *Evening News* (Portsmouth), January 20, 1944.

12. Barbanell, *The Case of Helen Duncan*, 22, 93, 143; Barbanell, "Editorial"; Gaskill, *Hellish Nell*, 188.

13. Price, *Search for Truth*, 180–182; Tabori, *Harry Price*, 139; Gaskill, *Hellish Nell*, 140.

14. Arthur West, letter to E. G. Robey, February 15, 1944, DPP 2/1204. My assumption based on this archival source and Price's subsequent involvement.

15. Price, *Search for Truth*, 180–182; Tabori, *Harry Price*, 133–140; Price, *The Duncan Mediumship*.

16. Cassirer, *Medium on Trial*, 40.

17. Cassirer, *Medium on Trial*, 32; Price, *The Duncan Mediumship*, 13; Gaskill, *Hellish Nell*, 130–134. These sources establish Mrs. Goldney's attendance at the London Spiritualist Alliance séances and her close association with Price.

18. Cassirer, *Medium on Trial*, 24–25.

19. London Spiritualist Alliance, "Report of the Happenings at Sittings with Mrs. Duncan," 1930–1931, College of Psychic Studies Archive, London; "Seven Sittings with Mrs. Duncan," 1930–1931, Society of Psychical Research Archive, London; "Sittings with Mrs. Duncan," *The Light*, 1930–1931. These eyewitness accounts describe Helen Duncan's 1930–1931 séances at the London Spiritualist Alliance in all their outrageous detail. In reconstructing these events, I also credit Cassirer and Gaskill, whose writings are more accessible.

20. Cassirer, *Medium on Trial*, 21; Gaskill, *Hellish Nell*, 117; "Sittings with Mrs. Duncan," *The Light*, February 28, 1931.

21. Cassirer, *Medium on Trial*, 163; Gaskill, *Hellish Nell*, 121.

22. Gaskill, *Hellish Nell*, 118; "Report of the Happenings at Sittings with Mrs. Duncan," 1930–1931, College of Psychic Studies Archive; "Sittings with Mrs. Duncan," *The Light*, 1930–1931.

23. Cassirer, *Medium on Trial*, 29; Gaskill, *Hellish Nell*, 119; "Report of the Happenings at Sittings with Mrs. Duncan," 1930–1931, College of Psychic Studies Archive; "Sittings with Mrs. Duncan," *The Light*, 1930–1931. Dialogue between Albert and his audience conforms to reports in these sources.

24. Gaskill, *Hellish Nell*, 119–120; "Report of the Happenings at Sittings with Mrs. Duncan," 1930–1931, College of Psychic Studies Archive; "Sittings with Mrs. Duncan," *The Light*, 1930–1931. Albert's assessment of Henry Duncan's theories is verbatim.

25. Gaskill, *Hellish Nell,* 120; "Report of the Happenings at Sittings with Mrs. Duncan," 1930–1931, College of Psychic Studies Archive; "Sittings with Mrs. Duncan," *The Light,* 1930–1931.

26. Price, *The Duncan Mediumship,* 42; Cassirer, *Medium on Trial,* 21.

27. Gaskill, *Hellish Nell,* 121; "Report of the Happenings at Sittings with Mrs. Duncan," 1930–1931, College of Psychic Studies Archive; "Sittings with Mrs. Duncan," *The Light,* 1930–1931.

28. Gaskill, *Hellish Nell,* 122; "Report of the Happenings at Sittings with Mrs. Duncan," 1930–1931, College of Psychic Studies Archive; "Sittings with Mrs. Duncan," *The Light,* 1930–1931.

29. Cassirer, *Medium on Trial,* 21, 161, 163; Gaskill, *Hellish Nell,* 119–122.

30. Gaskill, *Hellish Nell,* 122; "Report of the Happenings at Sittings with Mrs. Duncan," 1930–1931, College of Psychic Studies Archive; "Sittings with Mrs. Duncan," *The Light,* 1930–1931.

31. Cassirer, *Medium on Trial,* 28; Gaskill, *Hellish Nell,* 119–120; "Sittings with Mrs. Duncan," *The Light,* 1930–1931.

32. "Sittings with Mrs. Duncan," *The Light,* February 28, 1931.

33. Gaskill, *Hellish Nell,* 131.

34. Cassirer, *Medium on Trial,* 17.

35. Cassirer, *Medium on Trial,* 35; Gaskill, *Hellish Nell,* 129; *The Light,* July 17, 1931. Sources indicate a growing disaffection between the Duncans and the London Spiritualist Alliance.

36. Cassirer, *Medium on Trial,* 39–40; Price, *The Duncan Mediumship,* 13–14; Price, *Search for Truth,* 180; Tabori, *Harry Price,* 133–135.

37. Arthur West, letter to Harry Price, April 6, 1944, DPP 2/1204, Public Records Office, Kew, England. In this letter, West thanks Price for the loan of his book.

## Chapter 11

This chapter reconstructs Helen Duncan's imprisonment without bail and provides historical rationale, through flashbacks, for her attachment to her husband. To fully portray her prison experience, I place events reported by her biographers, relatives, and contemporaneous newspapers in the context of Holloway Prison—the building, its policies, and routines during the 1940s. Dialogue is constructed to reflect information as sourced below.

1. Maurice Barbanell, *The Case of Helen Duncan* (London: Psychic Press, 1945), 22, 93, 143; Maurice Barbanell, "Editorial," *Psychic News,* September 21, 1940; Malcolm Gaskill, *Hellish Nell* (London: Fourth Estate, 2001), 188; Ernest Oaten, "Law Relating to Mediumship," *Manual of Who's Who of Spiritualism and Psychic Research* (London: Spiritualist National Union, no date), 249.

2. Gena Brealey, *The Two Worlds of Helen Duncan* (London: Regency Press, 1985), 93.

3. Oaten, "Law Relating to Mediumship," 246.

4. Alan Crossley, *The Story of Helen Duncan* (Greenford: Psychic World Classic, 1999), 63. This reaction is consistent with Helen Duncan's personality.

5. Barbanell, *The Case of Helen Duncan,* 23; Brealey, *Two Worlds,* 93; "Medium's Body Endangered," *Evening News* (Portsmouth), January 25, 1944; Frederick Ford, report from Portsmouth City Police to the Under-Secretary of State, February 12, 1944, HO 144/22172, Public Records Office, Kew, England, 2.

6. Barbanell, *The Case of Helen Duncan*, 23; Brealey, *Two Worlds*, 93; "Medium's Body Endangered," *Evening News* (Portsmouth), January 25, 1944; Ford, report to the Under-Secretary of State, HO 144/22172, 2.

7. "Holloway Prison," www.richard.clarke32.btinternet.co.uk; "Holloway Prison," www.tchavalier.com.

8. Nick Walker, *Those Were The Days: British Police Cars* (London: Velco, 2001), photographs.

9. *Rex v. Duncan*, hearing transcript, February 1944, CRIM 1/1581, Public Records Office, Kew, England.

10. Albert Crew, *London Prisons Today and Yesterday* (London: Ivor, Nicholson and Watson, 1933), 137; Holloway Prison Photographs, PRI COM 9/1330, Public Records Office, Kew, England.

11. *Blue Guide to London* (London: A&C Black, 1998), 266.

12. Holloway Prison Photographs, PRI COM 9/1330.

13. R. G. Alford, *Notes on the Buildings of English Prisons*, vol. 1 (Parkhurst: H.M. Convict Prison, 1909), 21.

14. Holloway Prison Photographs, PRI COM 9/1330.

15. Holloway Prison photographs, HM Prison Service Museum Archives.

16. Holloway Prison photographs, HM Prison Service Museum Archives. Holloway Prison Photographs, PRI COM 9/1330; Crew, *London Prisons*, 141.

17. Crew, *London Prisons*, 141–142, 155.

18. Here I've constructed dialogue to represent Helen Duncan's consternation, in response to my assumed prejudice of the prison guard toward guilt.

19. "Helen Duncan's Wealth," *Daily Herald*, April 4, 1944; "Lies," *Daily Herald*, April 1, 1944; "Woman Medium's Trance," *Daily Herald*, March 28, 1944, photograph.

20. Holloway Prison Photographs, PRI COM 9/1330.

21. Ibid.

22. Brealey, *Two Worlds*, 98, 101; Gaskill, *Hellish Nell*, 197. The subsequent incident is constructed, including dialogue to reflect these sources in the context of Holloway prison routines, as documented below.

23. Crew, *London Prisons*, 140. This source describes reception and bath routine.

24. Holloway Prison Photographs, PRI COM 9/1330.

25. Brealey, *Two Worlds*, 98; Gaskill, *Hellish Nell*, 197.

26. Crew, *London Prisons*, 38–39.

27. Ibid., 140.

28. Ibid., 150. The dialogue here is used to communicate prison policy.

29. Felicity Ball, personal note on prison stationary, undated (1999).

30. Crew, *London Prisons*, 150. Given prison restrictions, I assume Helen wrote a letter.

31. "The Last Witch in England," interview with Shelia Downey and Ann Pooey, Helen Duncan's granddaughters, BBC Radio, London, August 13, 1998; Victoria Duncan, "Secrets of My Second Sight," *People's Journal*, October 2 and 17 and November 18, 1933.

32. Brealey, *Two Worlds*, 24–25; Duncan, "Secrets of My Second Sight," *People's Journal*, October 28, 1933.

33. Gaskill, *Hellish Nell*, 45–46.

34. Mary Armour, *Helen Duncan (1895–1956): My Living Has Not Been in Vain* (London: Pembridge, 2000), 24; anonymous, personal interview, December 19, 1999.

35. Brealey, *Two Worlds*, 20–21.

36. William Walker, *Juteopolis: Dundee and Its Textile Workers, 1885–1923* (Edinburgh: Scottish University Press, 1979), 12–22.

37. Richard van Emden, *Veterans: The Last Survivors of the Great War* (Yorkshire: Pen and Sword Books, 1998), 13–28.

38. Brealey, *Two Worlds*, 24–26; Duncan, "Secrets of My Second Sight," *People's Journal,* October 28, 1933.

39. Gaskill, *Hellish Nell,* 63.

40. Brealey, *Two Worlds*, 32–38; "Last Witch," interview with Downey and Pooey, BBC Radio, August 13, 1998.

41. Duncan, "Secrets of My Second Sight," *People's Journal,* October 7, 1933; Gaskill, *Hellish Nell,* 68.

42. Crew, *London Prisons,* 143.

43. R. G. Alford, *Notes on the Building of English Prisons* (Parkhurst: H.M. Convict Prison, 1909), 20.

44. Brealey, *Two Worlds*, 15; "Last Witch," interview with Downey and Pooey, BBC Radio, August 13, 1998; Gaskill, *Hellish Nell,* 35, 201.

45. Crew, *London Prisons,* 141–146. This source provides details of the daily routine at Holloway Prison.

46. Ibid., 150. Source describes the limits on communication and visitation.

47. Brealey, *Two Worlds*, 95; Gaskill, *Hellish Nell,* 193.

48. "Report on Arrest," *Psychic News,* January 29, 1944.

## Chapter 12

This scene begins with Chief Constable West examining the details of Operation Bodyguard, the military intelligence deception plan devised to mislead the Germans on the date, place, and strength of the Normandy Invasion. The likelihood that West received this document is evidenced below.

The chapter goes on to depict West's frustration at Helen Duncan's release on bail and his plan to secure her incarceration. The dialogue is designed to communicate factual information and foreshadow historical events.

1. Michael Howard, *British Intelligence in the Second World War,* vol. 5 (New York: Cambridge University Press, 1990), 247; "Plan Bodyguard," CAB 80/77, COS(43)799(o), January 23, 1944, Public Records Office, Kew, England.

2. F. H. Hinsley and C.A.G. Simkins, *British Intelligence in the Second World War,* vol. 4 (New York: Cambridge University Press, 1990), 73–74, 175, 179, 356; Howard, *British Intelligence,* vol. 5, 123. These sources document that, by 1944, the police were completely integrated into the security structure and that highly placed Chief Constables were privy to deception plans. Therefore, I assume that Chief Constable West received notice of Operation Bodyguard.

3. Howard, *British Intelligence,* vol. 5, 247. This quote appears on the first page of "Plan Bodyguard," CAB 80/77, COS(43)779(o) under the subheading "Present Situation."

4. "Blitz of Portsmouth: Lack of Water Killed Guildhall," *Evening News* (Portsmouth), January 1991; "January 10, 1941," *Evening News* (Portsmouth), D-Day Supplement, January 1991; Paul Jenkins, *Battle Over Portsmouth* (Midhurst, England: Middleton, 1998), 15; *World War II: Day by Day* (London: Dorling Kindersley, 2001), 153.

5. Jenkins, *Battle Over Portsmouth*, 15; Kelvin Shipp, e-mail to author, August 15, 2005; Terry Swetnam, personal interview, Portsmouth, England, November 3, 1999; Stanley Worth, personal interview, October 16, 2001.

6. *World War II: Day by Day*, 144–202.

7. "100 Tons a Minute on Berlin," *Evening News* (Portsmouth), January 20, 1944.

8. *World War II: Day by Day*, 259.

9. Ibid., 247.

10. "Russians Enter Poland," *Evening News* (Portsmouth), January 4, 1944; "Russian Armies Link Up," *Evening News* (Portsmouth), January 11, 1944.

11. "We're Toughening Up—Eisenhower Ground Work Done in Readiness for Invasion," *Evening News* (Portsmouth), January 16, 1944.

12. Hinsley, *British Intelligence*, vol. 4, 237–241; Howard, *British Intelligence*, vol. 5, 103–123; "Plan Bodyguard," CAB 80/77, COS(43)799(o), January 23, 1944. The preceding synopsis of Operation Bodyguard is based on these sources.

13. Hinsley and Simkins, *British Intelligence*, vol. 4, 237–241; Howard, *British Intelligence*, vol. 5, 103–123; "Plan Bodyguard," CAB 80/77, COS(43)799(o), January 23, 1944. The foregoing comparison of truth and acceptable gossip is based on these sources.

14. Maurice Barbanell, *The Case of Helen Duncan* (London: Psychic Press, 1945), 23; Gena Brealey, *The Two Worlds of Helen Duncan* (London: Regency Press, 1985), 93; Frederick Ford, report from Portsmouth City Police to Under-Secretary of State, February 12, 1944, HO 144/22172, Public Records Office, Kew, England, 2; "Medium's Body Endangered," *Evening News* (Portsmouth), January 25, 1944.

15. "The Last Witch in England," interview with Arthur West, BBC Radio. August 13, 1998.

16. Howard, *British Intelligence*, vol. 5, 115–118.

17. Ibid., 119.

18. Grimwood Mears, letter to Home Secretary, February 2, 1944, HO 144/22172, Public Records Office, Kew, England.

19. Ford, report to Under-Secretary of State, February 12, 1944, HO 144/22172, 2; Gaskill, *Hellish Nell*, 290; Mears, letter to Home Secretary, HO 144/22172. My conclusion that West planned to keep Helen Duncan under lock and key, delaying her appearance in court until Mears would be presiding, is derived from these sources.

20. Ford, report to Under-Secretary of State, February 12, 1944, HO 144/22172; Frederick Ford, report from Portsmouth City Police to Under-Secretary of State, April 5, 1944, HO 144/22172, Public Records Office, Kew, England; *Rex v. Duncan*, hearing transcript, February 1944, CRIM 1/1581, Public Records Office, Kew, England; C. E. Bechhofer Roberts, ed., *The Trial of Helen Duncan* (London: Jarrolds, 1945), 108–111; Swetnam, personal interview, November 3, 1999. Here and throughout this scene, my depiction of Fred Ford's affect and conversation reflects these sources.

21. Olive Cramer, telephone interview, October 25, 2005; Swetnam, personal interview, November 3, 1999; "Last Witch," interview with Arthur West, BBC Radio, August 13, 1998; Worth, personal interview, October 10, 2001. Here and throughout this scene, my depiction of West, his affect, and conversational style is based on these interviews.

22. Ford, report to Under-Secretary of State, February 12, 1944, HO 144/22172, 2; "Medium's Body Endangered."

23. Roberts, ed., *Trial of Helen Duncan*, photograph.

24. Barbanell, *The Case of Helen Duncan*, 22–24; "Medium's Body Endangered."

25. Barbanell, *The Case of Helen Duncan,* 23; Ford, report to Under-Secretary of State, February 12, 1944, HO 144/22172.

26. Barbanell, *The Case of Helen Duncan,* 23; Ford, report to the Under-Secretary of State, February 12, 1944, HO 144/22172, 3; Gaskill, *Hellish Nell,* 196–197; "Medium's Body Endangered."

27. "Medium's Body Endangered."

28. Barbanell, *The Case of Helen Duncan,* 23; Brealey, *Two Worlds,* 94; "Medium's Body Endangered."

29. Barbanell, *The Case of Helen Duncan,* 24; Ford, report to Under-Secretary of State, February 12, 1944, HO 144/22172, 3.

30. Barbanell, *The Case of Helen Duncan,* 24; Ford, report to Under-Secretary of State, February 12, 1944, HO 144/22172, 3.

31. Hinsley and Simkins, *British Intelligence,* vol. 4, 66, 73–74; Nigel West, *MI 5: British Security Operations, 1909–1945* (London: Triad Granada, 1983), 143.

32. Barbanell, *The Case of Helen Duncan,* 86; Roberts, ed., *Trial of Helen Duncan,* 337.

33. Herbert Morrison, letter to Winston Churchill, April 6, 1944, HO 144/22172. In this letter, Morrison offers this explanation to Churchill.

34. Ford, report to Under Secretary of State, February 12, 1944, HO 144/22172, 2; Gaskill, *Hellish Nell,* 290; Mears, letter to the Home Secretary, February 2, 1944, HO 144/22172. These sources provide evidence for concerns described in this paragraph.

35. Photograph of Frederick Ford, private collection, Terry Swetnam, letter to the author, February 16, 2000.

36. Ford, report to Under-Secretary of State, February 12, 1944, HO 144/22172; Ford, report to Under-Secretary of State, April 5, 1944, HO 144/22172. West's decision to keep Ford on the case is evidenced by Ford's own reports.

37. Ford, report to Under-Secretary of State, February 12, 1944, HO 144/22172.

38. Alex McCowan, Edinburgh Police Report to Portsmouth Police, February 1944, DDP 2/2104, Public Records Office, Kew, England.

39. *Rex v. Duncan,* Deponent(s), CRIM 1/1581, Public Records Office, Kew, England.

40. Worth, personal interview, October 10, 2001.

41. Roberts, ed., *Trial of Helen Duncan,* 16–17; Worth, personal interview, October 10, 2001.

42. Arthur West, letter to Director of Public Prosecutions, February 3, 1944, DPP 2/1204, Public Records Office, Kew, England.

43. Ford, report to Under-Secretary of State, February 12, 1944, HO 144/22172, 3.

## Chapter 13

This chapter reconstructs the opening of Helen Duncan's hearing, based entirely on contemporaneous reports and documents, including a transcript of the hearing.

1. *Evening News* (Portsmouth), February 2, 1944, photograph; HO 144/2272, Public Records Office, Kew, England, photograph.

2. Maurice Barbanell, *The Case of Helen Duncan* (London: Psychic Press, 1945), 90–91; "Freedom versus the Home Office," *Two Worlds,* February 1944.

3. Hugh Dowding, *Many Mansions* (London: Rider, 1943), 10–12; Michael Perry, ed., Foreward to *Special Report to the Archbishop of Canterbury* (London: CFPSS Press, 1999).

4. The Special Report to the Archbishop of Canterbury from his Special Committee on Spiritualism was submitted in 1937, but it was not released to the public until June 1979, according to Michael Perry, ed., *Special Report to the Archbishop of Canterbury,* 4.

5. Barbanell, *The Case of Helen Duncan,* 107–108.

6. Ibid., 151–152.

7. Ibid., 22–23.

8. "Helen Duncan's Wealth," *Daily Herald,* April 4, 1944; "Lies," *Daily Herald,* April 1, 1944; "Woman Medium's Trance," *Daily Herald,* March 28, 1944, photograph.

9. C. E. Bechhofer Roberts, ed., *The Trial of Helen Duncan* (London: Jarrolds, 1945), photograph.

10. *Evening News* (Portsmouth), February 2, 1944, photograph; HO 144/2272, photograph.

11. *Rex v. Duncan,* Deponent(s), CRIM 1/1581, Public Records Office, Kew, England; Frederick Ford, report from Portsmouth City Police to Under-Secretary of State, February 12, 1944, HO 144/22172, Public Records Office, Kew, England, 3.

12. John Sadden, ed., *The Archive Series: Portsmouth* (Stroud, England: Chalford, 1997), photograph, 21. The description of the interior of the court is based on this archival photograph.

13. *Rex v. Duncan,* hearing transcript, CRIM 1/1581.

14. *Rex v. Duncan,* copy of charge, CRIM 1/1581.

15. Barbanell, *The Case of Helen Duncan,* 24; *Rex v. Duncan,* copy of charge, CRIM 1/1581.

## Chapter 14

This chapter calls upon a variety of contemporaneous and background sources to reconstruct Helen Duncan's hearing; these are noted below.

1. Stanley Worth, personal interview, October 10, 2001.

2. "Edward George Robey," *Who Was Who* (London: A&C Black, 1985); Maurice Barbanell, *The Case of Helen Duncan* (London: Psychic Press, 1945), 24–25.

3. Malcolm Gaskill, *Hellish Nell* (London: Fourth Estate, 2001), 120; Harry Price, *Regurgitation and the Duncan Mediumship* (London: National Laboratory of Psychical Research, 1931), 31, 41; London Spiritualist Alliance, "Report of the Happenings at Sittings with Mrs. Duncan," 1930–1931, College of Psychic Studies Archive, London.

4. Barbanell, *The Case of Helen Duncan,* 24–25; *Rex v. Duncan,* brief for the Prosecution, 1944, DPP 2/1204, Public Records Office, Kew, England. Letters and references to Robey appear throughout this file.

5. "George Robey: The English Music Hall," www.amaranthdesign.ca.

6. "Edward George Robey," *Who Was Who.*

7. Barbanell, *The Case of Helen Duncan,* 24. Barbanell, a journalist present at the hearing, describes Robey's opening remarks. Here I transform that description into dialogue.

8. Barbanell, *The Case of Helen Duncan,* 25; "George Robey: The English Music Hall," www.amaranthdesign.ca; Stanley Worth, personal interview, October 10, 2001. Barbanell and Worth indicate that the solicitor's appearance and manner were similar to his famous father. Amaranth describes the father's stage affect.

9. Barbanell, *The Case of Helen Duncan,* 25.

10. Ibid.

11. Ibid.

12. Ibid.

13. Ibid. Here I have made Barbanell's paraphrase into a quote.

14. Ibid.

15. "Magic at War," *Channel 4's Portrait Gallery,* www.channel4.com; Michael Howard, *British Intelligence in the Second World War,* vol. 5 (New York: Cambridge University Press, 1990), 38.

16. Paul Jenkins, *Battle Over Portsmouth* (Midhurst, England: Middleton, 1998), 112.

17. C. E. Bechhofer Roberts, ed., *The Trial of Helen Duncan* (London: Jarrolds, 1945), 337.

18. "The Last Witch in England," interview with Arthur West, BBC Radio, August 13, 1998.

19. Barbanell, *The Case of Helen Duncan,* 25–26.

20. Ibid., 26.

21. Barbanell, *The Case of Helen Duncan,* 26; *Rex v. Duncan,* hearing transcript, February 1944, CRIM 1/1581, Public Records Office, Kew, England.

22. Stanley Worth, photograph.

23. Worth, personal interview, October 10, 2001.

24. Barbanell, *The Case of Helen Duncan,* 27; Gaskill, *Hellish Nell,* 204; *Rex v. Duncan,* hearing transcript, CRIM 1/1581; Worth, personal interview, October 10, 2001. The following depiction of Stanley Worth's testimony, including his affect, is based on these sources.

25. *Rex v. Duncan,* hearing transcript, CRIM 1/1581. The transcript does not include questions posed by Robey, the prosecutor. I have fashioned questions based on Worth's transcribed answers.

26. Barbanell, *The Case of Helen Duncan,* 33. Barbanell, a Spiritualist journalist, reported that piano tunes were heard in the background. This wartime song is representative of the historical atmosphere.

27. Frank Loesser, "Praise the Lord and Pass the Ammunition."

28. Barbanell, *The Case of Helen Duncan,* 33

29. Ibid., 38.

30. Gaskill, *Hellish Nell,* 204; *Rex v. Duncan,* hearing transcript, CRIM 1/1581; Worth, personal interview, October 10, 2001.

31. Barbanell, *The Case of Helen Duncan,* 27; *Rex v. Duncan,* hearing transcript, CRIM 1/1581.

32. *Rex v. Duncan,* hearing transcript, CRIM 1/1581.

33. Ibid.

34. Ibid.

35. Herbert Morrison, letter to Winston Churchill, April 6, 1944, HO 144/22172, Public Records Office, Kew, England.

36. *Rex v. Duncan,* hearing transcript, CRIM 1/1581. Here the judgment of the magistrates is paraphrased from court documents.

37. Barbanell, *The Case of Helen Duncan,* 34; Roberts, ed., *Trial of Helen Duncan,* 112.

38. Barbanell, *The Case of Helen Duncan,* 107; Gina Brealey, *The Two Worlds of Helen Duncan* (London: Regency Press, 1985), 95; "Last Witch," interview with Arthur West, BBC Radio, August 13, 1998. The view that Helen Duncan was a pawn is my interpretation of these sources.

39. Sir Grimwood Mears, letter to the Home Secretary, February 28, 1944, HO 144/22172, Public Records Office, Kew, England.

40. Arthur Sefton Cohen, letter to Chief Constable West, March 16, 1944, DPP 2/1204, Public Records Office, Kew, England; Frederick Ford, report from Portsmouth City Police to Under-Secretary of State, February 12, 1944, HO 144/22172, Public Records Office, Kew, England; *Rex v. Duncan*, brief for the Prosecution, DPP 2/1204; Arthur West, letter to Harry Price, April 6, 1944, DPP 2/1204, Public Records Office, Kew, England. These sources indicate that West sought Price's involvement.

## Chapter 15

The events in this chapter are preserved in archival documents and in transcripts of Helen Duncan's séances. I've incorporated my interpretation of Harry Price's motives, based on his own writings and those of his biographers and other researchers, as indicated below.

1. Arthur Sefton Cohen, letter to Chief Constable West, March 16, 1944, DPP 2/1204, Public Records Office, Kew, England; Arthur West, letter to Harry Price, April 6, 1944, DPP 2/1204, Public Records Office, Kew, England. These two letters give evidence of a sequence of events: Price sent a copy of his book to West; West delivered it to the Office of Public Prosecutions; the Assistant Director contacted Price.

2. Trevor Hall, *The Search for Harry Price* (London: Duckworth, 1978), 11, 101; Paul Tabori, *Harry Price: Biography of a Ghost Hunter* (London: Athenaeum Press, 1950), 2–3. These biographers agree on one point: Price loved publicity.

3. Malcolm Gaskill, *Hellish Nell* (London: Fourth Estate, 2001), 194.

4. Harry Price, *Regurgitation and the Duncan Mediumship* (London: National Laboratory of Psychical Research, 1931), 13–14, 25; Tabori, *Harry Price*, 134–135.

5. *Rex v. Duncan*, hearing transcript, February 29, 1944, CRIM 1/1581, Public Records Office, Kew, England.

6. Gaskill, *Hellish Nell*, 129; Price, *The Duncan Mediumship*, 81.

7. Price, *The Duncan Mediumship*, 13–48.

8. Ibid.,17, 18, 33, 43.

9. Ibid., 41.

10. Ibid., 56. The conversation between Albert and Price was recorded by a note-taker as it occurred.

11. Ibid.

12. Ibid.

13. Ibid.

14. Ibid.

15. Gaskill, *Hellish Nell*, 359. This source reports the rumor that Price and Goldney were lovers.

16. Price, *The Duncan Mediumship*, 56.

17. Ibid.

18. Ibid.

19. Ibid.

20. Ibid. I assume Price's reaction, given the reported conversation.

21. Ibid.

22. Ibid.

23. Ibid.

24. Price, *The Duncan Mediumship*, 56; Harry Price, *Search for Truth* (London: Collins, 1942). My interpretation is based on subsequent events, as reported in Price's books.

25. Cohen, letter to Chief Constable West, March 16, 1944, DPP 2/1204. This letter confirms the Office of Public Prosecution's invitation to Price.

26. Manfred Cassirer, *Medium on Trial* (Essex: PN Publishing, 1996), 40; Hall, *The Search for Harry Price*, 11, 101; Tabori, *Harry Price*, 2–3.

27. Cassirer, *Medium on Trial*, 41–48; Gena Brealey, *The Two Worlds of Helen Duncan* (London: Regency Press, 1985), 62–63; Price, *Search for Truth*, 180–182; Tabori, *Harry Price*, 134–140. These sources chronicle Price's ongoing efforts to debunk Helen Duncan.

## Chapter 16

To construct this scene, dates, places, and information gleaned from declassified documents have been combined with accounts of witnesses to Helen Duncan's trial. I have created dialogue that accurately communicates this information.

1. Arthur West, letter to E. G. Robey, March 4, 1944, DPP 2/1204, Public Records Office, Kew, England; site visit to Devonshire House, London, England. This letter confirms the date of this pre-arranged meeting and passes on instructions to use the east entrance of Devonshire House. Descriptive details are based on my visit to Devonshire House.

2. *Rex v. Duncan*, document folder, 1944, DPP 2/1204, Public Records Office, Kew, England; "The Last Witch in England," interview with Arthur West, BBC Radio, August 13, 1998. The document folder lists this event, indicating Atkinson's attendance, on a chronology of significant dates and meetings. In this BBC interview, West recalls meeting directly with Atkinson.

3. E. H. Tindall Atkinson, letter to Theo Mathew, Home Office, April 11, 1944, HO 144/22172, Public Records Office, Kew, England. In this letter, Atkinson denies any part in framing the charges against Helen Duncan. In contradiction, a notation on the official case folder (DPP 2/1204) indicates that he spent 1 1/4 hours with Counsel, one hour framing the indictment.

4. C. E. Bechhofer Roberts, ed., *The Trial of Helen Duncan* (London: Jarrolds, 1945), photograph; Donald Thomas, *An Underworld at War* (London: John Murray, 2003), 247.

5. Roberts, ed., *The Trial of Helen Duncan*, 21, photograph.

6. "John Cyril Maude," *Who Was Who* (London: A&C Black, 1897–1990); "Sir Tindall Atkinson," *Who Was Who* (London: A&C Black, 1897–1990).

7. A. B. Schofield, *Dictionary of Legal Biography*, 1845–1945 (Chichester: Barry Rose, 1998), 311.

8. Charles M. Yablon, "Wigs, Coifs and Other Idiosyncrasies of English Judicial Attire," www.cardozo.net.

9. "John Cyril Maude," *Who Was Who* (London: A&C Black, 1897–1990); Schofield, *Dictionary of Legal Biography*, 311.

10. Nigel West, *MI 5: British Security Operations, 1909–1945* (London: Triad Granada, 1983), 21.

11. Ibid., 171, 178.

12. E. Tindall Atkinson, nomination of prosecution counsel, March 1, 1944, DPP 2/1204, Public Records Office, Kew, England.

13. Malcolm Gaskill, *Hellish Nell* (London: Fourth Estate, 2001), 200.

14. Atkinson, nomination of prosecution counsel, March 1, 1944, DPP 2/1204.

15. Roberts, ed., *The Trial of Helen Duncan*, 21.

16. Ibid., photograph.

17. West, *MI 5*, 171, 178. I've inserted this bit of dialogue to remind readers of Maude's clandestine identity.

18. Arthur West, letter to E. G. Robey, March 4, 1944, DPP 2/1204. This letter indicates Robey's intention to be present.

19. Stanley Worth, personal interview, October 10, 2001.

20. Harry Price, *Regurgitation and the Duncan Mediumship* (London: National Laboratory of Psychical Research, 1931), 82. Price describes using a piece of Woolworth's cheesecloth, six feet long and thirty inches wide, to simulate a materialized spirit.

21. Hannen Swaffer, *My Greatest Story* (London: W. H. Allen, 1945), 221. Swaffer reports that the Prosecution's muslin was bought.

22. Ibid., 221, 227; Worth, personal interview, October 10, 2001.

23. Sir Gerald Dodson, *Consider Your Verdict* (London: Hutchinson and Co., 1967), 88–89.

24. Swaffer, *My Greatest Story*, 223.

25. "Sir Gerald Dodson," *Who Was Who* (London: A&C Black, 1897–1990). Dodson's bio gives evidence of his enthusiastic interest in theater.

26. "Cyril Maude," *Who Was Who* (London: A&C Black, 1897–1990).

27. *Rex v. Duncan*, prosecutors' notes, undated, DPP 2/1204, Public Records Office, Kew, England. This rational explanation is based on handwritten notes, presumably Maude's and Elam's.

28. "Last Witch," interview with Arthur West, BBC Radio, August 13, 1998. In this recorded interview, West recalls that the Director came up with idea to reframe the indictment.

29. Ernest Oaten, "Law Relating to Mediumship," *Manual of Who's Who of Spiritualism and Psychic Research* (London: Spiritualist National Union, no date), 246–247.

30. Ibid., 247.

## Chapter 17

This scene depicts Helen Duncan's initial appearance at the Old Bailey and in Courtroom #4. Details are sourced below.

1. "Lifted Heels over Head," *Psychic News*, December 29, 1956. I assume Helen Duncan took a cab to court, given that she was released on bail and was staying with friends in Merton Park.

2. Gena Brealey, *The Two Worlds of Helen Duncan* (London: Regency Press, 1985), 93. Helen Duncan's daughter reports that her father was present for the trial.

3. "'Lies' Cry by Medium," *Daily Herald*, April 1, 1944. This article describes Nan and reports her presence at the trial.

4. Site visit, Old Bailey, Central Criminal Court, London.

5. Brealey, *Two Worlds*, 96; C. E. Bechhofer Roberts, ed., *The Trial of Helen Duncan* (London: Jarrolds, 1945), 15.

6. Gerald Dodson, *Consider Your Verdict* (London: Hutchinson and Co., 1967), 109–110; Roberts, ed., *The Trial of Helen Duncan*, photograph.

7. Philip Zeigler, *London at War* (London: Arrow, 1998), 268–270.

8. Roberts, ed., *The Trial of Helen Duncan*, 15.

9. Site visit, Old Bailey, Central Criminal Court, London.

10. "'All Lies' Cry by Medium," *News of the World*, April 2, 1944. Supporter's comment reflects this report.

11. Site visit, Old Bailey, Central Criminal Court, London. My description is consistent with prisoner routine, as explained by security guards at the Old Bailey.

12. Ibid. Security guards described the ascent to Courtroom #4.

13. Dodson, *Consider Your Verdict*, 109–111.

14. Site visit, Old Bailey, Central Criminal Court, Courtroom #4. The courtroom and its routines have changed little.

15. "Lifted Heels over Head."

16. Brealey, *Two Worlds*, 95; Roberts, ed., *The Trial of Helen Duncan*, 15; "Woman Medium's Trance at Old Bailey," *Daily Herald*, March 28, 1944.

17. Site visit, Old Bailey, Central Criminal Court, Courtroom #4.

18. Roberts, ed., *The Trial of Helen Duncan*, photograph.

19. Malcolm Gaskill, *Hellish Nell* (London: Fourth Estate, 2001), 4.

20. *Rex v. Duncan*, trial transcript, DPP 2/1204, Public Records Office, Kew, England; Roberts, ed., *The Trial of Helen Duncan*, 26.

21. Brealey, *Two Worlds*, 15–16; "The Last Witch in England," interview with Shelia Downey and Ann Pooey, Helen Duncan's granddaughters, BBC Radio, August 13, 1998.

## Chapter 18

This chapter depicts Prosecutor Maude's opening remarks. His speech is abridged with only minor editing. A carbon copy of the trial transcript can be found in *Rex v. Duncan*, DPP 2/1204, Public Records Office, Kew, England. Maude's opening remarks are recorded verbatim in C. E. Bechhofer Roberts, editor, *The Trial of Helen Duncan* (London: Jarrolds, 1945). In narrating this scene, I have taken the Chief Constable's viewpoint, and the descriptions of the defendants, judge, and prosecutor conform with information in the sources below.

1. E. Tindall Atkinson, letter to Sir Gerald Dodson, undated, DPP 2/1204, Public Records Office, Kew, England.

2. Gerald Dodson, *Consider Your Verdict* (London: Hutchinson, 1967), photograph; C. E. Bechhofer Roberts, ed., *The Trial of Helen Duncan* (London: Jarrolds, 1945), photograph.

3. "Sir Gerald Dodson," *Who Was Who* (London: A&C Black, 1897–1990); John Maude, *Who Was Who* (London: A&C Black, 1897–1990); Hannen Swaffer, *My Greatest Story* (London: W. H. Allen, 1945), 223;

4. Maurice Barbanell, *The Case of Helen Duncan* (London: Psychic Press, 1945), 91–92; Gerald Dodson, *Consider Your Verdict* (London: Hutchinson, 1967), 135–136.

5. Dodson, *Consider Your Verdict*, Chapter 3, "Early Cases," 89–90.

6. Ibid., 23–24.

7. Roberts, ed., *The Trial of Helen Duncan*, 27.

8. Malcolm Gaskill, *Hellish Nell* (London: Fourth Estate, 2001), 4.

9. Donald Thomas, *An Underworld at War* (London: John Murray, 2003), 247.

10. *Rex v. Duncan*, trial transcript, DPP 2/1204, Public Records Office, Kew, England; Roberts, ed., *The Trial of Helen Duncan*, trial transcript, 27. Edited and abridged for clarity.

11. "'Lies' Cry by Medium," *Daily Herald*, April 1, 1944.

12. Barbanell, *The Case of Helen Duncan*, 37.

13. *Rex v. Duncan*, trial transcript, DPP 2/1204; Roberts, ed., *The Trial of Helen Duncan*, trial transcript, 27. Maude's remarks abridged.

14. Roberts, ed., *The Trial of Helen Duncan*, 16; Thomas, *Underworld at War*, 247; Stanley Worth, personal interview, October 10, 2001. I assume West's attitude based on sources and my own impressions of his opening remarks.

15. *Rex v. Duncan*, trial transcript, DPP 2/1204; Roberts, ed., *The Trial of Helen Duncan*, trial transcript, 27. Maude's remarks abridged.

16. *Rex v. Duncan*, trial transcript, DPP 2/1204; Roberts, ed., *The Trial of Helen Duncan*, trial transcript, 27. Maude's remarks abridged.

17. *Rex v. Duncan*, trial transcript, DPP 2/1204; Roberts, ed., *The Trial of Helen Duncan*, trial transcript, 27. Maude's remarks abridged.

18. Dodson, *Consider Your Verdict*, photograph; Roberts, ed., *The Trial of Helen Duncan*, photograph.

19. *Rex v. Duncan*, trial transcript, DPP 2/1204; Roberts, ed., *The Trial of Helen Duncan*, trial transcript, 27.

20. *Rex v. Duncan*, letters and petition to the Home Office and MP Rathborne, 1944, HO 144/22172, Public Records Office, Kew, England.

21. *Rex v. Duncan*, trial transcript, DPP 2/1204; Roberts, ed., *The Trial of Helen Duncan*, trial transcript, 28. Maude's remarks abridged.

22. *Rex v. Duncan*, trial transcript, DPP 2/1204; Roberts, ed., *The Trial of Helen Duncan*, trial transcript, 28. Maude's remarks abridged.

23. *Rex v. Duncan*, trial transcript, DPP 2/1204; Roberts, ed., *The Trial of Helen Duncan*, trial transcript, 28. Maude's remarks abridged.

24. *Rex v. Duncan*, trial transcript, DPP 2/1204; Roberts, ed., *The Trial of Helen Duncan*, trial transcript, 28–29. Maude's remarks abridged.

25. *Rex v. Duncan*, trial transcript, DPP 2/1204; Roberts, ed., *The Trial of Helen Duncan*, trial transcript, 30–36.

26. *Rex v. Duncan*, trial transcript, DPP 2/1204; Roberts, ed., *The Trial of Helen Duncan*, trial transcript, 36. Maude's remarks abridged.

## Chapter 19

This chapter reconstructs testimony from the first day in the witch trial of 1944. The narration, from the Chief Constable's viewpoint, is based on eyewitness sources. The testimony itself conforms closely to trial transcripts found in two sources (*Rex v. Duncan,* DPP 2/1204, Public Records Office, Kew, England; and C. E. Bechhofer Roberts, editor, *The Trial of Helen Duncan* (London: Jarrolds, 1945). Quotations from the examination and cross-examination of Stanley Worth are somewhat abridged for brevity and slightly edited for clarity.

1. C. E. Bechhofer Roberts, ed., *The Trial of Helen Duncan* (London: Jarrolds, 1945), 16.

2. "Loughans Tells Counsel, 'Police Are My Enemies,'" *Evening News* (Portsmouth), April 1, 1944.

3. *Rex v. Loughans*, CRIM 1/1583, Public Records Office, Kew, England; *Rex v. Loughans*, DPP 2/1192, Public Records Office, Kew, England.

4. "Declares Chief Constable Knew Him Innocent, City Murder Case," *Evening News* (Portsmouth), March 30, 1944.

5. "Loughans Tells Counsel 'Police Are My Enemies,'" *Evening News* (Portsmouth), April 1, 1944; *Rex v. Loughans*, DPP 2/1192.

6. Maurice Barbanell, *The Case of Helen Duncan* (London: Psychic Press, 1945), 38; Roberts, ed., *Trial of Helen Duncan*, 16.

7. "Says Dead Policeman and Cat Brought Back," *Daily Herald*, March 23, 1944.

8. Roberts, ed., *Trial of Helen Duncan*, 21, photograph.

9. Barbanell, *The Case of Helen Duncan*, 38; Roberts, ed., *Trial of Helen Duncan*, 16; Stanley Worth, personal interview, October 10, 2001.

10. *Rex v. Duncan*, trial transcript, DPP 2/1204; Roberts, ed., *Trial of Helen Duncan*, trial transcript, 38–40.

11. *Rex v. Duncan*, trial transcript, DPP 2/1204; Roberts, ed., *Trial of Helen Duncan*, trial transcript, 42–43.

12. *Rex v. Duncan*, trial transcript, DPP 2/1204; Roberts, ed., trial transcript, 43.

13. *Rex v. Duncan*, trial transcript, DPP 2/1204; Roberts, ed., *Trial of Helen Duncan*, trial transcript, 43. Worth's testimony abridged.

14. *Rex v. Duncan*, hearing transcript, DPP 2/1204; Roberts, ed., *Trial of Helen Duncan*, trial transcript, 43. Judge's questions abridged.

15. *Rex v. Duncan*, trial transcript, DPP 2/1204; Roberts, ed., *Trial of Helen Duncan*, trial transcript, 43.

16. *Rex v. Duncan*, trial transcript, DPP 2/1204; Roberts, ed., *Trial of Helen Duncan*, trial transcript, 44–53.

17. *Rex v. Duncan*, trial transcript, DPP 2/1204; Roberts, ed., *Trial of Helen Duncan*, trial transcript, 44–53; Worth, personal interview, October 10, 2001. Stan Worth told me that Elam had complimented him on being an extraordinarily effective witness.

18. Site visit; Charles M. Yablon, "Wigs, Coifs and Other Idiosyncrasies of English Judicial Attire," www.cardozo.net.

19. Roberts, ed., *Trial of Helen Duncan*, photograph.

20. Worth, personal interview, October 10, 2001.

21. *Rex v. Duncan*, trial transcript, DPP 2/1204; Roberts, ed., *Trial of Helen Duncan*, trial transcript, 53. Edited for clarity; Portsmouth séance replaces "Copnor Road."

22. Worth, personal interview, October 10, 2001.

23. *Rex v. Duncan*, trial transcript, DPP 2/1204; Roberts, ed., *Trial of Helen Duncan*, trial transcript, 53.

24. *Rex v. Duncan*, trial transcript, DPP 2/1204; Roberts, ed., *Trial of Helen Duncan*, trial transcript, 53. Edited for clarity.

25. *Rex v. Duncan*, trial transcript, DPP 2/1204; Roberts, ed., *Trial of Helen Duncan*, trial transcript, 53.

26. *Rex v. Duncan*, trial transcript, DPP 2/1204; Roberts, ed., *Trial of Helen Duncan*, trial transcript, 53. Worth's testimony slightly abridged.

27. *Rex v. Duncan*, trial transcript, DPP 2/1204; Roberts, ed., *Trial of Helen Duncan*, trial transcript, 54. Loseby's question abridged.

28. *Rex v. Duncan*, trial transcript, DPP 2/1204; Roberts, ed., *Trial of Helen Duncan*, trial transcript, 54. Stan Worth's response edited for clarity.

29. *Rex v. Duncan*, trial transcript, DPP 2/1204; Roberts, ed., *Trial of Helen Duncan*, trial transcript, 54.

30. *Rex v. Duncan*, trial transcript, DPP 2/1204; Roberts, ed., *Trial of Helen Duncan*, trial transcript, 54. Stan Worth's response abridged.

31. *Rex v. Duncan*, trial transcript, DPP 2/1204; Roberts, ed., *Trial of Helen Duncan*, trial transcript, 54.

32. *Rex v. Duncan,* trial transcript, DPP 2/1204; Roberts, ed., *Trial of Helen Duncan,* trial transcript, 55.

33. *Rex v. Duncan,* trial transcript, DPP 2/1204; Roberts, ed., *Trial of Helen Duncan,* trial transcript, 55. Worth's answer abridged.

34. "Helen Duncan's Wealth," *Daily Herald,* April 4, 1944; "Mrs. Duncan's 100 Pounds," *Evening News* (Portsmouth), April 4, 1944.

35. *Rex v. Duncan,* trial transcript, DPP 2/1204; Roberts, ed., *Trial of Helen Duncan,* trial transcript, 55.

36. *Rex v. Duncan,* trial transcript, DPP 2/1204; Roberts, ed., *Trial of Helen Duncan,* trial transcript, 55.

37. *Rex v. Duncan,* trial transcript, DPP 2/1204; Roberts, ed., *Trial of Helen Duncan,* trial transcript, 55.

38. *Rex v. Duncan,* trial transcript, DPP 2/1204; Roberts, ed., *Trial of Helen Duncan,* trial transcript, 55.

39. *Rex v. Duncan,* trial transcript, DPP 2/1204; Roberts, ed., *Trial of Helen Duncan,* trial transcript, 56. Edited for clarity; "Master Temple" replaces "Copnor Road."

40. *Rex v. Duncan,* trial transcript, DPP 2/1204; Roberts, ed., *Trial of Helen Duncan,* trial transcript, 56.

41. *Rex v. Duncan,* trial transcript, DPP 2/1204; Roberts, ed., *Trial of Helen Duncan,* trial transcript, 56. Loseby's questioning abridged.

42. *Rex v. Duncan,* trial transcript, DPP 2/1204; Roberts, ed., *Trial of Helen Duncan,* trial transcript, 56.

43. *Rex v. Duncan,* trial transcript, DPP 2/1204; Roberts, ed., *Trial of Helen Duncan,* trial transcript, 56.

44. *Rex v. Duncan,* trial transcript, DPP 2/1204; Roberts, ed., *Trial of Helen Duncan,* trial transcript, 56. Stan Worth's response abridged.

45. *Rex v. Duncan,* trial transcript, DPP 2/1204; Roberts, ed., *Trial of Helen Duncan,* trial transcript, 56. Loseby's remark abridged and edited for clarity.

46. *Rex v. Duncan,* trial transcript, DPP 2/1204; Roberts, ed., *Trial of Helen Duncan,* trial transcript, 56.

47. *Rex v. Duncan,* trial transcript, DPP 2/1204; Roberts, ed., *Trial of Helen Duncan,* trial transcript, 56–57. Loseby's cross-examination abridged.

48. *Rex v. Duncan,* trial transcript, DPP 2/1204; Roberts, ed., *Trial of Helen Duncan,* trial transcript, 57.

49. *Rex v. Duncan,* trial transcript, DPP 2/1204; Roberts, ed., *Trial of Helen Duncan,* trial transcript, 57. Loseby's explanation abridged.

50. *Rex v. Duncan,* trial transcript, DPP 2/1204; Roberts, ed., *Trial of Helen Duncan,* trial transcript, 57. Loseby's statements abridged slightly.

51. *Rex v. Duncan,* trial transcript, DPP 2/1204; Roberts, ed., *Trial of Helen Duncan,* trial transcript, 57.

52. *Rex v. Duncan,* trial transcript, DPP 2/1204; Roberts, ed., *Trial of Helen Duncan,* trial transcript, 57.

53. *Rex v. Duncan,* trial transcript, DPP 2/1204; Roberts, ed., *Trial of Helen Duncan,* trial transcript, 57.

54. *Rex v. Duncan,* trial transcript, DPP 2/1204; Roberts, ed., *Trial of Helen Duncan,* trial transcript, 57–60.

55. *Rex v. Duncan,* trial transcript, DPP 2/1204; Roberts, ed., *Trial of Helen Duncan,* trial transcript, 60.

56. *Rex v. Duncan,* trial transcript, DPP 2/1204; Roberts, ed., *Trial of Helen Duncan,* trial transcript, 60.

57. *Rex v. Duncan,* trial transcript, DPP 2/1204; Roberts, ed., *Trial of Helen Duncan,* trial transcript, 60.

58. *Rex v. Duncan,* trial transcript, DPP 2/1204; Roberts, ed., *Trial of Helen Duncan,* trial transcript, 64.

59. *Rex v. Duncan,* trial transcript, DPP 2/1204; Roberts, ed., *Trial of Helen Duncan,* trial transcript, 64.

60. *Rex v. Duncan,* trial transcript, DPP 2/1204; Roberts, ed., *Trial of Helen Duncan,* trial transcript, 64.

61. *Rex v. Duncan,* trial transcript, DPP 2/1204; Roberts, ed., *Trial of Helen Duncan,* trial transcript, 64.

62. *Rex v. Duncan,* trial transcript, DPP 2/1204; Roberts, ed., *Trial of Helen Duncan,* trial transcript, 65. Loseby's questioning abridged.

63. *Rex v. Duncan,* trial transcript, DPP 2/1204; Roberts, ed., *Trial of Helen Duncan,* trial transcript, 65.

64. *Rex v. Duncan,* trial transcript, DPP 2/1204; Roberts, ed., *Trial of Helen Duncan,* trial transcript, 65.

65. *Rex v. Duncan,* trial transcript, DPP 2/1204; Roberts, ed., *Trial of Helen Duncan,* trial transcript, 65.

66. *Rex v. Duncan,* trial transcript, DPP 2/1204; Roberts, ed., *Trial of Helen Duncan,* trial transcript, 65.

67. *Rex v. Duncan,* trial transcript, DPP 2/1204; Roberts, ed., *Trial of Helen Duncan,* trial transcript, 65.

68. *Rex v. Duncan,* trial transcript, DPP 2/1204; Roberts, ed., *Trial of Helen Duncan,* trial transcript, 69.

69. *Rex v. Duncan,* trial transcript, DPP 2/1204; Roberts, ed., *Trial of Helen Duncan,* trial transcript, 69.

70. *Rex v. Duncan,* trial transcript, DPP 2/1204; Roberts, ed., *Trial of Helen Duncan,* trial transcript, 69.

## Chapter 20

In this chapter, the Prosecution concludes its case. Examination, cross-examination, and testimony are taken from verbatim transcripts, edited minimally for clarity and abridged for brevity. The chapter also includes a flashback to the bizarre and pitiless research experiments conducted on Helen Duncan. My reconstruction is based primarily on observational notes of these investigations reported in Harry Price's book on the Duncan mediumship.

1. Malcolm Gaskill, *Hellish Nell* (London: Fourth Estate, 2001), 2.

2. Manfred Cassirer, *Medium on Trial* (Essex: PN Publishing, 1996), 44–45; Harry Price, *Regurgitation and the Duncan Mediumship* (London: National Laboratory of Psychical Research, 1931), 16, 30–31. These sources indicate the close relationship between Molly Goldney and Harry Price. I assume Mrs. Goldney's presence in court would unsettle Helen Duncan.

3. Price, *The Duncan Mediumship,* 16, 30–31.

4. Cassirer, *Medium on Trial,* 66; C. E. Bechhofer Roberts, ed., *The Trial of Helen Duncan* (London: Jarrolds, 1945), 108.

5. Stanley Worth, personal interview, October 10, 2001.

6. Maurice Barbanell, *The Case of Helen Duncan* (London: Psychic Press, 1945), 30; Terry Swetnam, letter to author, February 16, 2000, photograph of Frederick Ford.

7. *Rex v. Duncan*, trial transcript, DPP 2/1204, Public Records Office, Kew, England; Roberts, ed., *Trial of Helen Duncan*, trial transcript, 110. Loseby's cross-examination abridged.

8. Swetnam, letter to author, February 16, 2000, photograph of Frederick Ford.

9. *Rex v. Duncan*, trial transcript, DPP 2/1204; Roberts, ed., *Trial of Helen Duncan*, trial transcript, 110.

10. *Rex v. Duncan*, trial transcript, DPP 2/1204; Roberts, ed., *Trial of Helen Duncan*, trial transcript, 110. Loseby's remarks abridged.

11. *Rex v. Duncan*, trial transcript, DPP 2/1204; Roberts, ed., *Trial of Helen Duncan*, trial transcript, 110.

12. *Rex v. Duncan*, trial transcript, DPP 2/1204; Roberts, ed., *Trial of Helen Duncan*, trial transcript, 110.

13. *Rex v. Duncan*, trial transcript, DPP 2/1204; Roberts, ed., *Trial of Helen Duncan*, trial transcript, 110.

14. *Rex v. Duncan*, trial transcript, DPP 2/1204; Roberts, ed., *Trial of Helen Duncan*, trial transcript, 110.

15. *Rex v. Duncan*, trial transcript, DPP 2/1204; Roberts, ed., *Trial of Helen Duncan*, trial transcript, 110.

16. *Rex v. Duncan*, trial transcript, DPP 2/1204; Roberts, ed., *Trial of Helen Duncan*, trial transcript, 110.

17. *Rex v. Duncan*, trial transcript, DPP 2/1204; Roberts, ed., *Trial of Helen Duncan*, trial transcript, 110. Ford's answer abridged.

18. Price, *The Duncan Mediumship*, 30–31, 55–64.

19. Gena Brealey, *The Two Worlds of Helen Duncan* (London: Regency Press, 1985), 57; Price, *The Duncan Mediumship*, 39.

20. Paul Tabori, *Harry Price: Biography of a Ghost Hunter* (London: Athenaeum Press, 1950), 135.

21. Cassirer, *Medium on Trial*, 44; Price, *The Duncan Mediumship*, 30–31.

22. Price, *The Duncan Mediumship*, photographs; Cassirer, *Medium on Trial*, photograph.

23. Price, *The Duncan Mediumship*, 30. The following description of Helen Duncan's vaginal and rectal exam is based on Harry Price's own account.

24. Price, *The Duncan Mediumship*, photographs.

25. Ibid., 30. While these events are based on Price's account, I assume Helen Duncan's viewpoint.

26. Ibid., 31.

27. Ibid., 34.

28. Brealey, *Two Worlds*, 121; Cassirer, *Medium on Trial*, 164; Gaskill, *Hellish Nell*, 329. These sources establish Helen Duncan's alcohol use.

29. Price, *The Duncan Mediumship*, 31.

30. Ibid., 32.

31. Ibid., 32–34.

32. Ibid., 41–45.

33. Ibid., 59.

34. Ibid., 60–61.

35. Ibid., 61.

36. Ibid., 61. Quote is based on information in this source.

37. Brealey, *Two Worlds*, 59; Price, *The Duncan Mediumship*, 61.

38. Brealey, *Two Worlds*, 59; Price, *The Duncan Mediumship*, 61.

39. Price, *The Duncan Mediumship*, 61.

40. Ibid.

41. Brealey, *Two Worlds*, 59; Price, *The Duncan Mediumship*, 61.

42. Site visit, 13 Rolland Gardens, London, address of Price's National Laboratory of Psychical Research.

43. Ibid.

44. Price, *The Duncan Mediumship*, 61.

45. Tabori, *Harry Price*, 136.

46. Ibid.

47. Price, *The Duncan Mediumship*, 61.

48. Ibid., 69.

49. *Rex v. Duncan*, trial transcript, DPP 2/1204; Roberts, ed., *Trial of Helen Duncan*, hearing transcript, 111.

50. *Rex v. Duncan*, hearing transcript, DPP 2/1204; Roberts, ed., *Trial of Helen Duncan*, hearing transcript, 111.

51. *Rex v. Duncan*, hearing transcript, DPP 2/1204; Roberts, ed., *Trial of Helen Duncan*, hearing transcript, 111.

52. *Rex v. Duncan*, hearing transcript, DPP 2/1204; Roberts, ed., *Trial of Helen Duncan*, hearing transcript, 111.

53. *Rex v. Duncan*, hearing transcript, DPP 2/1204; Roberts, ed., *Trial of Helen Duncan*, hearing transcript, 111.

54. *Rex v. Duncan*, hearing transcript, DPP 2/1204; Roberts, ed., *Trial of Helen Duncan*, hearing transcript, 111.

55. *Rex v. Duncan*, hearing transcript, DPP 2/1204; Roberts, ed., *Trial of Helen Duncan*, hearing transcript, 111.

56. *Rex v. Duncan*, hearing transcript, DPP 2/1204; Roberts, ed., *Trial of Helen Duncan*, hearing transcript, 111.

57. *Rex v. Duncan*, hearing transcript, DPP 2/1204; Roberts, ed., *Trial of Helen Duncan*, hearing transcript, 111. Ford's response abridged.

58. *Rex v. Duncan*, hearing transcript, DPP 2/1204; Roberts, ed., *Trial of Helen Duncan*, hearing transcript, 111.

## Chapter 21

This depiction of the Defense's opening remarks is based on verbatim trial transcripts found in *Rex v. Duncan*, DPP 2/1204 and C. E. Bechhofer Roberts, editor, *The Trial of Helen Duncan*. I describe the scene assuming Chief Constable Arthur West's viewpoint. Background information is supplied as noted below.

1. Honourable Society of the Middle Temple, *Middle Temple Ordeal* (London: Sir Isaac Pitman and Sons, 1948), 44–45.

2. "John Cyril Maude," *Who Was Who* (London: A&C Black, 1897–1990).

3. "Middle Temple," www.wikipedia.org.

4. "Charles Loseby, " *Who Was Who* (London: A&C Black, 1897–1990).

5. Society of the Middle Temple, *Middle Temple Ordeal,* 44–45.

6. "Bombs Start London Fires," *Daily Herald,* March 25, 1944; "Longest Raid in a Year," *Daily Express,* March 25, 1944; "*Luftwaffer* Made Big Attempt to Burn London," *Evening News* (Portsmouth), March 25, 1944.

7. "Crowds Jam Tube," *Daily Express,* March 27, 1944; "Hyde Park Puts on a Pageant," *Daily Express,* March 27, 1944; "Salute Crowds," *Daily Herald,* March 27, 1944.

8. "Invasion: British in Equal Numbers to US," *Daily Express,* March 27, 1944.

9. Michael Howard, *British Intelligence in the Second World War,* vol. 5 (New York: Cambridge University Press, 1990), 247; "Plan Bodyguard," January 23, 1944, CAB 80/77, COS(43)799(o), Public Records Office, Kew, England.

10. "Spy Raiders Over London, Night Fighters Tailed Spy Planes from South Coast," *Daily Express,* March 23, 1944.

11. In Britain, it's the usual practice for defendants to testify.

12. Gena Brealey, *The Two Worlds of Helen Duncan* (London: Regency Press, 1985), 89, 97.

13. Maurice Barbanell, *The Case of Helen Duncan* (London: Psychic Press, 1945), 99.

14. C. E. Bechhofer Roberts, ed., *The Trial of Helen Duncan* (London: Jarrolds, 1945), 114.

15. Ibid., 337. West's testimony.

16. *Rex v. Duncan,* trial transcript, DPP 2/1204, Public Records Office, Kew, England; Roberts, ed., *The Trial of Helen Duncan,* trial transcript, 111.

17. "Charles Loseby," *Who Was Who.*

18. "Bosworth Market," www.britannia-bosworth.activehostels.com.

19. "Gray's Inn-Virtual Tour," www.graysinn.org.uk.

20. "Charles Loseby," *Who Was Who.*

21. Malcolm Gaskill, *Hellish Nell* (London: Fourth Estate, 2001), 194–195.

22. Ibid., 194–195.

23. "Use of Poison Gas in World War I," www.wikipedia.org.; "Facts about Sulfur Mustard," Centers for Disease Control, www.cdc.gov.

24. *Rex v. Duncan,* trial transcript, DPP 2/1204; Roberts, ed., *The Trial of Helen Duncan,* trial transcript, 111–112.

25. *Rex v. Duncan,* trial transcript, DPP 2/1204; Roberts, ed., *The Trial of Helen Duncan,* trial transcript, 112. Loseby's remarks abridged.

26. *Rex v. Duncan,* trial transcript, DPP 2/1204; Roberts, ed., *The Trial of Helen Duncan,* trial transcript, 112. Loseby's remarks edited slightly for clarity.

27. "Medium's Body Endangered," *Evening News* (Portsmouth), January 25, 1944.

28. "Sir Grimwood Mears," *Who Was Who* (London: A&C Black, 1897–1990).

29. Grimwood Mears, letter to Home Secretary Morrison, February 2, 1944, HO 144/22172, Public Records Office, Kew, England.

30. Site visit, Meonstoke House, Meonstoke, England.

31. K. M. Burrell, personal interview, Portsmouth, England, November 3, 1999.

32. Mears, letter to Home Secretary Morrison, February 2, 1944, HO 144/22172.

33. "Sir Grimwood Mears," *Who Was Who.*

34. "The Dardanelles Commission," www.firstworldwar.com.

35. Mears, letter to Home Secretary Morrison, February 2, 1944, HO 144/22172; J.A.R. Pimbott, Private Secretary to Home Secretary Morrison, letter to Sir Grimwood Mears, February 25, 1944, HO 144/22172, Public Records Office, Kew, England.

36. "Charles Loseby," *Who Was Who;* "John Cyril Maude," *Who Was Who;* "E. G. Robey," *Who Was Who.*

37. Author site visit; "The Garrick Club," www.ken.co.uk.

38. *Rex v. Duncan*, trial transcript, DPP 2/1204; Roberts, ed., *The Trial of Helen Duncan*, trial transcript, 112. Loseby's remarks edited slightly and abridged for clarity.

39. *Rex v. Duncan*, trial transcript, DPP 2/1204; Roberts, ed., *The Trial of Helen Duncan*, trial transcript, 112.

40. *Rex v. Duncan*, trial transcript, DPP 2/1204; Roberts, ed., *The Trial of Helen Duncan*, trial transcript, 112. Loseby's remarks edited slightly for clarity.

41. *Rex v. Duncan*, trial transcript, DPP 2/1204; Roberts, ed., *The Trial of Helen Duncan*, trial transcript, 112. Loseby's remarks edited slightly and abridged for clarity.

42. *Rex v. Duncan*, trial transcript, DPP 2/1204; Roberts, ed., *The Trial of Helen Duncan*, trial transcript, 113.

43. *Rex v. Duncan*, trial transcript, DPP 2/1204; Roberts, ed., *The Trial of Helen Duncan*, trial transcript, 113.

44. *Rex v. Duncan*, trial transcript, DPP 2/1204; Roberts, ed., *The Trial of Helen Duncan*, trial transcript, 114. Edited slightly for brevity and clarity.

45. *Rex v. Duncan*, trial transcript, DPP 2/1204; Roberts, ed., *The Trial of Helen Duncan*, trial transcript, 114. Edited slightly for brevity and clarity.

46. *Rex v. Duncan*, trial transcript, DPP 2/1204; Roberts, ed., *The Trial of Helen Duncan*, trial transcript, 120–121.

47. *Rex v. Duncan*, trial transcript, DPP 2/1204; Roberts, ed., *The Trial of Helen Duncan*, trial transcript, 119. Slightly abridged.

48. *Rex v. Duncan*, trial transcript, DPP 2/1204; Roberts, ed., trial transcript, 119. Slightly abridged.

49. *Rex v. Duncan*, trial transcript, DPP 2/1204; Roberts, ed., *The Trial of Helen Duncan*, trial transcript, 119.

50. Cassirer, *Medium on Trial*, 123, 159.

51. Gerald Dodson, *Consider Your Verdict* (London: Hutchinson, 1967), 111.

## Chapter 22

The bulk of this chapter returns to Harry Price's obsession with Helen Duncan's mediumship. The reconstruction of scenes is based primarily on eyewitness accounts recorded in Price's exposé of the Duncan mediumship.

1. Arthur Sefton Cohen, Assistant Director of Public Director of Public Prosecutions, letter to Chief Constable West, March 16, 1944, DPP 2/1204, Public Records Office, Kew, England.

2. Trevor Hall, *The Search for Harry Price* (London: Duckworth, 1978). Hall exposes a series of untruths and exaggerations.

3. Cohen, letter to West, March 16, 1944, DPP 2/1204.

4. Hall, *The Search for Harry Price*, 11, 101; Paul Tabori, *Harry Price: Biography of a Ghost Hunter* (London: Athenaeum Press, 1950), 2–3. Biographers agree that Price loved publicity.

5. Harry Price, *Search for Truth* (London: Collins, 1942), 180–182.

6. Harry Price, *Regurgitation and the Duncan Mediumship* (London: National Laboratory of Psychical Research, 1931), 56.

7. Price, *The Duncan Mediumship*, 61; Price, *Search for Truth*, 180–182; Tabori, *Harry Price*, 136.

8. Price, *The Duncan Mediumship,* 59.

9. Ibid., 62–63.

10. Ibid., 63.

11. Ibid. Dialogue is derived from Price's account.

12. Ibid., 69.

13. Harry Price, "Dr. X's Report on His Examination of Medium at Fifth Séance," in *The Duncan Mediumship,* 106–107.

14. Price, *The Duncan Mediumship,* 70–72. Dialogue and interaction are based on Price's account.

15. Ibid., 72. Dialogue is derived from Price's account and reflects my understanding of the people involved.

16. Ibid., 79.

17. Ibid., 96. Mr. Bois's question is abridged.

18. Ibid., 97. Henry Duncan's response is abridged.

19. Robert Fielding-Ould, Editorial, *Two Worlds,* June 21, 1931.

20. Price, *The Duncan Mediumship,* 97.

21. Ibid.

22. Ibid., 97–98. Mr. Bois's questions are abridged.

23. Ibid., 98–99." Henry Duncan's response is abridged.

24. Ibid., 99. Henry's response is edited for clarity.

25. Ibid. Mr. Bois's responses are combined.

26. Ibid. Henry's responses are combined.

27. Ibid., 100.

28. Ibid.

29. Ibid.

30. Ibid., 96–104. "Appendix B" is a verbatim transcript of Henry Duncan's interrogation by Price and his colleagues.

31. Maurice Barbanell, *The Case of Helen Duncan* (London: Psychic Press, 1945), 99–103.

## Chapter 23

This chapter recalls the losses and challenges that led up to Helen Duncan's becoming a professional medium. In depicting these emotionally devastating events, I find understanding of Helen Duncan's character and motivation.

1. Gena Brealey, *The Two Worlds of Helen Duncan* (London: Regency Press, 1985), 97.

2. Ibid., 95.

3. *Rex v. Duncan,* trial transcript, DPP 2/1204, Public Records Office, Kew, England; C. E. Bechhofer Roberts, ed., *The Trial of Helen Duncan* (London: Jarrolds, 1945), trial transcript, 122.

4. *Rex v. Duncan,* trial transcript, DPP 2/1204; Roberts, ed., *The Trial of Helen Duncan,* trial transcript, 122.

5. *Rex v. Duncan,* trial transcript, DPP 2/1204; Roberts, ed., *The Trial of Helen Duncan,* trial transcript, 122.

6. *Rex v. Duncan,* trial transcript, DPP 2/1204; Roberts, ed., *The Trial of Helen Duncan,* trial transcript, 122. Loseby's explanation is minimally edited for clarity.

7. *Rex v. Duncan,* trial transcript, DPP 2/1204; Roberts, ed., *The Trial of Helen Duncan,* trial transcript, 122.

8. *Rex v. Duncan*, trial transcript, DPP 2/1204; Roberts, ed., *The Trial of Helen Duncan*, trial transcript, 122.

9. *Rex v. Duncan*, trial transcript, DPP 2/1204; Roberts, ed., *The Trial of Helen Duncan*, trial transcript, 122.

10. *Rex v. Duncan*, trial transcript, DPP 2/1204; Roberts, ed., trial transcript, 122. Loseby's explanation is minimally edited for clarity.

11. "The Right to Silence," www.wikipedia.org.

12. Stanley Worth, personal interview, October 15, 2001.

13. *Rex v. Duncan*, trial transcript, DPP 2/1204; Roberts, ed., *The Trial of Helen Duncan*, trial transcript, 123–141.

14. *Rex v. Duncan*, trial transcript, DPP 2/1204; Roberts, ed., *The Trial of Helen Duncan*, trial transcript, 142.

15. *Rex v. Duncan*, trial transcript, DPP 2/1204; Roberts, ed., *The Trial of Helen Duncan*, trial transcript, 142.

16. *Rex v. Duncan*, trial transcript, DPP 2/1204; Roberts, ed., *The Trial of Helen Duncan*, trial transcript, 142. Interchange between Loseby and Dodson is minimally abridged.

17. *Rex v. Duncan*, trial transcript, DPP 2/1204; Roberts, ed., *The Trial of Helen Duncan*, trial transcript, 142. Judge's statements are abridged.

18. *Rex v. Duncan*, trial transcript, DPP 2/1204; Roberts, ed., *The Trial of Helen Duncan*, trial transcript, 142–155.

19. Alan Crossley, *The Story of Helen Duncan* (Greenford: Psychic World Classic, 1999), 19–22; Brealey, *Two Worlds*, 34–38. The following scenes from Helen Duncan's life rely primarily on the accounts of her friend (Alan Crossley) and her daughter (Gena Brealey). I call upon other sources for detail and context.

20. Crossley, *The Story of Helen Duncan*, 19; Brealey, *Two Worlds*, 34.

21. WebMD, "Symptoms of Eclampsia," www.webmd.com. Helen Duncan suffered from eclampsia during her third pregnancy. I depict the symptoms of this disease in the context of her early marriage.

22. Roberts, ed., *The Trial of Helen Duncan*, 96.

23. WebMD, "Symptoms of Eclampsia," www.webmd.com.

24. Brealey, *Two Worlds*, 34.

25. Ibid.

26. Ibid., 34–35.

27. Ibid., 35.

28. Ibid.

29. Ibid.

30. Crossley, *The Story of Helen Duncan*, 20.

31. Brealey, *Two Worlds*, 37.

32. Ibid., 35–36.

33. Malcolm Gaskill, *Hellish Nell* (London: Fourth Estate, 2001), 46.

34. Mary Armour, *Helen Duncan (1895–1956): My Living Has Not Been in Vain* (London: Pembridge, 2000), 24; Anonymous, personal interview, December 19, 1999.

35. Brealey, *Two Worlds*, 36.

36. Ibid.

37. Ibid., 36–37.

38. Ibid., 39.

39. Ibid., 37.

40. Brealey, *Two Worlds*, 37; Crossley, *The Story of Helen Duncan*, 22–23.

41. Brealey, *Two Worlds*, 44–54; "The Last Witch in England," interview with Shelia Downey and Ann Pooey, Helen Duncan's granddaughters, BBC Radio, London, August 13, 1998.

42. "'All Lies' Cry by Medium," *News of the World*, April 2, 1944.

43. Ibid.

## Chapter 24

This chapter depicts testimony given over a three-day period. For clarity, brevity, and impact, I've abridged and edited the trial transcript while maintaining Chief Constable West's point of view.

1. Gerald Dodson, *Consider Your Verdict* (London: Hutchinson, 1967), 111.

2. Gena Brealey, *The Two Worlds of Helen Duncan* (London: Regency Press, 1985), 96–97; Dodson, *Consider Your Verdict,* 112.

3. *Rex v. Duncan*, trial transcript, DPP 2/1204, Public Records Office, Kew, England; C. E. Bechhofer Roberts, ed., *The Trial of Helen Duncan* (London: Jarrolds, 1945), trial transcript, 149.

4. *Rex v. Duncan*, trial transcript, DPP 2/1204; Roberts, ed., *The Trial of Helen Duncan,* trial transcript, 148.

5. *Rex v. Duncan*, trial transcript, DPP 2/1204; Roberts, ed., *The Trial of Helen Duncan,* trial transcript, 149. Maude's questions are combined and abridged.

6. *Rex v. Duncan*, trial transcript, DPP 2/1204; Roberts, ed., *The Trial of Helen Duncan,* trial transcript, 149–150. Mr. Gill's responses are combined and abridged.

7. *Rex v. Duncan*, trial transcript, DPP 2/1204; Roberts, ed., *The Trial of Helen Duncan,* trial transcript, 150.

8. *Rex v. Duncan*, trial transcript, DPP 2/1204; Roberts, ed., *The Trial of Helen Duncan,* trial transcript, 150.

9. *Rex v. Duncan*, trial transcript, DPP 2/1204; Roberts, ed., *The Trial of Helen Duncan,* trial transcript, 150.

10. *Rex v. Duncan*, trial transcript, DPP 2/1204; Roberts, ed., *The Trial of Helen Duncan,* trial transcript, 150.

11. *Rex v. Duncan*, trial transcript, DPP 2/1204; Roberts, ed., *The Trial of Helen Duncan,* trial transcript, 150.

12. *Rex v. Duncan*, trial transcript, DPP 2/1204; Roberts, ed., *The Trial of Helen Duncan,* trial transcript, 150; Stanley Worth, personal interview, October 15, 2001.

13. *Rex v. Duncan*, trial transcript, DPP 2/1204; Roberts, ed., *The Trial of Helen Duncan,* trial transcript, 148.

14. Site visit.

15. *Rex v. Duncan*, trial transcript, DPP 2/1204; Roberts, ed., *The Trial of Helen Duncan,* trial transcript, 151.

16. *Rex v. Duncan*, trial transcript, DPP 2/1204; Roberts, ed., *The Trial of Helen Duncan,* trial transcript, 151.

17. *Rex v. Duncan*, trial transcript, DPP 2/1204; Roberts, ed., *The Trial of Helen Duncan,* trial transcript, 151.

18. *Rex v. Duncan*, trial transcript, DPP 2/1204; Roberts, ed., *The Trial of Helen Duncan,* trial transcript, 152.

19. *Rex v. Duncan*, trial transcript, DPP 2/1204; Roberts, ed., *The Trial of Helen Duncan,* trial transcript, 152.

20. *Rex v. Duncan*, trial transcript, DPP 2/1204; Roberts, ed., *The Trial of Helen Duncan*, trial transcript, 152.

21. *Rex v. Duncan*, trial transcript, DPP 2/1204; Roberts, ed., *The Trial of Helen Duncan*, trial transcript, 152.

22. *Rex v. Duncan*, trial transcript, DPP 2/1204; Roberts, ed., *The Trial of Helen Duncan*, trial transcript, 152.

23. *Rex v. Duncan*, trial transcript, DPP 2/1204; Roberts, ed., *The Trial of Helen Duncan*, trial transcript, 143.

24. *Rex v. Duncan*, trial transcript, DPP 2/1204; Roberts, ed., *The Trial of Helen Duncan*, trial transcript, 143.

25. *Rex v. Duncan*, trial transcript, DPP 2/1204; Roberts, ed., *The Trial of Helen Duncan*, trial transcript, 203.

26. *Rex v. Duncan*, trial transcript, DPP 2/1204; Roberts, ed., *The Trial of Helen Duncan*, trial transcript, 206.

27. *Rex v. Duncan*, trial transcript, DPP 2/1204; Roberts, ed., *The Trial of Helen Duncan*, trial transcript, 206.

28. *Rex v. Duncan*, trial transcript, DPP 2/1204; Roberts, ed., *The Trial of Helen Duncan*, trial transcript, 206.

29. *Rex v. Duncan*, trial transcript, DPP 2/1204; Roberts, ed., *The Trial of Helen Duncan*, trial transcript, 206.

30. *Rex v. Duncan*, trial transcript, DPP 2/1204; Roberts, ed., *The Trial of Helen Duncan*, trial transcript, 206.

31. *Rex v. Duncan*, trial transcript, DPP 2/1204; Roberts, ed., *The Trial of Helen Duncan*, trial transcript, 206.

32. *Rex v. Duncan*, trial transcript, DPP 2/1204; Roberts, ed., *The Trial of Helen Duncan*, trial transcript, 229.

33. *Rex v. Duncan*, trial transcript, DPP 2/1204; Roberts, ed., *The Trial of Helen Duncan*, trial transcript, 229.

34. *Rex v. Duncan*, trial transcript, DPP 2/1204; Roberts, ed., *The Trial of Helen Duncan*, trial transcript, 229.

35. *Rex v. Duncan*, trial transcript, DPP 2/1204; Roberts, ed., *The Trial of Helen Duncan*, trial transcript, 229.

36. *Rex v. Duncan*, trial transcript, DPP 2/1204; Roberts, ed., *The Trial of Helen Duncan*, trial transcript, 229. Mrs. Blackwell's answers are combined and abridged.

37. *Rex v. Duncan*, trial transcript, DPP 2/1204; Roberts, ed., *The Trial of Helen Duncan*, trial transcript, 230–231. Blackwell's answers are combined and abridged.

38. *Rex v. Duncan*, trial transcript, DPP 2/1204; Roberts, ed., *The Trial of Helen Duncan*, trial transcript, 232.

39. *Rex v. Duncan*, trial transcript, DPP 2/1204; Roberts, ed., *The Trial of Helen Duncan*, trial transcript, 232.

40. *Rex v. Duncan*, trial transcript, DPP 2/1204; Roberts, ed., *The Trial of Helen Duncan*, trial transcript, 232.

41. *Rex v. Duncan*, trial transcript, DPP 2/1204; Roberts, ed., *The Trial of Helen Duncan*, trial transcript, 232.

42. *Rex v. Duncan*, trial transcript, DPP 2/1204; Roberts, ed., *The Trial of Helen Duncan*, trial transcript, 232.

43. *Rex v. Duncan*, trial transcript, DPP 2/1204; Roberts, ed., *The Trial of Helen Duncan*, trial transcript, 232.

44. *Rex v. Duncan*, trial transcript, DPP 2/1204; Roberts, ed., *The Trial of Helen Duncan*, trial transcript, 232.

45. *Rex v. Duncan*, trial transcript, DPP 2/1204; Roberts, ed., *The Trial of Helen Duncan*, trial transcript, 232.

46. *Rex v. Duncan*, trial transcript, DPP 2/1204; Roberts, ed., *The Trial of Helen Duncan*, trial transcript, 232.

47. *Rex v. Duncan*, trial transcript, DPP 2/1204; Roberts, ed., *The Trial of Helen Duncan*, trial transcript, 232.

48. *Rex v. Duncan*, trial transcript, DPP 2/1204; Roberts, ed., *The Trial of Helen Duncan*, trial transcript, 232.

49. *Rex v. Duncan*, trial transcript, DPP 2/1204; Roberts, ed., *The Trial of Helen Duncan*, trial transcript, 232.

50. *Rex v. Duncan*, trial transcript, DPP 2/1204; Roberts, ed., *The Trial of Helen Duncan*, trial transcript, 232.

51. *Rex v. Duncan*, trial transcript, DPP 2/1204; Roberts, ed., *The Trial of Helen Duncan*, trial transcript, 232.

52. *Rex v. Duncan*, trial transcript, DPP 2/1204; Roberts, ed., *The Trial of Helen Duncan*, trial transcript, 232.

53. *Rex v. Duncan*, trial transcript, DPP 2/1204; Roberts, ed., *The Trial of Helen Duncan*, trial transcript, 232.

54. *Rex v. Duncan*, trial transcript, DPP 2/1204; Roberts, ed., *The Trial of Helen Duncan*, trial transcript, 232.

55. *Rex v. Duncan*, trial transcript, DPP 2/1204; Roberts, ed., *The Trial of Helen Duncan*, trial transcript, 232.

56. *Rex v. Duncan*, trial transcript, DPP 2/1204; Roberts, ed., *The Trial of Helen Duncan*, trial transcript, 232.

57. *Rex v. Duncan*, trial transcript, DPP 2/1204; Roberts, ed., *The Trial of Helen Duncan*, trial transcript, 232.

58. *Rex v. Duncan*, trial transcript, DPP 2/1204; Roberts, ed., *The Trial of Helen Duncan*, trial transcript, 233.

59. *Rex v. Duncan*, trial transcript, DPP 2/1204; Roberts, ed., *The Trial of Helen Duncan*, trial transcript, 234.

60. *Rex v. Duncan*, trial transcript, DPP 2/1204; Roberts, ed., *The Trial of Helen Duncan*, trial transcript, 234.

61. *Rex v. Duncan*, trial transcript, DPP 2/1204; Roberts, ed., *The Trial of Helen Duncan*, trial transcript, 234. Mrs. Blackwell's answer is minimally edited for clarity.

62. *Rex v. Duncan*, trial transcript, DPP 2/1204; Roberts, ed., *The Trial of Helen Duncan*, trial transcript, 234.

63. *Rex v. Duncan*, trial transcript, DPP 2/1204; Roberts, ed., *The Trial of Helen Duncan*, trial transcript, 234.

64. *Rex v. Duncan*, trial transcript, DPP 2/1204; Roberts, ed., *The Trial of Helen Duncan*, trial transcript, 233.

65. *Rex v. Duncan*, trial transcript, DPP 2/1204; Roberts, ed., *The Trial of Helen Duncan*, trial transcript, 232.

66. *Rex v. Duncan*, trial transcript, DPP 2/1204; Roberts, ed., *The Trial of Helen Duncan*, trial transcript, 232.

67. *Rex v. Duncan*, trial transcript, DPP 2/1204; Roberts, ed., *The Trial of Helen Duncan*, trial transcript, 229–234. Mrs. Blackwell's testimony is abridged and reordered for clarity and impact.

## Chapter 25

This chapter recollects Helen Duncan's history as a medium in the context of testimony at her 1944 witch trial. My depiction of events is based primarily on her daughter's book, *The Two Worlds of Helen Duncan*, supplemented by sources noted below. I have constructed dialogue to reflect these accounts. My examination of her emotional state draws on these same sources.

1. *Rex v. Duncan*, trial transcript, DPP 2/1204, Public Records Office, Kew, England; C. E. Bechhofer Roberts, ed., *The Trial of Helen Duncan* (London: Jarrolds, 1945), trial transcript, 212.

2. *Rex v. Duncan*, trial transcript, DPP 2/1204; Roberts, ed., *The Trial of Helen Duncan*, trial transcript, 212.

3. *Rex v. Duncan*, trial transcript, DPP 2/1204; Roberts, ed., *The Trial of Helen Duncan*, trial transcript, 212.

4. *Rex v. Duncan*, trial transcript, DPP 2/1204; Roberts, ed., *The Trial of Helen Duncan*, trial transcript, 212.

5. *Rex v. Duncan*, trial transcript, DPP 2/1204; Roberts, ed., *The Trial of Helen Duncan*, trial transcript, 212.

6. *Rex v. Duncan*, trial transcript, DPP 2/1204; Roberts, ed., *The Trial of Helen Duncan*, trial transcript, 212.

7. *Rex v. Duncan*, trial transcript, DPP 2/1204; Roberts, ed., *The Trial of Helen Duncan*, trial transcript, 212.

8. *Rex v. Duncan*, trial transcript, DPP 2/1204; Roberts, ed., *The Trial of Helen Duncan*, trial transcript, 213. Mr. Kirby's answers are combined and abridged.

9. *Rex v. Duncan*, trial transcript, DPP 2/1204; Roberts, ed., *The Trial of Helen Duncan*, trial transcript, 213.

10. *Rex v. Duncan*, trial transcript, DPP 2/1204; Roberts, ed., *The Trial of Helen Duncan*, trial transcript, 213.

11. *Rex v. Duncan*, trial transcript, DPP 2/1204; Roberts, ed., *The Trial of Helen Duncan*, trial transcript, 213.

12. *Rex v. Duncan*, trial transcript, DPP 2/1204; Roberts, ed., *The Trial of Helen Duncan*, trial transcript, 213.

13. Gena Brealey, *The Two Worlds of Helen Duncan* (London: Regency Press, 1985), 32–33; Alan Crossley, *The Story of Helen Duncan* (Greenford: Psychic World Classic, 1999), 27–28.

14. Harry Price, *Regurgitation and the Duncan Mediumship* (London: National Laboratory of Psychical Research, 1931), 99. Henry Duncan states his opinion that his wife was immature.

15. Brealey, *Two Worlds*, 32.

16. Ibid.

17. Ibid., 33.

18. Ibid., 39.

19. Ibid., 42.

20. Brealey, *Two Worlds*, 48; "The Last Witch in England," interviews with Shelia Downey and Ann Pooey, Helen Duncan's granddaughters, BBC Radio, August 13, 1999.

21. Brealey, *Two Worlds*, 48.

22. Brealey, *Two Worlds*, 48; Crossley, *The Story of Helen Duncan*, 25.

23. Brealey, *Two Worlds,* 48–49; Crossley, *The Story of Helen Duncan,* 25–27; Helen Duncan, "Secrets of My Second Sight," *People's Journal,* October 7, 1933.

24. Brealey, *Two Worlds,* 49; Crossley, *The Story of Helen Duncan,* 27; Duncan, "Secrets of My Second Sight."

25. Brealey, *Two Worlds,* 53–54. Helen Duncan's daughter describes the outrageous personality and events in the following scene. I add dialogue consistent with her account.

26. Ibid., 54.

27. "'All Lies' Cry by Medium," *News of the World,* April 2, 1944.

28. Brealey, *Two Worlds,* 56–57.

29. Ibid., 55–56.

30. Malcolm Gaskill, *Hellish Nell* (London: Fourth Estate, 2001), 103. I depict "Uncle Albert's" playful relationship with the Duncan children, adding dialogue.

31. Ibid., 114.

32. Ibid., 103.

33. Gaskill, *Hellish Nell,* 103.

34. Manfred Cassirer, *Medium on Trial* (Essex: PN Publishing, 1996), 166.

35. "Fairy Form at Séance," *Daily Sketch,* March 25, 1944.

36. Roberts, ed., *The Trial of Helen Duncan,* 45.

37. Gaskill, *Hellish Nell,* 257–258.

38. Brealey, *Two Worlds,* 48.

39. James Souter, letter to the editor, *The Light,* June 1929.

40. Cassirer, *Medium on Trial,* 122–123; "Materialization Medium," *The Scotsman,* May 5, 1933.

41. Brealey, *Two Worlds,* 64; "Materialization Medium."

42. Brealey, *Two Worlds,* 64.

43. Gaskill, *Hellish Nell,* 103.

44. Brealey, *Two Worlds,* 57; Cassirer, *Medium on Trial,* 17–18.

45. *Rex v. Duncan,* trial transcript, DPP 2/1204; Roberts, ed., *The Trial of Helen Duncan,* trial transcript, 218. Loseby's question is edited minimally for clarity.

46. *Rex v. Duncan,* trial transcript, DPP 2/1204; Roberts, ed., *The Trial of Helen Duncan,* trial transcript, 218.

## Chapter 26

This chapter revisits some of the most colorful testimony of Helen Duncan's 1944 witch trial. It also returns to 1931 for her final encounter with Harry Price. My depiction of events calls upon trial transcripts, newspaper reports, and other supplemental sources.

1. *Rex v. Duncan,* trial transcript, DPP 2/1204, Public Records Office, Kew, England; C. E. Bechhofer Roberts, ed., *The Trial of Helen Duncan* (London: Jarrolds, 1945), trial transcript, 218.

2. Trevor Hall, *The Search for Harry Price* (London: Duckworth, 1978), photographs; Paul Tabori, *Harry Price: Biography of a Ghost Hunter* (London: Athenaeum Press, 1950), photographs.

3. Harry Price, *Regurgitation and the Duncan Mediumship* (London: National Laboratory of Psychical Research, 1931), 79–83, 96–104.

4. Robert Fielding-Ould, Editorial, *Two Worlds,* June 21, 1931.

5. Henry Duncan, "Letter to Robert Fielding-Ould," *Two Worlds*, June 15, 1931.

6. Fielding-Ould, Editorial, *Two Worlds*, June 21, 1931. I've added dialogue that reflects Fielding-Ould's account.

7. Price, *The Duncan Mediumship*, 81.

8. Ibid.

9. Ibid.

10. Ibid.

11. Gena Brealey, *The Two Worlds of Helen Duncan* (London: Regency Press, 1985), 60–61.

12. *Rex v. Duncan*, trial transcript, DPP 2/1204; Roberts, ed., *The Trial of Helen Duncan*, trial transcript, 239.

13. Edgar Wallace, "Foreword: The Plague of Swafferism," in *Hannen Swaffer's Who's Who*, by Hannen Swaffer (London, no date), 5–6.

14. Hannen Swaffer, *My Greatest Story* (London: W. H. Allen, 1945), 223.

15. Ibid., photograph.

16. Roberts, ed., *The Trial of Helen Duncan*, 20.

17. Wallace, "Foreward: The Plague of Swafferism," 5.

18. Photograph, source unknown.

19. Roberts, ed., *The Trial of Helen Duncan*, 20.

20. "Medium Defied Sashcord," *New Chronicle*, March 30, 1944.

21. Roberts, ed., *The Trial of Helen Duncan*, trial transcript, 239.

22. *Rex v. Duncan*, trial transcript, DPP 2/1204; Roberts, ed., *The Trial of Helen Duncan*, trial transcript, 239.

23. *Rex v. Duncan*, trial transcript, DPP 2/1204; Roberts, ed., *The Trial of Helen Duncan*, trial transcript, 239.

24. *Rex v. Duncan*, trial transcript, DPP 2/1204; Roberts, ed., *The Trial of Helen Duncan*, trial transcript, 239.

25. *Rex v. Duncan*, trial transcript, DPP 2/1204; Roberts, ed., *The Trial of Helen Duncan*, trial transcript, 242.

26. Swaffer, *My Greatest Story*, 223.

27. *Rex v. Duncan*, trial transcript, DPP 2/1204; Roberts, ed., *The Trial of Helen Duncan*, trial transcript, 242.

28. *Rex v. Duncan*, trial transcript, DPP 2/1204; Roberts, ed., *The Trial of Helen Duncan*, trial transcript, 242.

29. *Rex v. Duncan*, trial transcript, DPP 2/1204; Roberts, ed., *The Trial of Helen Duncan*, trial transcript, 242.

30. *Rex v. Duncan*, trial transcript, DPP 2/1204; Roberts, ed., *The Trial of Helen Duncan*, trial transcript, 242.

31. *Rex v. Duncan*, trial transcript, DPP 2/1204; Roberts, ed., *The Trial of Helen Duncan*, trial transcript, 245.

32. *Rex v. Duncan*, trial transcript, DPP 2/1204; Roberts, ed., *The Trial of Helen Duncan*, trial transcript, 245.

33. Swaffer, *Hannen Swaffer's Who's Who* (London, no date), 64.

34. *Rex v. Duncan*, trial transcript, DPP 2/1204; Roberts, ed., *The Trial of Helen Duncan*, trial transcript, 245.

35. *Rex v. Duncan*, trial transcript, DPP 2/1204; Roberts, ed., *The Trial of Helen Duncan*, trial transcript, 246.

36. Price, *The Duncan Mediumship*, 79–83.

37. *Rex v. Duncan*, trial transcript, DPP 2/1204; Roberts, ed., *The Trial of Helen Duncan*, trial transcript, 245.

38. Malcolm Gaskill, *Hellish Nell* (London: Fourth Estate, 2001), 145.

## Chapter 27

This chapter depicts a dramatic turning point in the 1944 witch trial. During the testimony of Alfred Dodd, Helen Duncan's previous brush with the law comes to light. My portrayal of Dodd's testimony is based on the trial transcripts, newspaper reports, and Maurice Barbanell's account. My rendering of Helen Duncan's entrapment by the feisty feminist, Miss Esson Maule, depends largely on newspaper reports dating back to 1933.

1. "Paralyzed Ghost Appears, Judge Wishes He Had a Spirit Guide," *Evening News* (Portsmouth), March 31, 1944.

2. *Rex v. Duncan*, trial transcript, DPP 2/1204, Public Records Office, Kew, England; C. E. Bechhofer Roberts, ed., *The Trial of Helen Duncan* (London: Jarrolds, 1945), trial transcript, 256.

3. Percy Wilson, "Lifted Heels over Head," *Psychic News,* December 15, 1956.

4. Maurice Barbanell, *The Case of Helen Duncan* (London: Psychic Press, 1945), 69; *Rex v. Duncan*, trial transcript, DPP 2/1204; Roberts, ed., *The Trial of Helen Duncan*, trial transcript, 256.

5. "Says Hand Ached for Hours," *Daily Herald,* March 31, 1944.

6. Alfred Dodd, *The Secret Shakespeare* (London: Rider, 1941), photograph.

7. Barbanell, *The Case of Helen Duncan,* 69; Dodd, *The Secret Shakespeare.*

8. *Rex v. Duncan*, trial transcript, DPP 2/1204; Roberts, ed., *The Trial of Helen Duncan*, trial transcript, 257–260. Dodd's answers are combined and abridged with minimal editing for clarity. The language is his own.

9. *Rex v. Duncan*, trial transcript, DPP 2/1204; Roberts, ed., *The Trial of Helen Duncan*, trial transcript, 261.

10. *Rex v. Duncan*, trial transcript, DPP 2/1204; Roberts, ed., *The Trial of Helen Duncan*, trial transcript, 261.

11. *Rex v. Duncan*, trial transcript, DPP 2/1204; Roberts, ed., *The Trial of Helen Duncan*, trial transcript, 261.

12. *Rex v. Duncan*, trial transcript, DPP 2/1204; Roberts, ed., *The Trial of Helen Duncan*, trial transcript, 261.

13. *Rex v. Duncan*, trial transcript, DPP 2/1204; Roberts, ed., *The Trial of Helen Duncan*, trial transcript, 261.

14. *Rex v. Duncan*, trial transcript, DPP 2/1204; Roberts, ed., *The Trial of Helen Duncan*, trial transcript, 261.

15. "Spirit Gave Husband's Ring," *New Chronicle,* March 31, 1944.

16. *Rex v. Duncan*, trial transcript, DPP 2/1204; Roberts, ed., *The Trial of Helen Duncan*, trial transcript, 262.

17. "Charge Against a Medium," *The Scotsman,* May 4, 1944.

18. Site visit, Stafford Street, Edinburgh, Scotland, December 16, 1999.

19. Esson Maule, "A Dream of the Past," *People's Journal,* November 10, 1944. This article includes a photograph of Miss Maule at the desk with another woman, presumably her secretary.

20. Gena Brealey, *The Two Worlds of Helen Duncan* (London: Regency Press, 1985), 68; "Charge Against a Medium."

21. Esson Maule, "Weird Figure that Haunted My House," *People's Journal*, December 22, 1934.

22. Esson Maule, "I Have Lived a Strange Life," *People's Journal*, October 13, 1933; Maule, "A Dream of the Past"; Esson Maule, "A Queer Vision," *People's Journal*, November 24, 1934. The photographs in these three articles chronicle Miss Maule's change of style. In the first, she appears in Victorian dress, long shirt and high collar. In the second, she wears a suit, tie, and trilby hat and looks exactly like a man. In the third, she sports a man's short haircut.

23. Helen Duncan, "Secrets of My Second Sight," *People's Journal*, October 7 to December 16, 1933. Malcolm Gaskill, *Hellish Nell* (London: Fourth Estate, 2001), 17, photograph.

24. "Charge Against a Medium"; Gaskill, *Hellish Nell*, 155.

25. "Charge Against a Medium."

26. Gaskill, *Hellish Nell*, 155.

27. "Charge Against a Medium"; "Materialization Medium," *The Scotsman*, May 5, 1944.

28. "Charge Against a Medium."

29. Ibid.

30. Ibid. This quote reflects Miss Maule's testimony.

31. Ibid. Helen Duncan's threat conforms to Miss Maule's reported testimony.

32. Gaskill, *Hellish Nell*, 157. The dialogue and action in this and the previous paragraph are based on Gaskill's description.

33. "Charge Against a Medium." Helen Duncan's statement conforms with Miss Maule's reported testimony.

34. Gaskill, *Hellish Nell*, 157. I assume Nell's reasoning.

35. Ibid.

36. "Charge Against a Medium."

37. Gaskill, *Hellish Nell*, 157.

38. Gaskill, *Hellish Nell*, 158; "Charge Against a Medium." I try to reconcile these accounts and represent Helen Duncan's viewpoint.

39. "Charge Against a Medium"; Gaskill, *Hellish Nell*, 154–162; "Materialization Medium"; "Medium Fined," *The Scotsman*, May 12, 1933. My depiction of Miss Maule's testimony builds upon these accounts and is consistent with her personality as expressed in a series of articles she wrote for the *People's Journal* between October 13 and December 22, 1934.

40. Maule, "I Have Lived a Strange Life."

41. "Charge Against a Medium."

42. Ibid.

43. Ibid.

44. Maule, "A Dream of the Past." This article is accompanied by a photograph of Miss Maule at the desk with another woman, presumably her secretary.

45. "Charge Against a Medium."

46. "Charge Against a Medium"; "Medium Fined."

47. *Rex v. Duncan*, trial transcript, DPP 2/1204; Roberts, ed., *The Trial of Helen Duncan*, trial transcript, 261–265.

48. *Rex v. Duncan*, trial transcript, DPP 2/1204; Roberts, ed., *The Trial of Helen Duncan*, trial transcript, 265.

49. "Alleged Séance Deceptions," *The Times* (London), March 31, 1944; *Rex v. Duncan*, trial transcript, DPP 2/1204; Roberts, ed., *The Trial of Helen Duncan*, trial transcript, 265.

50. "Alleged Séance Deceptions"; *Rex v. Duncan*, trial transcript, DPP 2/1204; Roberts, ed., *The Trial of Helen Duncan*, trial transcript, 265.

51. *Rex v. Duncan*, trial transcript, DPP 2/1204; Roberts, ed., *The Trial of Helen Duncan*, trial transcript, 265–266. Mr. Dodd's testimony is abridged and slightly edited.

## Chapter 28

This chapter depicts the celebratory dinner that preceded final arguments in the witch trial of 1944. The scene is based primarily on the report of Percy Wilson, who was present at the event. Contextual details are gleaned from supplementary sources, as credited below. The embedded flashback to Helen Duncan's childhood experience calls upon her daughter's account, augmented by site visits and interviews, itemized below.

1. Percy Wilson, "Lifted Heels over Head," *Psychic News,* October 28, 1956.

2. Site visit, Bonnington Hotel, Southampton Row, London.

3. "U.S. Salute to Our Soldiers," *The Times* (London), March 30, 1944.

4. Michael Howard, *British Intelligence in the Second World War,* vol. 5 (New York: Cambridge University Press, 1990), 251, 253; "Plan Bodyguard," CAB 80/77, COS(43)799(o), January 23, 1944, Public Records Office, Kew, England.

5. Philip Zeigler, *London at War* (London: Arrow, 1998), 267–281.

6. Site visit, Bonnington Hotel, Southampton Row, London.

7. Wilson, "Lifted Heels over Head."

8. Maurice Barbanell, *The Case of Helen Duncan* (London: Psychic Press, 1945), 35–36, 58. This conversation is constructed to communicate the Spiritualist viewpoint.

9. C. E. Bechhofer Roberts, ed., *The Trial of Helen Duncan* (London: Jarrolds, 1945), 305. Loseby's comment is designed to foreshadow subsequent events.

10. Wilson, "Lifted Heels over Head." Dialogue reflects description by this eyewitness.

11. Helen Duncan, "My Second Sight," *People's Journal,* November 18 and 25, 1933. Portrait of Helen Duncan's adolescent personality is consistent with her own writing.

12. Site visit, Callander, Scotland, December 18, 1999.

13. J. K. Dunn, personal interview, Callander, Scotland, December 18, 1999. In this personal interview, Mr. Dunn described Callander Primary School and its routines.

14. Photograph of Callander Primary School in early 1900s, Harvey MacNaughton's personal collection, Callander, Scotland.

15. Dunn, personal interview, December 18, 1999.

16. Gena Brealey, *The Two Worlds of Helen Duncan* (London: Regency Press, 1985), 17.

17. Dunn, personal interview, December 18, 1999.

18. Brealey, *Two Worlds,* 17.

19. Dunn, personal interview, December 18, 1999.

20. Brealey, *Two Worlds,* 17; Duncan, "My Second Sight," November 18 and 25, 1933.

21. Dunn, personal interview, December 18, 1999.

22. Brealey, *Two Worlds,* 17. Mr. Cummings's instruction reflects description in the account by Helen Duncan's daughter.

23. Ibid. Mr. Cummings's accusation is consistent with the account by Helen Duncan's daughter.

24. Ibid.

25. Ibid. Mr. Cummings's further accusation reflects the description by Helen Duncan's daughter.

26. Ibid. Young Helen Duncan's response is consistent with her daughter's retelling of the story.

27. Dunn, personal interview, December 18, 1999. Mr. Dunn provided the description of Mr. Cummings's hair.

28. Brealey, *Two Worlds*, 17–18.

29. Ibid., 19.

30. Wilson, "Lifted Heels over Head." The remainder of this scene is constructed based on this eyewitness report.

## Chapter 29

This scene depicts closing arguments and the verdict in England's 1944 witch trial, based on trial transcripts and contemporaneous reports.

1. Gerald Dodson, *Consider Your Verdict* (London: Hutchinson, 1967), 111.

2. C. E. Bechhofer Roberts, ed., *The Trial of Helen Duncan* (London: Jarrolds, 1945), "Contents."

3. Maurice Barbanell, *The Case of Helen Duncan* (London: Psychic Press, 1945), 101–104.

4. *Rex v. Duncan*, trial transcript, DPP 2/1204, Public Records Office, Kew, England; Roberts, ed., *The Trial of Helen Duncan*, trial transcript, 305.

5. Barbanell, *The Case of Helen Duncan*, 105–108; *Rex v. Duncan*, letters and petition to the Home Office and MP Rathborne, 1944, HO 144/22172, Public Records Office, Kew, England.

6. *Rex v. Duncan*, trial transcript, DPP 2/1204; Roberts, ed., *The Trial of Helen Duncan*, trial transcript, 305.

7. *Rex v. Duncan*, trial transcript, DPP 2/1204; Roberts, ed., *The Trial of Helen Duncan*, trial transcript, 305.

8. Roberts, ed., *The Trial of Helen Duncan*, 22.

9. *Rex v. Duncan*, trial transcript, DPP 2/1204; Roberts, ed., *The Trial of Helen Duncan*, trial transcript, 307.

10. *Rex v. Duncan*, trial transcript, DPP 2/1204; Roberts, ed., *The Trial of Helen Duncan*, trial transcript, 308. Loseby's remarks are abridged.

11. *Rex v. Duncan*, trial transcript, DPP 2/1204; Roberts, ed., *The Trial of Helen Duncan*, trial transcript, 309. Loseby's remarks are abridged.

12. *Rex v. Duncan*, trial transcript, DPP 2/1204; Roberts, ed., *The Trial of Helen Duncan*, trial transcript, 320.

13. Donald Thomas, *An Underworld at War* (London: John Murray, 2003), 247. Thomas describes Maude's typical affect and gestures.

14. Barbanell, *The Case of Helen Duncan*, 83; *Rex v. Duncan*, trial transcript, DPP 2/1204.

15. Roberts, ed., *The Trial of Helen Duncan*, trial transcript, 321. Maude's closing is abridged.

16. *Rex v. Duncan*, trial transcript, DPP 2/1204; Roberts, ed., *The Trial of Helen Duncan*, trial transcript, 320–321. Judge's summation and instructions are abridged.

17. *Rex v. Duncan*, trial transcript, DPP 2/1204; Roberts, ed., *The Trial of Helen Duncan*, trial transcript, 335.

18. *Rex v. Duncan*, trial transcript, DPP 2/1204; Roberts, ed., *The Trial of Helen Duncan*, trial transcript, 335–336. Judge's responses are combined and abridged.

19. *Rex v. Duncan*, trial transcript, DPP 2/1204; Roberts, ed., *The Trial of Helen Duncan*, trial transcript, 336.

20. "'All Lies,'" *News of the World*, April 2, 1944.

21. Roberts, ed., *The Trial of Helen Duncan*, trial transcript, 336.

22. "Coast Ban Lifted for Sweethearts," *Evening News* (Portsmouth), March 29, 1944.

23. Michael Howard, *British Intelligence in the Second World War*, vol. 5 (New York: Cambridge University Press, 1990), 254, 257–258.

24. Site visit, Courtroom #4, Old Bailey, Central Criminal Court, London.

25. Roberts, ed., *The Trial of Helen Duncan*, trial transcript, 336.

26. Site visit, Courtroom #4, Old Bailey, Central Criminal Court, London.

27. "'All Lies.'"

28. Roberts, ed., *The Trial of Helen Duncan*, trial transcript, 336.

29. Ibid.

30. Ibid. Clerk's question is abridged.

31. Ibid.

32. "'Lies' Cry by Medium," *Daily Herald*, April 1, 1944.

33. Ibid.

## Chapter 30

Based primarily on trial transcripts and eyewitness and newspaper accounts, this chapter depicts Chief Constable West and His Lordship Sir Gerald Dodson in a testy interchange. These along with ancillary sources are noted below.

1. *Rex v. Duncan*, Prosecutors' notes, undated, DPP 2/1204, Public Records Office, Kew, England.

2. Site visit, Courtroom #4, Old Bailey, Central Criminal Court, London.

3. *Rex v. Duncan*, trial transcript, DPP 2/1204, Public Records Office, Kew, England; C. E. Bechhofer Roberts, ed., *The Trial of Helen Duncan* (London: Jarrolds, 1945), trial transcript, 336.

4. *Rex v. Duncan*, trial transcript, DPP 2/1204; Roberts, ed., *The Trial of Helen Duncan*, trial transcript, 336.

5. *Rex v. Duncan*, trial transcript, DPP 2/1204; Roberts, ed., *The Trial of Helen Duncan*, trial transcript, 336.

6. Stanley Worth, personal interview, October 15, 2001.

7. Manfred Cassirer, *Medium on Trial* (Essex: PN Publishing, 1996), 111; Roberts, ed., *The Trial of Helen Duncan*, 13.

8. "Says He Heard Row Between Ghost and Medium," *Daily Mirror*, March 24, 1944. Photographs in this article give the impression of contrition.

9. "'All Lies!'" *News of the World*, April 2, 1944. This article describes Helen Duncan's haughty stance at certain times during the trial.

10. Percy Wilson, "Lifted Heels over Head," *Psychic News*, October 28, 1956. This article suggests that Helen Duncan believed, based on a clairvoyant message, that she would be set free.

11. *Rex v. Duncan*, trial transcript, DPP 2/1204; Roberts, ed., *The Trial of Helen Duncan*, trial transcript, 337.

12. *Rex v. Duncan*, trial transcript, DPP 2/1204; Roberts, ed., *The Trial of Helen Duncan*, trial transcript, 337.

13. *Rex v. Duncan*, trial transcript, DPP 2/1204; Roberts, ed., *The Trial of Helen Duncan*, trial transcript, 337.

14. *Rex v. Duncan*, trial transcript, DPP 2/1204; Roberts, ed., *The Trial of Helen Duncan*, trial transcript, 337.

15. *Rex v. Duncan*, trial transcript, DPP 2/1204; Roberts, ed., *The Trial of Helen Duncan*, trial transcript, 337—338. Chief Constable's answer is abridged.

16. *Rex v. Duncan*, trial transcript, DPP 2/1204; Roberts, ed., *The Trial of Helen Duncan*, trial transcript, 336.

17. *Rex v. Duncan*, trial transcript, DPP 2/1204; Roberts, ed., *The Trial of Helen Duncan*, trial transcript, 336–337.

18. "Mrs. Duncan, 'A Humbug,'" *Daily Mail*, April 4, 1944.

19. "Medium Weeps and Shouts," *New Chronicle*, April 1, 1944.

20. *Rex v. Duncan*, trial transcript, DPP 2/1204; Roberts, ed., *The Trial of Helen Duncan*, trial transcript, 337.

21. *Rex v. Duncan*, trial transcript, DPP 2/1204; Roberts, ed., *The Trial of Helen Duncan*, trial transcript, 337.

22. *Rex v. Duncan*, trial transcript, DPP 2/1204; Roberts, ed., *The Trial of Helen Duncan*, trial transcript, 337.

23. *Rex v. Duncan*, trial transcript, DPP 2/1204; Roberts, ed., *The Trial of Helen Duncan*, trial transcript, 337.

24. *Rex v. Duncan*, trial transcript, DPP 2/1204; Roberts, ed., *The Trial of Helen Duncan*, trial transcript, 337.

25. *Rex v. Duncan*, trial transcript, DPP 2/1204; Roberts, ed., *The Trial of Helen Duncan*, trial transcript, 337.

26. *Rex v. Duncan*, trial transcript, DPP 2/1204; Roberts, ed., *The Trial of Helen Duncan*, trial transcript, 337.

27. *Rex v. Duncan*, trial transcript, DPP 2/1204; Roberts, ed., *The Trial of Helen Duncan*, trial transcript, 337. Chief Constable's disclosure is abridged.

28. Worth, personal interview, October 15, 2001.

29. *Rex v. Duncan*, trial transcript, DPP 2/1204; Roberts, ed., *The Trial of Helen Duncan*, trial transcript, 337.

30. *Rex v. Duncan*, trial transcript, DPP 2/1204; Roberts, ed., trial transcript, 337.

31. *Rex v. Duncan*, trial transcript, DPP 2/1204; Roberts, ed., *The Trial of Helen Duncan*, trial transcript, 339.

## Chapter 31

This depiction of the sentencing of Helen Duncan calls upon vivid and detailed newspaper accounts, along with the trial transcript and supplementary sources.

1. Malcolm Gaskill, *Hellish Nell* (London: Fourth Estate, 2001), 216.

2. "Helen Duncan's Wealth," *Daily Herald*, April 4, 1944.

3. "We Will Fight to the End for Her," *Sunday Pictorial*, April 2, 1944.

4. "Helen Duncan's Wealth."

5. Ibid.

6. Gaskill, *Hellish Nell*, 216. These statements are written to reflect the Spiritualists' responses to the verdict, as reported by Gaskill.

7. Percy Wilson, "Lifted Heels over Head," *Psychic News*, October 28, 1956.

8. Gina Brealey, *The Two Worlds of Helen Duncan* (London: Regency Press, 1985), 97.

9. *Rex v. Duncan*, trial transcript, DPP 2/1204, CRIM 1/1581, Public Records Office, Kew, England; C. E. Bechhofer Roberts, ed., *The Trial of Helen Duncan* (London: Jarrolds, 1945), trial transcript, 339–340. Judge's remarks upon sentencing are abridged.

10. "Helen Duncan's Wealth."

11. "Mrs. Duncan, 'A Humbug,'" *Daily Mail*, April 1, 1944. This article contains a photograph of Helen Duncan.

12. "Helen Duncan's Wealth."

13. *Rex v. Duncan*, trial transcript, DPP 2/1204; Roberts, ed., *The Trial of Helen Duncan*, trial transcript, 341.

14. *Rex v. Duncan*, trial transcript, DPP 2/1204; Roberts, ed., *The Trial of Helen Duncan*, trial transcript, 341.

## Chapter 32

This chapter returns to Portsmouth and the duties of Chief Constable West. The depiction of his activities and concerns is gleaned from local newspaper accounts, personal interviews, and site visits. I am especially indebted to Stanley Worth for telling me about his visit with Chief Constable and Ida West on the eve of D-Day.

1. *Rex v. Duncan*, trial transcript, DPP 2/1204 Public Records Office, Kew, England; C. E. Bechhofer Roberts, ed., *The Trial of Helen Duncan* (London: Jarrolds, 1945), trial transcript, 340.

2. F. H. Hinsley and C.A.G. Simkins, *British Intelligence in the Second World War,* vol. 4 (New York: Cambridge University Press, 1990), 251–255.

3. Ursula Norton, "Life Inside Fortress Southsea," *Evening News* (Portsmouth), D-Day Supplement, June 1984.

4. John Stedman, ed., *People of Portsmouth: The 20th Century in Their Own Words* (Derby, England: Breedon Books, 2002), 117–118.

5. Site visit, Byculla House, Portsmouth, England.

6. Norton, "Life Inside Fortress Southsea."

7. Site visit, Southsea, Portsmouth, England.

8. Norton, "Life Inside Fortress Southsea." The following vignette is based on a retrospective article written by the little girl in the story. In my retelling, I assume the Chief Constable's viewpoint.

9. Ibid.

10. Ibid.

11. Stanley Worth, personal interview, October 16, 2001.

12. *World War II: Day by Day* (London: Dorling Kindersley, 2001), 522; Worth, personal interview, October 16, 2001. I assume that Stanley Worth visited the Wests in the late afternoon, given that the decision to launch the D-Day invasion was reportedly made at 4 PM.

13. Olive and Jim Cramer, personal interview, May 12, 2005; Worth, personal interview, October 16, 2001. The Chief Constable's wife was similarly described by all interviewees.

14. D-Day Supplement, *Evening News* (Portsmouth), June 1984. Source describes weather based on eyewitnesses.

15. Anthony Kemp, *D-Day: The Normandy Landings and the Liberation of Europe* (London: Thames and Hudson, 1994), 53; D-Day Supplement, *Evening News* (Portsmouth), June 1984. Sources describe weather.

16. Worth, personal interview, October 16, 2001. Conversation is designed to communicate information and reflect Ida West's personality.

17. Olive and Jim Cramer, personal interview, May 12, 2005; Worth, personal interview, October 16, 2001. The Chief Constable's wife is portrayed as described in personal interviews.

18. Worth, personal interview, October 15, 2001. In my telephone interview with Worth, he mentioned his visit to the Wests. Here I assume the local custom.

19. Jim Cramer, personal interview, May 12, 2005; Terry Swetnam, personal interview, November 3, 1999. My impression of Chief Constable West is based on these interviews.

20. Worth, personal interview, October 16, 2001.

21. Ibid.

22. Hinsley and Simkins, *British Intelligence*, vol. 4, 238–242, 257–257; *Rex v. Duncan*, extract of criminal appeal cases, June 8, 9, 19, 1944, HO 144/22172, Public Records Office, Kew, England. Hinsley and Simkins report that authorities wanted to maintain secrecy in coastal areas until the end of the summer. Court documents confirm date of appeal.

23. Worth, personal interview, October 16, 2001.

24. Kemp, *D-Day*, 53; D-Day Supplement, *Evening News* (Portsmouth), June 1984; *World War II: Day by Day*, 522.

25. Kemp, *D-Day*, 53; D-Day Supplement, *Evening News* (Portsmouth), June 1984.

26. Norton, "Life Inside Fortress Southsea." In this article, Ursula Norton describes her own experience. I assume the Chief Constable's viewpoint.

27. *World War II: Day by Day*, 522–523; D-Day Supplement, *Evening News* (Portsmouth), June 1984.

28. Worth, personal interview, October 15, 2001.

## Chapter 33

This chapter recounts the appeal of the 1944 witch trial convictions to the Supreme Court of Britain. Since no verbatim transcript of the proceedings survives, I am particularly indebted to the eyewitness account of Maurice Barbanell in *The Case of Helen Duncan* (London: Psychic Press, 1945). His report is replete with detail and color.

The flashback to Helen Duncan's childhood experience calls upon her daughter's account, site visits, and personal interviews.

1. Anthony Kemp, *D-Day: The Normandy Landings and the Liberation of Europe* (London: Thames and Hudson, 1994), 90–91; *World War II: Day by Day* (London: Dorling Kindersley, 2001), 253–257.

2. *Rex v. Duncan*, extract of criminal appeal cases, June 8, 9, 19, 1944, HO 144/22172, Public Records Office, Kew, England.

3. Site visit, Royal Courts of Justice, London. Interview with security guards about procedure for the arrival of prisoners.

4. Mary Armour, *Helen Duncan (1895–1956): My Living Has Not Been in Vain* (London: Pembridge, 2000), 22. Helen Duncan's relatives claim that she always carried two large hankies.

5. *Rex v. Duncan*, extract of criminal appeal cases, June 8, 9, 19, 1944, HO 144/22172.

6. Site visit, Royal Courts of Justice, Bell Yard, London. Interview with security guards about procedure for the arrival of prisoners.

7. Site visit, Royal Courts of Justice, London. Interview with security guards about procedure for the arrival of prisoners.

8. Site visit, Court of the Chief Justice, Royal Courts of Justice, London.

9. Ibid.

10. Maurice Barbanell, *The Case of Helen Duncan* (London: Psychic Press, 1945), 113; *Rex v. Duncan*, extract of criminal appeal cases, June 8, 9, 19, 1944, HO 144/22172.

11. Site visit, Court of the Chief Justice in the Royal Courts of Justice. Procedural details based on my observation of the appeal process, a process that has not changed for centuries.

12. Barbanell, *The Case of Helen Duncan*, 114.

13. Ibid., 115.

14. C. E. Bechhofer Roberts, ed., *The Trial of Helen Duncan* (London: Jarrolds, 1945), "Grounds for Appeal," 242; Barbanell, *The Case of Helen Duncan*, 112–114. Loseby's reading of the "Grounds for Appeal" is abridged.

15. Donald Thomas, *An Underworld at War* (London: John Murray, 2003), 247; Nigel West, *MI 5: British Security Operations, 1909–1945* (London: Triad Granada, 1983), 21; Stanley Worth, personal interview, October 15, 2001. Maude's demeanor is described by Thomas.

16. Site visit, Royal Courts of Justice, portrait of Chief Justice Caldecote.

17. Barbanell, *The Case of Helen Duncan*, 114; *Rex v. Duncan*, extract of criminal appeal cases, June 8, 9, 19, 1944, HO 144/22172. Interchanges between counsel and the Appeals Court Justices are designed to communicate information and demeanor reported in Barbanell's eyewitness account and in official extracts.

18. Barbanell, *The Case of Helen Duncan*, 114, 113; *Rex v. Duncan*, extract of criminal appeal cases, June 8, 9, 19, 1944, HO 144/22172, 2.

19. Gena Brealey, *The Two Worlds of Helen Duncan* (London: Regency Press, 1985), 15; "The Last Witch in England," interview with Shelia Downey and Ann Pooey, Helen Duncan's granddaughters, BBC Radio, August 13, 1998.

20. Armour, *Helen Duncan*, 16; Malcolm Gaskill, *Hellish Nell* (London: Fourth Estate, 2001), 35.

21. Harvey MacNaughton, personal interview, Callander, Scotland, December 19, 1999.

22. Brealey, *Two Worlds*, 16.

23. MacNaughton, personal interview, December 19, 1999. In my interview with Harvey MacNaughton, he told the villagers' version of the story about the doctor's death and young Nell's prophecy. Helen Duncan's daughter briefly touches on the subject in *The Two Worlds of Helen Duncan*. The details provided by Mr. MacNaughton lend greater veracity to his telling of the tale. I have depicted events and conversation consistent with the oral history of the village, my site visit, and sources as detailed.

24. Site visit, Bridgend, Callander, Scotland, December 19, 1999.

25. Brealey, *Two Worlds*, 18.

26. Brealey, *Two Worlds*, 16; MacNaughton, personal interview, December 19, 1999. Brealey provided a general outline. Mr. MacNaughton gave details, including names and locations.

27. MacNaughton, personal interview, December 19, 1999. In Brealey's version, the doctor lives. In Mr. MacNaughton's telling, Dr. Todd dies. To this day, the villagers continue to call that spot in the road "the Doctor's Corner"; this convinced me that Mr. MacNaughton's version has greater credibility.

28. Anonymous, personal interview, Callander, Scotland, December 19, 1999; "The Last Witch," interview with Downey and Pooey, BBC Radio, August 13, 1999; Gaskill, *Hellish Nell*, 35. This dialogue is designed to communicate the sentiments expressed by multiple sources.

29. Dorothy Mahoney, personal interview, Callander, Scotland, December 18, 1999; J. K. Dunn, personal interview, Callander, Scotland, December 18, 1999; MacNaughton, personal

interview, December 19, 1999; Morag Lloyds, *Images of Scotland: Around Callander and the Trossachs* (Stroud, Gloucestershire: Tempus, 1999), 26–27. Callander residents all told me that Helen Duncan was called "Hellish Nell." Morag provides names and occupations of villagers who lived in Callander at the time Dr. Todd died.

30. Armour, *Helen Duncan,* 24.

31. Brealey, *Two Worlds,* 95; Barbanell, *The Case of Helen Duncan,* 120.

32. Barbanell, *The Case of Helen Duncan,* 114–121; *Rex v. Duncan,* extract of criminal appeal cases, June 8, 9, 19, 1944, HO 144/22172. With the return to the appeal, the interchanges between counsel and the Appeals Court Justices are based on this eyewitness account and on the official extract. I have communicated the content of the proceedings through constructed dialogue.

33. Barbanell, *The Case of Helen Duncan,* 121.

34. *Rex v. Duncan,* extract of criminal appeal cases, June 8, 9, 19, 1944, HO 144/22172, 6.

35. Barbanell, *The Case of Helen Duncan,* 121,

36. Barbanell, *The Case of Helen Duncan,* 120; *Rex v. Duncan,* extract of criminal appeal cases, June 8, 9, 19, 1944, HO 144/22172, 2.

37. Barbanell, *The Case of Helen Duncan,* 120.

38. Barbanell, *The Case of Helen Duncan,* 118; *Rex v. Duncan,* extract of criminal appeal cases, June 8, 9, 19, 1944, HO 144/22172, 5.

39. Barbanell, *The Case of Helen Duncan,* 120; *Rex v. Duncan,* extract of criminal appeal cases, June 8, 9, 19, 1944, HO 144/22172, 1.

40. Barbanell, *The Case of Helen Duncan,* 121.

41. Ibid.

42. *Rex v. Duncan,* extract of criminal appeal cases, June 8, 9, 19, 1944, HO 144/22172, 4; Barbanell, *The Case of Helen Duncan,* 115.

43. Barbanell, *The Case of Helen Duncan,* 116.

44. Ibid.

45. Ibid.

46. Ibid.

47. Ibid.

48. Ibid.

49. Ibid., 117.

50. Ibid.

51. *Rex v. Duncan,* extract of criminal appeal cases, June 8, 9, 19, 1944, HO 144/22172; Barbanell, *The Case of Helen Duncan,* 121.

52. Barbanell, *The Case of Helen Duncan,* 122; Bob Ogley, *Doodlebugs and Rockets: Battle of the Flying Bombs* (Westerham, Kent: Froglets, 1992), 107, photograph; Philip Zeigler, *London at War* (London: Arrow, 1998), 283.

53. Ogley, *Doodlebugs and Rockets,* 34.

54. Ibid., 107, photograph.

55. Ibid., 33.

56. Ibid., 106–107.

57. *World War II: Day by Day,* 533.

58. Ogley, *Doodlebugs and Rockets,* 38.

59. Barbanell, *The Case of Helen Duncan,* 122; Ylva French, *London Blue Guide* (London: A&C Black, 1998), 232. Barbanell reports that the Appeals Court decision was read in a crypt turned bomb shelter; French reports that the crypt beneath Lincoln's Inn Chapel

served as a bomb shelter in World War II. Given these two pieces of information, I assume this location.

60. Barbanell, *The Case of Helen Duncan*, 122.
61. Site visit, Crypt, Royal Courts of Justice, London.
62. Barbanell, *The Case of Helen Duncan*, 123.
63. Barbanell, *The Case of Helen Duncan*, 129; *Rex v. Duncan*, extract of criminal appeal cases, June 8, 9, 19, 1944, HO 144/22172, 7.
64. Barbanell, *The Case of Helen Duncan*, 129.

## Chapter 34

In the summer of 1944, during Helen Duncan's incarceration, a V-1 bomb—one of the world's first rocket-powered missiles—hit Holloway Prison. I owe a real debt to Felicity Ball, at the H.M. Prison Museum in Rugby, England, for helping me to uncover documents and photographs chronicling the massive destruction. None of Helen Duncan's biographers had unearthed this event. Given her mother's prophecy—"You'll be burnt as witch"—I reconstruct this scene and assume its importance. To support my depiction and its transformational effect, I piece together details from a variety of historical sources.

1. Gena Brealey, *The Two Worlds of Helen Duncan* (London: Regency Press, 1985), 101; M. M. Rougie, Medical Officer, Enclosure, Form 1012, H.M. Prison, August 8, 1944, HO 144/22172, Public Records Office, Kew, England.

2. "Minutes of Voluntary Advisory Nursing Board, September 4, 1944," H.M.S. Prison Museum Archives, Rugby, England. This archival document provides the date of the Holloway Prison V-1 attack on Cell Block B.

3. Brealey, *Two Worlds*, 101; Henry Duncan, letter to His Majesty, August 8, 1944, HO 144/22172, Public Records Office, Kew, England; Henry Duncan, letter to Under-Secretary of State, June 29, 1944, HO 144/22172, Public Records Office, Kew, England; Henry Duncan, letter to Right Honourable Winston Churchill, August 8, 1944, HO 144/22172, Public Records Office, Kew, England.

4. Bob Ogley, *Doodlebugs and Rockets: Battle of the Flying Bombs* (Westerham, Kent: Froglets, 1992), 34. Description of the fear that accompanied the silence when a V-1 "cut out."

5. "The Last Witch in England," interview with Shelia Downey and Ann Pooey, Helen Duncan's granddaughters, BBC Radio, August 13, 1998; Malcolm Gaskill, *Hellish Nell* (London: Fourth Estate, 2001), 35.

6. "Minutes of Voluntary Advisory Nursing Board, September 4, 1944"; Photograph of V-1 bomb damage, H.M.S. Prison Museum Archives, Rugby, England.

7. Rougie, Medical Officer, Enclosure, Form 1012, H.M. Prison, August 8, 1944, HO 144/22172. Rougie describes Helen Duncan's "emotionally unstable" and "hysterical" reaction to bomb attacks.

8. I assume that the attack must have re-ignited the memory of her mother's prophecy, a prophecy mentioned by her granddaughters in "The Last Witch," BBC Radio, August 13, 1998, and reported by historian Malcolm Gaskill in *Hellish Nell*, page 35.

9. Brealey, *Two Worlds*, 16–17, 102. Helen Duncan's daughter reports that her mother reminisced about her childhood after her imprisonment and told the following story. I have constructed dialogue consistent with Brealey's version and added details based on additional sources.

10. J. K. Dunn, personal interview, December 18, 1999; Harvey Duncan, contemporaneous journal describing Callander and its townfolk in the early 1900s, Harvey MacNaughton's private collection, Callander, Scotland.

11. Dorothy Mahoney, letter to author, October 28, 1999; Dunn, personal interview, December 18, 1999. To reconstruct the tale of little Hellish Nell scaling the schoolhouse, I have combined Dorothy Mahoney's letter with J. K. Dunn's information about school rules, uniforms, and routines.

12. Dunn, personal interview, December 18, 1999.

13. Mahoney, letter to author, October 28, 1999.

14. Dunn, personal interview, December 18, 1999.

15. Mahoney, letter to author, October 28, 1999.

16. Dunn, personal interview, December 18, 1999.

17. Mahoney, letter to author, October 28, 1999.

18. Brealey, *Two Worlds*, 16–17. The dialogue in the remainder of this scene conforms with Brealey's description.

19. Ibid., 17.

20. Ibid., 18.

21. Brealey, *Two Worlds*, 16–19; Dunn, personal interview, December 18, 1999; MacNaughton, personal interview, December 19, 1999; Mahoney, letter to author, October 28, 1999.

22. Brealey, *Two Worlds*, 17.

23. Ibid., 102.

24. Photograph of Holloway prisoners in capes, H.M.S. Prison Museum Archives, Rugby, England.

25. Photograph of visitors' room at Holloway Prison, H.M.S. Prison Museum Archives, Rugby, England.

26. Brealey, *Two Worlds*, 102.

27. Albert Crew, *London Prisons of Today and Yesterday* (London: Ivor, Nicholson and Watson, 1933), 150. Wardress reflects prison routines.

28. Brealey, *Two Worlds*, 102.

29. Crew, *London Prisons*, 150.

30. Brealey, *Two Worlds*, 102.

31. Ibid., 101.

32. Gaskill, *Hellish Nell*, 218.

33. Brealey, *Two Worlds*, 102.

34. Photograph of Holloway Prison's Infirmary cells, H.M.S. Prison Museum Archives, Rugby, England.

35. Crew, *London Prisons*, 133–134, 145.

36. Crew, *London Prisons*, 143; Photograph of Holloway Prison's Infirmary nursing station, H.M.S. Prison Museum Archives, Rugby, England.

37. Brealey, *Two Worlds*, 102.

## Chapter 35

This chapter brings the *Witch Trial of World War II* to its conclusion. Helen Duncan's release from prison, Chief Constable West's transformed responsibilities, and Harry Price's reaction are placed in their historical context.

1. *World War II: Day by Day* (London: Dorling Kindersley, 2001), 560.

2. M. M. Rougie, Medical Officer, Enclosure, Form 1012, H.M. Prison, August 8, 1944, HO 144/22172, Public Records Office, Kew, England.

3. Albert Crew, *London Prisons of Today and Yesterday* (London: Ivor, Nicholson and Watson, 1933), 141.

4. Philip Zeigler, *London at War* (London: Arrow, 1998), 295.

5. Ibid., 296.

6. Bob Ogley, *Doodlebugs and Rockets: Battle of the Flying Bombs* (Westerham, Kent: Froglets, 1992), 143.

7. Ibid.

8. Zeigler, *London at War,* 297.

9. Ogley, *Doodlebugs and Rockets,* 145.

10. Ibid., 142.

11. Ibid., 143.

12. Rougie, Medical Officer, Enclosure, Form 1012, H.M. Prison, August 8, 1944, HO 144/22172.

13. Maurice Barbanell, *The Case of Helen Duncan* (London: Psychic Press, 1945), 153; Gena Brealey, *The Two Worlds of Helen Duncan* (London: Regency Press, 1985), 100, 101. Assumptions about Helen Duncan's state of mind are based on these sources and subsequent actions.

14. Brealey, *Two Worlds,* 100.

15. Rougie, Medical Officer, Enclosure, Form 1012, H.M. Prison, August 8, 1944, HO 144/22172.

16. Photographs of Holloway prisoners, H.M.S. Prison Museum Archives, Rugby, England.

17. Photographs of Holloway Prison Gate, H.M.S. Prison Museum Archives, Rugby, England.

18. Barbanell, *The Case of Helen Duncan,* 153; Brealey, *Two Worlds,* 100.

19. Barbanell, *The Case of Helen Duncan,* 153; Brealey, *Two Worlds,* 100.

20. Brealey, *Two Worlds,* 100.

21. *World War II: Day by Day,* photograph and caption, 566.

22. John Stedman, ed., *People of Portsmouth: The 20th Century in Their Own Words* (Derby, England: Breedon Books, 2002), 121; John Stedman, *Portsmouth Reborn* (Portsmouth: Portsmouth City Council, 1995), 7.

23. *World War II: Day by Day,* 558.

24. Ibid., 562.

25. Ibid., 561.

26. D-Day Supplement, *Evening News* (Portsmouth), June 1984; *World War II: Day by Day,* 522.

27. *World War II: Day by Day,* 565.

28. F. H. Hinsley and C.A.G. Simkins, *British Intelligence in the Second World War,* vol. 4 (New York: Cambridge University Press, 1990), 258.

29. Ursula Norton, "Life Inside Fortress Southsea," *Evening News* (Portsmouth), D-Day Supplement, June 1984.

30. Olive Cramer, personal interview, October 25, 2005.

31. Stanley Worth, personal interview, October 16, 2001.

32. Hinsley and Simkins, *British Intelligence,* vol. 4, 258.

33. Brealey, *Two Worlds,* 101–102.

34. Harry Price, *Search for Truth* (London: Collins, 1942), 111.

35. Trevor Hall, *The Search for Harry Price* (London: Duckworth, 1978), photograph; Paul Tabori, *Harry Price: Biography of a Ghost Hunter* (London: Athenaeum Press, 1950), photograph.

36. Barbanell, *The Case of Helen Duncan*, 153; Brealey, *Two Worlds*, 100.

37. Malcolm Gaskill, *Hellish Nell* (London: Fourth Estate, 2001), 326.

## Epilogue

Scenes in this epilogue depict life going on: Chief Constable West presides over peacetime Portsmouth; Harry Price and Helen Duncan die. Their continued stories are based on sources noted below.

1. Gena Brealey, *The Two Worlds of Helen Duncan* (London: Regency Press, 1985), 106–119.

2. Ibid., 105.

3. Ibid., 103.

4. Ibid., 111.

5. Ibid., 118.

6. Ibid., 106–107.

7. Ibid., 111.

8. Mary Armour, *Helen Duncan (1895–1956): My Living Has Not Been in Vain* (London: Pembridge, 2000), 98.

9. Brealey, *Two Worlds*, 106.

10. Site visit, 36 Rankeiler Street, Edinburgh; Armour, *Helen Duncan*, 98; Brealey, *Two Worlds*, 120.

11. Brealey, *Two Worlds*, 111–112.

12. Malcolm Gaskill, *Hellish Nell* (London: Fourth Estate, 2001), 334.

13. Brealey, *Two Worlds*, 111.

14. Ibid.

15. Ibid., 111–112.

16. "June 27, 1947," Foxworth and History Society, www.foxworth.org.uk.

17. Paul Tabori, *Harry Price: Biography of a Ghost Hunter* (London: Athenaeum Press, 1950), 1.

18. Trevor Hall, *The Search for Harry Price* (London: Duckworth, 1978), 101.

19. Tabori, *Harry Price*, 1; Peter Underwood, "Harry Price: An Introduction," www.harryprice.co.uk, photograph.

20. Hall, *The Search for Harry Price*, 14; Tabori, *Harry Price*, 254–256.

21. National Heart, Lung, and Blood Institute, "Diseases Index: Heart Attack, Angina," www.nih.com.

22. Hall, *The Search for Harry Price*, 14. Hall quotes from *Evening News* (Portsmouth), March 30, 1948.

23. Underwood, "Harry Price: An Introduction," www.harryprice.co.uk., photograph.

24. Hall, *The Search for Harry Price*, 14. Hall quotes from *Evening News* (Portsmouth), March 30, 1948.

25. Ibid., 51–53.

26. Ibid., 14. Hall quotes from *Evening News* (Portsmouth), March 30, 1948.

27. Alan Crossley, *The Story of Helen Duncan* (Greenford: Psychic World Classic, 1999), 168–169; Gaskill, *Hellish Nell*, 346.

28. Brealey, *Two Worlds*, 113.

29. Ibid., 112, "The Last Witch in England," interview with Shelia Downey and Ann Pooey, Helen Duncan's granddaughters, BBC Radio, London, August 13, 1998.

30. Manfred Cassirer, *Medium on Trial* (Essex: PN Publishing, 1996), 164.

31. Brealey, *Two Worlds*, 115.

32. Brealey, *Two Worlds*, 115; "Last Witch," interview with Downey and Pooey, BBC Radio, August 13, 1998.

33. Brealey, *Two Worlds*, 121.

34. Portsmouth City Police, "Unveiling and Dedication of Memorial Plaque," November 16, 1952, Terry Swetnam's personal collection, Portsmouth, England.

35. Site visit to Byculla House.

36. Portsmouth City Police, "Unveiling and Dedication of Memorial Plaque," November 16, 1952.

37. Brealey, *Two Worlds*, 9–10.

38. Ibid., 120–121.

39. Ibid., 123.

# Bibliography

I list these resources with gratitude for the information provided by each and every one.

## Books

Alford, R. G. *Notes on the Building of English Prisons*. Parkhurst: H.M. Convict Prison, 1909.

Armour, Mary. *Helen Duncan (1895–1956): My Living Has Not Been in Vain*. London: Pembridge, 2000.

Barbanell, Maurice. *The Case of Helen Duncan*. London: Psychic Press, 1945.

Beesley, Patrick. *Very Special Intelligence*. London: Sphere Books, 1977.

Brealey, Gena. *The Two Worlds of Helen Duncan*. London: Regency Press, 1985.

Campbell, A. M. *Let's See Callander and the Trossachs*. Fort William, 1951.

Cassirer, Manfred. *Medium on Trial*. Essex: PN Publishing, 1996.

Collier, Basil. *Leader of the Few*. London: Jarrolds, 1957.

Crew, Albert. *London Prisons of Today and Yesterday*. London: Ivor, Nicholson and Watson, 1933.

Crossley, Alan. *The Story of Helen Duncan*. Greenford: Psychic World Classic, 1999.

Dodd, Alfred. *The Secret Shakespeare*. London: Rider, 1941.

Dodson, Gerald. *Consider Your Verdict*. London: Hutchinson, 1967.

Dowding, Hugh. *Many Mansions*. London: Rider, 1943.

Dowding, Muriel. *Beauty, Not the Beast*. London: Rider, 1968.

French, Ylva. *London Blue Guide*. London: A&C Black, 1998.

Gaskill, Malcolm. *Hellish Nell*. London: Fourth Estate, 2001.

Hall, Trevor. *The Search for Harry Price*. London: Duckworth, 1978.

Hinsley, F. H., and C.A.G. Simkins. *British Intelligence in the Second World War*, vol. 4. New York: Cambridge University Press, 1990.

Honourable Society of the Middle Temple. *Middle Temple Ordeal*. London: Sir Isaac Pitman & Sons, 1948.

Howard, Michael. *British Intelligence in the Second World War*, vol.5. New York: Cambridge University Press, 1990.

Jenkins, Paul. *Battle Over Portsmouth*. Midhurst: Middleton Press, 1998.

Jones, Kevin. *Conan Doyle and the Spirits*. Wellingborough: Aquarian, 1998.

Kemp, Anthony. *D-Day: The Normandy Landings*. London: Thames and Hudson, 1994.

Lloyds, Morag. *Images of Scotland: Around Callander and the Trossachs*. Stroud: Tempus, 1999.

Oaten, Ernest. "Law Relating to Mediumship," *Manual of Who's Who of Spiritualism and Psychic Research*. London: Spiritualist National Union, no date.

Ogley, Bob. *Doodlebugs and Rockets: Battle of the Flying Bombs*. Westerham, Kent: Froglets, 1992.

Perry, Michael, ed. Special Report to the Archbishop of Canterbury. London, CFPSS Press, 1999.

Price, Harry. *The End of Borley Rectory*. London: George G. Harrap, 1946.

_____. *The Most Haunted House in England*. London: Longmans, 1940.

_____. *Poltergeist Over England*. London: Country Life, 1945.

_____. *Regurgitation and the Duncan Mediumship*. London: National Laboratory of Psychical Research, 1931.

_____. *Search for Truth*. London: Collins, 1942.

Roberts, C. E. Bechhofer, ed. *The Trial of Helen Duncan*. London: Jarrolds, 1945.

Roskill, Stephen. *The Navy at War, 1939–1945*. London: Collins, 1960.

Ross, David. *The Story of Rob Roy*. New Lanark: Corbie, 1998.

Sadden, John, ed. *The Archive Series: Portsmouth*. Stroud, England: Chalford, 1997.

Schofield, A. B. *Dictionary of Legal Biography, 1845–1945*. Chichester: Barry Rose, 1998.

Stedman, John. *Portsmouth Reborn*. Portsmouth: Portsmouth City Council, 1995.

Stedman, John, ed. *People of Portsmouth: The 20th Century in Their Own Words*. Derby, England: Breedon Books, 2002.

Swaffer, Hannen. *Hannen Swaffer's Who's Who*. London: Hutchinson, 1945.

Swaffer, Hannen. *My Greatest Story*. London: W. H. Allen, 1945.

Tabori, Paul. *Harry Price: The Biography of a Ghost Hunter*. London: Athenaeum Press, 1950.

Thomas, Donald. *An Underworld at War*. London: John Murray, 2003.

*The War Cabinet Rooms*. London: Imperial War Museum Publication, 1996.

van Emden, Richard. *Veterans: The Last Survivors of the Great War*. Yorkshire: Pen & Sword Books, 1998.

Walker, Nick. *Those Were the Days: British Police Cars*. London: Velco, 2001.

Walker, William. *Juteopolis: Dundee and Its Textile Workers, 1885–1923*. Edinburgh: Scottish University Press, 1979.

Watson, Mark. *Jute Mills of Dundee*. Hull: Hutton Press, 1990.

West, Nigel. *MI 5: British Security Operations, 1909–1945*. London: Triad Granada, 1983.

*Who Was Who*. London: A&C Black, 1897–1990.

*World War II: Day by Day*. London: Dorling Kindersley, 2001.

Zeigler, Philip. *London at War*. London: Arrow, 1998.

## Archival Materials

"Arthur Charles West," service record. Private collection, Terry Swetnam, Portsmouth, England.

Atkinson, E. Tindall. Letter to Sir Gerald Dodson. Undated. DPP 2/1204. Public Records Office, Kew, England.

Atkinson, E. Tindall. Nomination of prosecution counsel. March 1, 1944. DPP 2/1204. Public Records Office, Kew, England.

Churchill, Winston. Letter to Home Secretary. April 3, 1944. HO 144/22172. Public Records Office, Kew, England.

Cohen, Arthur Sefton. Letter to Chief Constable West. March 16, 1944. DPP 2/1204. Public Records Office, Kew, England.

Duncan, Harvey. Contemporaneous journal describing Callander and its townfolk in early 1900s. Harvey MacNaughton's private collection, Callander, Scotland.

Duncan, Henry. Letter to the Honourable Winston Churchill. June 29, 1944. HO 144/22172. Public Records Office, Kew, England.

Duncan, Henry. Letter to Your Majesty. June 29, 1944. HO 144/22172. Public Records Office, Kew, England.

Duncan, Henry. Letter to the Under-Secretary of State. June 29, 1944. HO 144/22172. Public Records Office, Kew, England.

Ford, Frederick. Report from Portsmouth City Police to Under-Secretary of State. February 12, 1944. HO 144/22172. Public Records Office, Kew, England.

Ford, Frederick. Report from Portsmouth City Police to Under-Secretary of State. April 5, 1944. HO 144/22172. Public Records Office, Kew, England.

"Frederick David Ford," service record. Private collection, Terry Swetnam, Portsmouth, England.

"HM Prison Auxiliary Meeting Notes." August 1944. HM Prison Service Museum Archives. Rugby, Warwickshire, England.

Holloway Prison photographs. July 1944 bomb damage to Cell Block B. HM Prison Service Museum Archives. Rugby, Warwickshire, England.

Holloway Prison photographs. HM Prison Service Museum Archives. Rugby, Warwickshire, England.

London Spiritualist Alliance. "Report of the Happenings at Sittings with Mrs. Duncan." 1930–1931. College of Psychic Studies Archive, London.

McCowan, Alex. Edinburgh Police Report to Portsmouth Police, Feb, 1944, DDP 2/2104, Public Records Office, Kew, England.

Mears, Grimwood. Letter to Home Secretary. February 2, 1944. HO 144/22172, Public Records Office, Kew, England.

Mears, Grimwood. Letter to Home Secretary. February 28, 1944. HO 144/22172. Public Records Office: Kew England.

Minutes of Voluntary Advisory Nursing Board. September 4, 1944. HM Prison Service Museum Archives, Rugby, Warwickshire, England.

Morrison, Herbert. Letter to Winston Churchill. April 6, 1944. HO 144/22172. Public Records Office, Kew, England.

"Most Secret: Loss of *Barham*—Board of Inquiry." April 28, 1942. ADM. 1/11948. Public Records Office, Kew, England.

Pimbott, J.A.R., Private Secretary to Home Secretary Morrison. Letter to Sir Grimwood Mears. February 25, 1944. HO 144/22172. Public Records Office, Kew, England.

Plan Bodyguard. CAB 80/77. COS(43)799(o). January 23, 1944. Public Records Office, Kew, England.

Police Minutes. February 1944. HO 144/22172. Public Records Office, Kew, England.

Portsmouth City Police, "Unveiling and Dedication of Memorial Plaque." November 16, 1952. Terry Swetnam's private collection, Portsmouth, England.

"Operation Bodyguard, Overall Deception Police for the War against Germany." [January 23, 1944] CAB 80/77, Public Records Office, Kew, England.

*Rex v. Duncan.* Brief for the Prosecution. DPP 2/1204. Public Records Office, Kew, England.

*Rex v. Duncan.* Copy of charge. February 8, 1944. Portsmouth Magistrates Court. CRIM 1/1581. Public Records Office, Kew, England.

*Rex v. Duncan.* Deponent(s). CRIM 1/1581. Public Records Office, Kew, England.

*Rex v. Duncan.* Extract of criminal appeal cases, June 8, 9, 19, 1944. HO 144/22172. Public Records Office, Kew, England.

*Rex v. Duncan.* Hearing transcript. February 29, 1944. Portsmouth Magistrates' Court. CRIM 1/1581. Public Records Office, Kew, England.

*Rex v. Duncan.* Letters and petition to the Home Office and MP Rathborne. 1944. HO 144/22172. Public Records Office, Kew, England.

*Rex v. Duncan.* Prosecutors' notes. Undated. DPP 2/1204. Public Records Office, Kew, England.

*Rex v. Duncan.* Trial transcript. 1944. DPP 2/1234. Public Records Office, Kew, England.

*Rex v. Loughans.* CRIM 1/1583. Public Records Office, Kew, England.

*Rex v. Loughans.* DPP 2/1192. Public Records Office, Kew, England.

*Rex v. Duncan.* Letters and petition to the Home Office and MP Rathborne, 1944. HO 144/22172, Public Records Office, Kew, England.

Rougie, M. M., Medical Officer. Enclosure, Form 1012, HM Prison. August 8, 1944. HO 144/22172. Public Records Office, Kew, England.

"Seven Sittings with Mrs. Duncan." 1930–1931. Society of Psychical Research Archive, London.

West, Arthur. Letter to Francis Graham-Harrison. February 14, 1944. HO 144/22172. Public Records Office, Kew, England.

West, Arthur. Letter to Harry Price. April 6, 1944. DPP 2/1204. Public Records Office, Kew, England.

West, Arthur. Letter to E. G. Robey. February 15, 1944. DPP 2/1204. Public Records Office, Kew, England.

West, Arthur. Letter to E. G. Robey. March 4, 1944. DPP 2/1204. Public Records Office, Kew, England.

## Newspaper and Magazine Articles

"100 Tons a Minute on Berlin." *Evening News* (Portsmouth), January 20, 1944.

"600 Bombers Warn Berlin, 'We're Coming.'" *Daily Herald* (London), March 23, 1944.

"2,000 Ton Blitz Hits Nuremberg." *Evening News* (Portsmouth), March 29, 1944.

"Air War Gigantic—4 German Cities Ablaze." *Sunday Pictorial* (London), March 26, 1944.

"'All Lies' Cries Medium." *Daily Express* (London), April 1, 1944.

"'All Lies' Cry by Medium." *News of the World* (London), April 2, 1944.

"Alleged Séance Deceptions." *The Times* (London), March 31, 1944.

Barbanell, Maurice. "Editorial." *Psychic News* (London), September 21, 1940

"Blitz of Portsmouth: Lack of Water Killed Guildhall." *Evening News* (Portsmouth), January 1991.

"Bombs Start London Fires." *Daily Herald* (London), March 25, 1944.

"Charge Against a Medium." *Scotsman* (Edinburgh), May 4, 1944.

"Constable Grabs 'Spirit': Shocking Things Divulged." *Evening News* (Portsmouth), January 20, 1944.

"Coast Ban Lifted for Sweethearts." *Evening News* (Portsmouth), March 29, 1944.

"Crowds Jam Tube—Biggest Rush since Coronation, Salute to Soldiers." *Daily Express* (London), March 27, 1944.

D-Day Supplement. *Evening News* (Portsmouth), June 1984.

Duncan, Madame Victoria. "Secrets of My Second Sight." *People's Journal* (Aberdeen), October 7, 1933.

Duncan, Madame Victoria. "Secrets of My Second Sight: Terrifying Visitors from the Beyond." *People's Journal* (Aberdeen), October 14, 1933.

Duncan, Madame Victoria. "Secrets of My Second Sight: Scottish Youth's Plight." *People's Journal* (Aberdeen), October 21, 1933.

Duncan, Madame Victoria. "Secrets of My Second Sight: Husband's Dramatic Homecoming." *People's Journal* (Aberdeen), October 28, 1933.

Duncan, Madame Victoria. "Secrets of My Second Sight: Girls I Have Helped to Find Happiness." *People's Journal* (Aberdeen), November 4, 1933.

Duncan, Madame Victoria. "Secrets of My Second Sight: Missing from Home." *People's Journal* (Aberdeen), November 11, 1933.

Duncan, Madame Victoria. "Secrets of My Second Sight: My First Experiences in Trance." *People's Journal* (Aberdeen), November 18, 1933.

Duncan, Madame Victoria. "Secrets of My Second Sight: Girls Who Laughed at My Second Sight." *People's Journal* (Aberdeen), November 25, 1933.

Duncan, Madame Victoria. "Secrets of My Second Sight: Saved Man from Committing a Terrible Crime." *People's Journal* (Aberdeen), December 2, 1933.

Duncan, Madame Victoria. "Secrets of My Second Sight: Knots I have Unraveled." *People's Journal* (Aberdeen), December 9, 1933.

Duncan, Madame Victoria. "Secrets of My Second Sight: Mending Broken Hearts." *People's Journal* (Aberdeen), December 16, 1933.

"Fairy Form at Séance." *Daily Sketch*, March 25, 1944.

Fielding-Ould, Robert. Editorial. *Two Worlds* (London), June 21, 1931.

"Helen Duncan's Wealth." *Daily Herald* (London), April 4, 1944.

"Invasion: British in Equal Numbers to US." *Daily Express* (London), March 27, 1944.

"January 10, 1941." *Evening News* (Portsmouth), D-Day Supplement, January 1991.

"'Lies' Cry by Medium." *Daily Herald* (London), April 1, 1944.

"Longest Raid in a Year." *Daily Express* (London), March 25, 1944.

"Loughans Tells Counsel, 'Police Are My Enemies.'" *Evening News* (Portsmouth), April 1, 1944.

"*Luftwaffer* Made Big Attempt to Burn London." *Evening News* (Portsmouth), March 25, 1944.

"Materialization Medium." *The Scotsman* (Edinburgh), May 5, 1933.

Maule, Esson. "I Have Lived a Strange Life." *People's Journal* (Aberdeen), October 13, 1933.

Maule, Esson. "A Dream of the Past." *People's Journal* (Aberdeen), November 10, 1944.

Maule, Esson. "A Queer Vision." *People's Journal* (Aberdeen), November 24, 1934.

Maule, Esson. "Weird Figure that Haunted My House." *People's Journal* (Aberdeen), December 22, 1934.

"Medium Defied Handcuffs and Sashcord." *New Chronicle* (London), March 30, 1944.

"Medium Weeps and Shouts at Verdict." *New Chronicle* (London), April 1, 1944.

"Medium's Body Endangered." *Evening News* (Portsmouth), January 25, 1944.
"MP's Queue to Vote for Churchill, Undid Equal Pay." *Daily Express* (London), March 31, 1944.
"Mrs. Duncan, 'A Humbug.'" *Daily Mail* (London), April 4, 1944.
"Mrs. Duncan's 100 Pounds." *Evening News* (Portsmouth), April 4, 1944.
"Police Revelations Do Not Shake Followers." *News of the World* (London), March 30, 1944.
"Premier Challenges Equal Pay Rebels." *Evening News* (Portsmouth), March 29, 1944.
"Prime Minister Issues Ultimatum—Rose to Cheers from House of Commons." *Daily Herald* (London), March 30, 1944.
"Reversal of Equal Pay: MP's Cancel Vote." *Daily Herald* (London), March 31, 1944.
"Russian Armies Link Up." *Evening News* (Portsmouth), January 11, 1944.
"Russians Enter Poland." *Evening News* (Portsmouth), January 4, 1944.
"Salute Crowds." *Daily Herald* (London), March 27, 1944.
"Salute to Soldier Previewed." *The Times* (London), March 24, 1944.
"Says Dead Policeman and Cat Brought Back." *Daily Herald* (London), March 23, 1944.
"Says Hand Ached for Hours." *Daily Herald* (London), March 31, 1944.
"Says He Heard Row Between Ghost and Medium." *Daily Mirror* (London), March 24, 1944.
"Seaside Has 7 Day Holiday Boom." *Sunday Pictorial* (London), March 26, 1944.
"Sittings with Mrs. Duncan." *The Light* (London), 1930–1931.
Souter, James. "Letter to the editor." *The Light* (London), June 19, 1929.
"Special Cabinet Summoned: One Vote Defeat for Government on Equal Pay." *Daily Herald* (London), March 29, 1944.
"Spirit Gave Husband's Ring." *New Chronicle* (London), March 31, 1944.
"Spy Raiders Over London, Night Fighters Tailed Spy Planes from South Coast." *Daily Express* (London), March 23, 1944.
Stevenson, Jason. "The *Barham* Conspiracy." *World War II Magazine*, December 2, 2004, 62–68.
"Story of Ghost." *Daily Express* (London), March 25, 1944.
"Story of Mrs. Duncan 100 Pounds a Week." *Evening News* (Portsmouth), April 2, 1944.
"Two Allied Victories: Italy and Russia." *Evening News* (Portsmouth), January 22, 1944.
Ursula Norton. "Life Inside Fortress Southsea." *Evening News* (Portsmouth), D-Day Supplement, June 1984.
"U.S. Salute to Our Soldier." *The Times* (London), March 30, 1944.
"Warning to Home Guards: Careless Talk and Second Front." *Evening News* (Portsmouth), January 22, 1944.
"We Will Fight for Her to the End." *Sunday Pictorial* (London), April 2, 1944.
"'We're Toughening Up,'—Eisenhower." *Evening News* (Portsmouth), January 16, 1944.
Wilson, Percy. "Lifted Heels over Head." *Psychic News* (London), December 29, 1956.
"Witchcraft Act Offences." *The Times* (London), April 1, 1944.
"Woman Medium's Trance at Old Bailey." *Daily Herald* (London), March 28, 1944.

## Personal Communications

Burrell, R. C., and K. M. Personal interview. Portsmouth, England, November 3, 1999.
Cramer, Jim. Telephone interview. May 12, 2005.
Cramer, Jim. Telephone interview. Oct. 25, 2005.
Cramer, Olive. Telephone interview. Portsmouth, England. May 12, 2005.

Cramer, Olive. Telephone interview. Portsmouth, England. October 25, 2005.
Dunn, J. K. Personal interview. Callander, Scotland. December 10, 1999.
Lewis-Proudlock, Logan. Personal interview. College of Psychic Studies, London. April 7, 2005.
MacNaughton, Harvey. Personal interview. Callander, Scotland. December 11, 1999.
Mahoney, Dorothy. Personal interview. Callander, Scotland. December 10, 1999.
Mahoney, Dorothy. Personal letter. Callander, Scotland. October 28, 1999.
Mahoney, Dorothy. Personal letter. Callander, Scotland. November 2, 1999.
Mahoney, Dorothy. Personal letter. Callander, Scotland. November 19, 1999.
Mahoney, Dorothy. Personal letter. Callander, Scotland. November 29, 1999.
Mahoney, Dorothy. Personal letter. Callander, Scotland. December 16, 1999.
Shipp, Kelvin. Personal e-mail. August 15, 2005.
Swetnam, Terry. Personal interview. Portsmouth, England. November 3, 1999.
Swetnam, Terry. Personal letter. Portsmouth, England. February 16, 2000.
Worth, Stanley. Telephone interview. Auckland, New Zealand. October 10, 2001.
Worth, Stanley. Telephone interview. Auckland, New Zealand. October 16, 2001.

## Television and Radio

"The Last Witch in England." BBC Radio, London, August 13, 1998.
"Weekend Edition with Scott Simon." National Public Radio, Washington, D.C., January 31, 1998.
"Witch Hunt." Channel 4, London, July 13, 1999.

## Web Sites

Bevand, Paul, and Frank Allen. "The Pursuit of the *Bismarck* and Sinking of the *Hood*." www.hmshood.com.
"Bosworth Market." www.britannia-bosworth.activehostels.com.
"The Dardanelles Commission," www.firstworldwar.com.
"Disease and Conditions Index." National Institutes of Health. www.nih.com.
"Facts about Sulfur Mustard." Centers for Disease Control. www.cdc.gov.
"George Robey: The English Music Hall." www.amaranthdesign.ca.
"Gray's Inn-Virtual Tour." www.graysinn.org.uk.
"Holloway Prison." www.richard.clarke32.btinternet.co.uk.
"Holloway Prison." www.tchavalier.com.
"June 27, 1947." Foxworth and History Society, www.foxworth.org.uk.
"Magic at War." Channel 4's Portrait Gallery. www.channel4.com.
"Portsmouth Guildhall." www.portsmouth-guide.co.uk.
"The Right to Silence." www.wikipedia.org.
"South of the Border," by Chris Isaak. Baja Sessions. www.allthelyrics.com.
"Symptoms of Eclampsia." WebMD. www.webmd.com.
"Transport." Hampshire Constabulary Historical Society, Netley, England. www.hants.gov.uk.
Underwood, Peter. "Harry Price: An Introduction." www.harryprice.co.uk.
"Use of Poison Gas in World War I." www.wikipedia.org.
Yablon, Charles M. "Wigs, Coifs and Other Idiosyncrasies of English Judicial Attire." www.cardozo.net.

# Index